SPIRAL UP!

BOOKS BY CHLOE FAITH WORDSWORTH

Resonance Repatterning® Books

Quantum Change Made Easy

Spiral Up! 127 Energizing Options to be your best right now

Commitment to Life: A program for super health and vitality

The Resonance Repatterning® Series

The Fundamentals of Resonance Repatterning –
includes Empowering Yourself with Resonance Repatterning

Transforming Primary Patterns

Transforming Unconscious Patterns

Resonance Repatterning Process Guide

Transforming Chakra Patterns

Transforming Five Element and Meridian Patterns

Inner Cultivation through the Twelve Meridians – The Five Essences

Principles of Relationship

A New Vision

Energetics of Relationship

A RESONANCE REPATTERNING® BOOK

SPIRAL UP!
127
ENERGIZING OPTIONS TO BE YOUR BEST RIGHT NOW

CHLOE FAITH WORDSWORTH

Founder and Developer of the Resonance Repatterning® System

Resonance Publishing
A Division of the Resonance Repatterning Institute, LLC
P.O. Box 4578
Scottsdale, Arizona 85261, USA
ResonanceRepatterning.net
info@ResonanceRepatterning.net

The information in this self-help book is intended for research and educational purposes only. **The author does not present any part of this work, directly or indirectly, for the diagnosis or prescription of any disease or condition. People who use the information in this book or receive sessions from Resonance Repatterning practitioners take responsibility for consulting the health professional of their choice regarding all matters pertaining to their physical and mental health.**

Cover Design: Carol White *carol@saltriverpublishing.com* and
George Foster *george@fostercovers.com*

Previous editions were called SELF-HEALING MODALITIES FOR QUANTUM CHANGE USED IN THE RESONANCE REPATTERNING SYSTEM.

Seventh Edition 2014 Paperback
17 16 15 14 9 8 7 6 5 4 3 VIII VII
ISBN 978-1-937710-03-3
Printed in USA

CONTENTS

A BALL OF LIGHT AND FOUR TRUTHS **vii–xxiv**

WAYS TO USE SPIRAL UP **1–8**

INDEX OF 127 ENERGIZING OPTIONS **9–12** / *blue pages*

- **A. Process Options** 13
- **B. Sound Options** 27
- **C. Color and Light Options** 75
- **D. Movement Options** 107
- **E. Breath Options** 163
- **F. Energy Contact Options** 189
- **G. Essential Oil Options** 233

POSITIVE ACTIONS **243–264**

- Index of Positive Actions 245 / *yellow page*
- Positive Actions 247

A SCIENTIST SPEAKS **265–293**

- The Science of Spirals: A thirty-year adventure by James L. Oschman, PhD 267
- Afterword by James L. Oschman, PhD 283

RESOURCES 295–324

- Understanding the formatting prompts 297
- CD suggestions for free movement 300
- References and further reading for SPIRAL UP! 301
- What can I do next? 302
- Training in Resonance Repatterning 303
- Seminar descriptions 305
- Eight points of interest to clients 308
- Repatterning Practitioners Association USA 309
- The Vision of the Resonance Repatterning® Institute 310
- The Mission of the Resonance Repatterning® Institute 311
- Spiral Up supplies 312
- LIVING IN TUNE – TURN YOUR PROBLEMS INTO JOY 316
  52 Web radio shows with Chloe Faith Wordsworth
- The story behind SPIRAL UP! 320
- About the author 321
- Acknowledgments 322

A BALL OF LIGHT AND FOUR TRUTHS

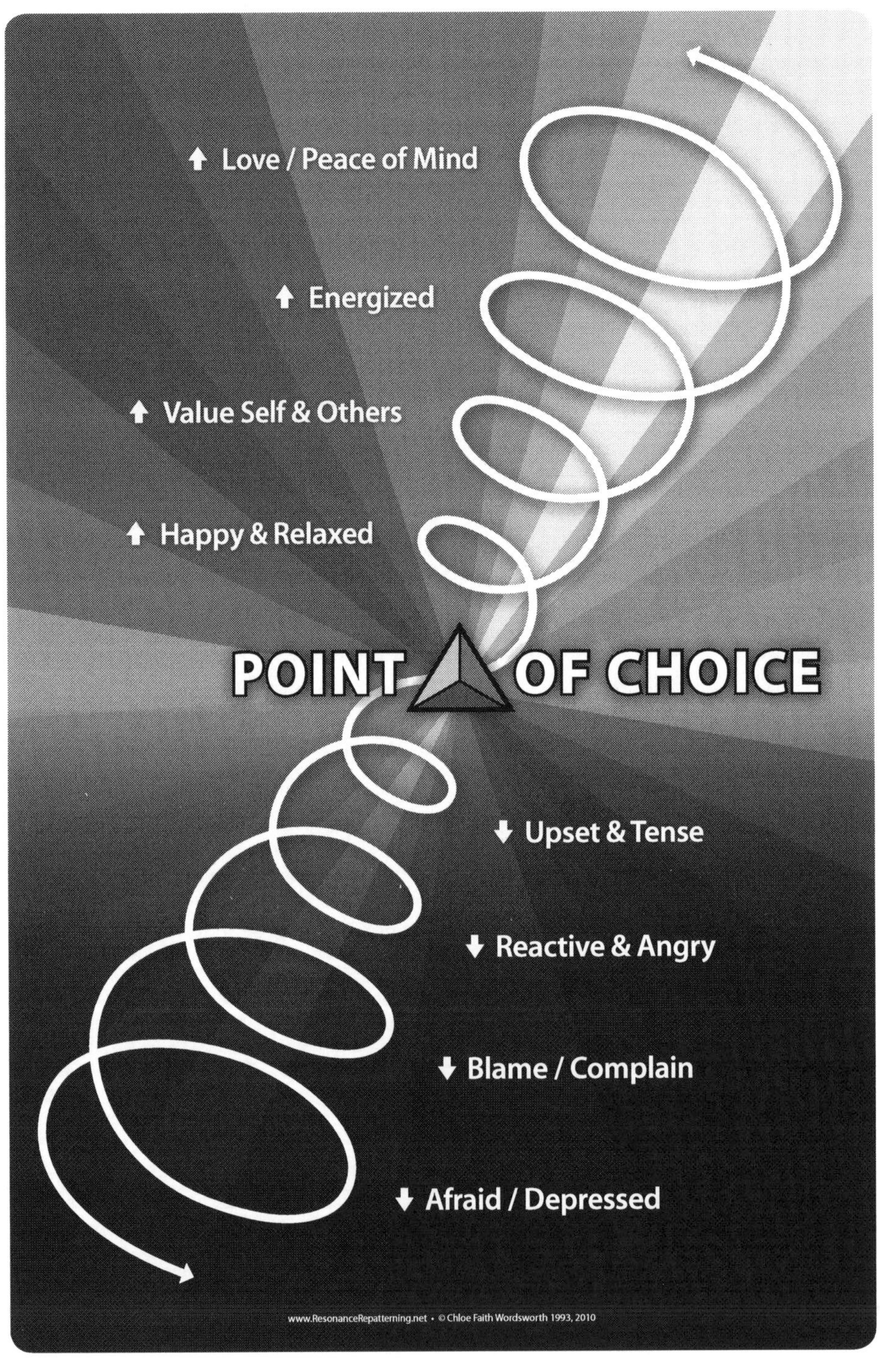

Love / Peace of Mind
Energized
Value Self & Others
Happy & Relaxed
POINT OF CHOICE
Upset & Tense
Reactive & Angry
Blame / Complain
Afraid / Depressed
www.ResonanceRepatterning.net • © Chloe Faith Wordsworth 1993, 2010

A BALL OF LIGHT AND FOUR TRUTHS

In an African village a group of women had an idea about how to handle their husbands when they returned home drunk and beat their wives and children. Whenever the abuse began, a child would run to all the surrounding huts. Within minutes the women of the village were standing outside the hut of the drunken husband, calling out "We love you, we love you," over and over, laughing and singing. And the abuse stopped.

These women were at their best, 'right now,' in the moment – the spiral up state. The drunken abusive husband, in a spiral down state, was not at his best. But in the middle of his drunkenness and abuse, something changed for him and his wife. The input of loving energy from the women shifted his resonance with violence and his wife's resonance with being abused. And in that moment everyone was empowered to spiral up to their best.

Spiraling up means we help ourselves and others move through any problem, trauma or shock by resonating with the optimal frequency range that supports living the best of who we are.

At our optimal frequency range we experience deep relaxation, a sense of lightness and peace, self-confidence, trust, compassion, love, integrity and a happiness from within ourselves that has no external cause. Physical health, and going into action to do those things that make health possible, is also a characteristic of this spiral up frequency range.

When we don't resonate with our optimal frequency range, we automatically experience its shadow – the life-depleting characteristics, actions, attitudes and life of a spiral down state of being.

We know when we are not resonating at our best frequency range: irritation, impatience, lack of self-confidence, fear, anger, disharmonious relationships, negative habits we can't break, positive habits we can't sustain, addictions, eating processed junk food, depression, a lack of joy and humor, worry, dishonesty, exhaustion, stress we can't handle – these are just a few signs that tell us we are no longer resonating or vibrating at our optimal frequency range. They let us know that our energy needs to spiral up.

What is hopeful is that being at our best frequency range is built in to who we are. It is a law of nature that there is a range of frequencies where we naturally function well. We know, for example:

- When our blood pressure is 120/90 to 100/60, we function at our best. Out of this range, and we get sick or we die.
- When our body temperature hovers around 98.6 degrees Fahrenheit, we are healthy. Two degrees higher than this, and we go to bed. Eight degrees higher for more than a day or two usually leads to death.
- The pH of our blood has a tiny range of frequencies that are optimal for supporting life: slightly alkaline at 7.365 to 7.4. Below this range leads to acidity. Acidity is followed by decreased oxygen levels (cancer cells survive without oxygen), joint inflammation, muscle tension, pain and weakness, heart and pancreatic problems, the death of our cells (old age), and in fact almost all illness. Our body will even remove calcium from our bones and teeth to maintain this optimal alkaline pH range in our blood.
- On the mental and emotional level, there is a best frequency range for positive thoughts, attitudes and feelings. Out of this range we have negative thoughts, attitudes and feelings that have an instantaneous negative effect on each of our trillions of cells, including the DNA within the nucleus of each cell. The experiment in which participants had either loving, appreciative thoughts or negative, critical thoughts illustrates this effect: appreciation and gratitude lengthened the DNA strands and made more codes available, whereas criticism and negative thoughts shorten the DNA strands and turned off some of its codes.

Disease and any negative state of mind is simply a sign that an organ or a way of thinking and feeling have lost their optimal vibration. As a result our natural capacity to function well is impaired.

Most of us spend our life randomly shuttling in and out of our optimal frequency range. One day we may be at our best and the next day, or hour, we may be at our worst. The question is why is positive change like a heavy piano we are trying to heave upstairs? It's exhausting, takes a lot of time, and often results in our giving up or not even trying. Positive change is built in to who we are; it should be like a ramp that allows us to move a piano up the stairs with ease and pleasure.

So what does this ramp that supports ease and joyful change consist of? Four truths.

Living these four truths helps us move effortlessly with strength and resilience through the challenges of life. Living these truths helps us realign ourselves with nature's law. Nature's law supports us in accessing our optimal frequency range and regaining our sense of well-being.

The four truths of positive change

- Resonance
- Point of Choice
- An input of coherent energy
- A system that works

RESONANCE

The first truth of positive change is Resonance. All positive change is based on transforming what we resonate with, because what we resonate with is what we experience. What we don't resonate with, we don't experience.

For instance, if we resonate with the frequency of health and vitality, we will want to eat healthy life-giving food, and we will be motivated to transform any negative attitudes and habits that lead to poor health.

Using joy as an example, we can see from the simplified diagram that follows what resonance, or being in sync, looks like. If our frequencies are in sync with the frequencies of joy, we have more energy and joy in our life because **frequencies that are in sync are amplified** (known as constructive interference).

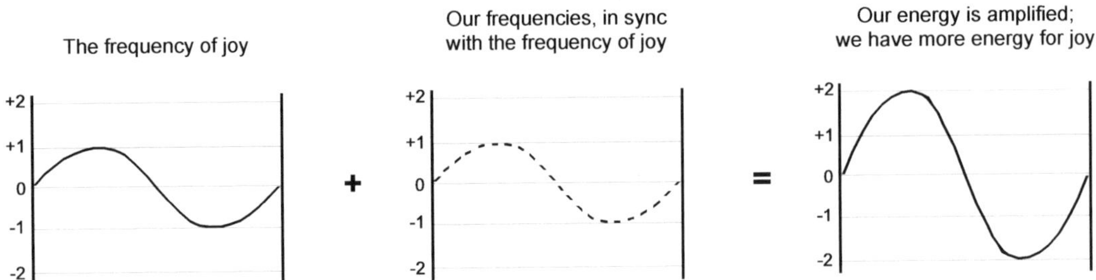

If our frequencies are out of sync with the frequency of joy, we don't resonate with joy. We then have less energy for joy because **out-of-sync frequencies are diminished** (known as destructive interference). As a result, we may experience sadness, discontent, lethargy, upset, moodiness or depression.

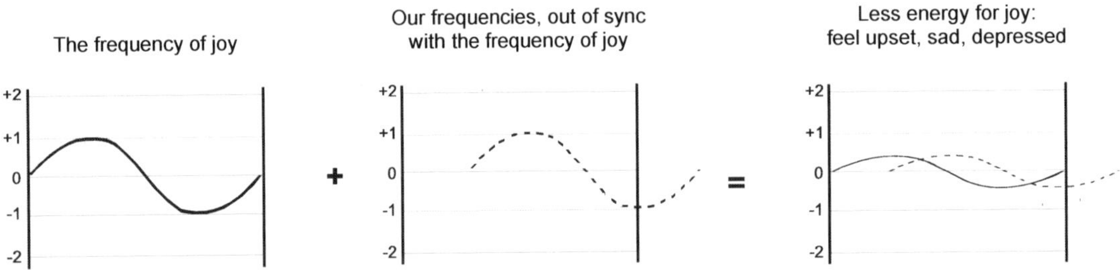

Resonance is about recognizing that when 'good' things happen to us, it is because we resonate with positive feelings, thoughts and situations (constructive interference). And when 'bad' things happen, it is because we no longer resonate with positive feelings, thoughts and situations (destructive interference).

A professor in the early 1900s is said to have asked his students a question: "Do you believe in God?" The students said yes. Then he asked, "Do you believe in evil?" Again they said yes. He then said, "If God created everything, it follows that God is evil."

The next day one of the students put his hand up and asked the professor a question: "Do you believe in light?" The professor said yes. The student then asked, "Do you believe in darkness?" Again the professor said yes. The student finished: "Darkness does not exist. It is simply a word we use to denote the absence of light. Similarly, evil is a word we use to denote the absence of God's love in our heart." The student, it is said, was Einstein.

There is only the positive. When we are out of sync with the positive, we don't resonate with the positive and we experience 'the dark'. Being our best means we resonate with our optimal frequency range, the 'light'. If we don't resonate with that range, we experience an absence of our best.

Like a radio receiver, we tune in to specific frequency vibrations and the information or programs they carry.
The frequency range we resonate with attunes us either to health or disease, success or failure, joy or misery, and to positive or negative ways of thinking, feeling and acting.
The quality of our life, down to the smallest detail, depends on the kind of frequencies we resonate with.

POINT OF CHOICE

The second truth is that at every moment we have a choice: If I am angry, do I want to be calm? If I am nervous before a test, interview or speaking in public, do I want to think clearly and be confident, inspired and relaxed? If I am overwhelmed by too many things on my To Do list, do I want to be focused so I easily complete each project, with energy to spare at the end of the day?

If we want to be our best, our first step is to make the choice for something better. In Resonance Repatterning we call this the Point of Choice: "I want, choose and am ready for (*name the positive state of mind and action you want*)." In other words, we say strongly and with conviction that we want to come back into sync with our optimal vibration.

The Point of Choice is about recognizing that we have a problem and then making the first move towards resonance with wanting, choosing and being ready for something different from our problem.

This choosing of the positive is the first step in all self-healing. No one can force healing or positive change on us. Something within us, with help from others and life, drives us to recognize that we have a problem. And if we want something more positive, life moves us in that direction.

For instance, if I am feeling overwhelmed by how much I have to do and I am rushing around feeling inefficient and unfocused:

- My first step is to stop and recognize that I have a problem: I resonate with being overwhelmed.

- Now I am at my Point of Choice: Do I want something different or do I want to stay as I am? If I want something different, I say the Point of Choice statement: "Yes, I want, choose and am ready (*and I name what I want: to be clear about my priorities and calmly focus on one priority at a time*)."

- I then use an Energizing Option to resonate with the optimal frequency range of my intention.

This one small step of making our Point of Choice can initiate a life change because it amplifies our energy for what is positive. *See #3 Ways to use Spiral Up*

As you can see from the Power of Your Point of Choice diagram, life is a constant wobble between coherence and non-coherence, order and chaos, equilibrium and disequilibrium, good things happening and not-so-good things happening, between trust and fear. We need to remember that we always have a Point of

The Power of *Your* Point of Choice

Do you want to continue being immersed in your problems or do you want to make a quantum leap to a higher state of consciousness and well-being?

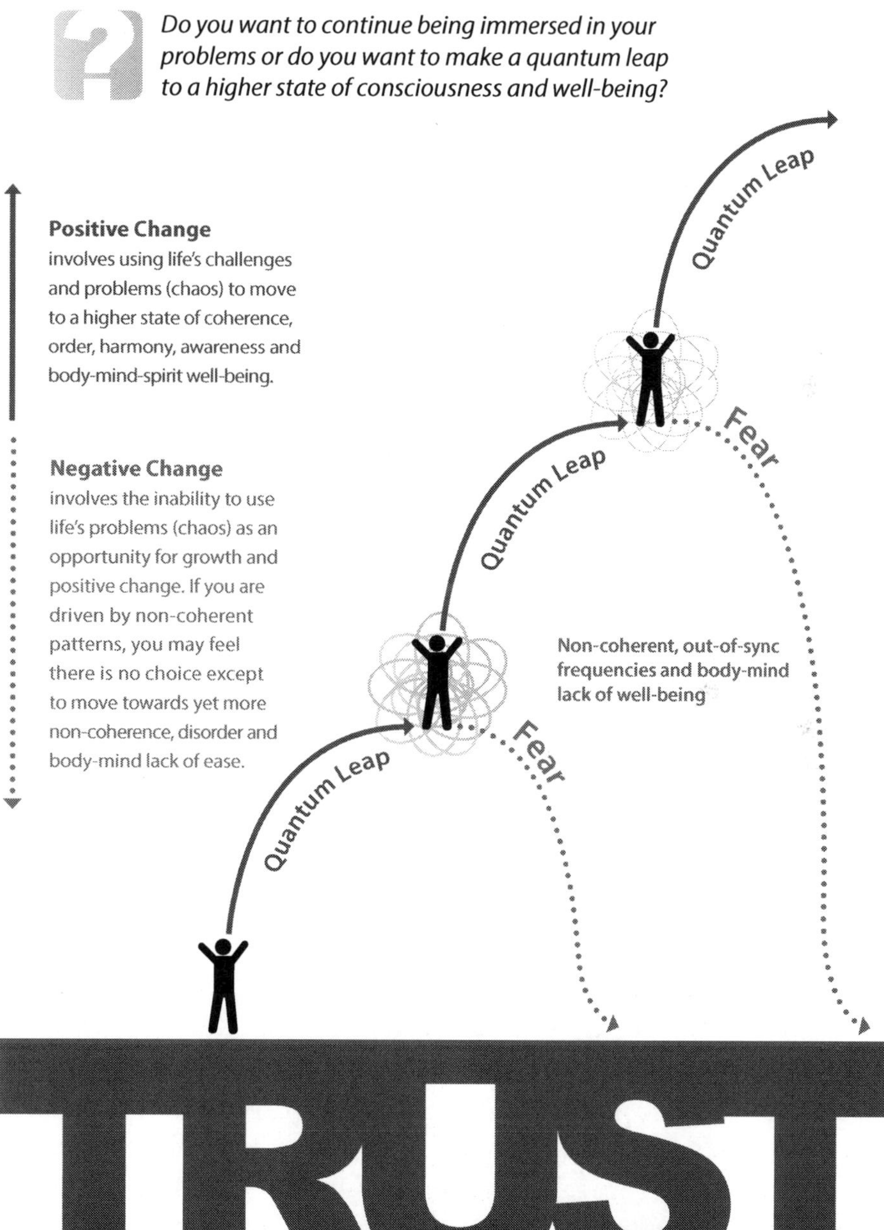

Positive Change
involves using life's challenges and problems (chaos) to move to a higher state of coherence, order, harmony, awareness and body-mind-spirit well-being.
Negative Change
involves the inability to use life's problems (chaos) as an opportunity for growth and positive change. If you are driven by non-coherent patterns, you may feel there is no choice except to move towards yet more non-coherence, disorder and body-mind lack of ease.
Quantum Leap
Quantum Leap
Quantum Leap
Fear
Fear
Non-coherent, out-of-sync frequencies and body-mind lack of well-being
TRUST

Choice – that we can choose to resonate with our best, especially when we are facing the chaotic, not-so-good happenings of life. The moment we resonate with our Point of Choice, we immediately become receptive to spiraling up once more to our optimal frequency range and to a positive state of body, emotions and mind.

Trust is the foundation for making a Point of Choice for something better. When we resonate with trusting that positive change is possible for us, no matter how desperate our state of mind or the circumstances of our life, we become receptive to the field of limitless possibilities that physicists (and spiritual adepts since ancient times) talk about.

Fear-based words and thoughts like "It's impossible; I can't; I'll never be able to do it; if that's true, why hasn't the government done something about it; he/she/ it won't change; it's his/her fault; I just have to live with it" give the message to our limbic brain and cerebral cortex that what we want is impossible. Our brain then does its best to make it difficult, exhausting or impossible to manifest our goals.

When we resonate with our optimal frequency range, we make our Point of Choice for something better and move forward with trust in spite of our fears. In fact our fears force us to face our trust issues. Unhesitating positive action aligned with our Point of Choice intention gives the message to our limbic brain and cerebral cortex that anything is possible; and our limbic brain and cerebral cortex then do their best to make our Point of Choice possible.

The upward spiral towards our best begins to happen automatically when we reframe our way of thinking and resonate with "Anything is possible; I can do this; I will go into action for what is true for me; I can change how I see this situation; I make the Point of Choice to be (*honest, loving, compassionate, courageous, respectful, humorous, etc.*); I am ready to explore new possibilities with optimism."

An airplane never flies directly from point A to point B. The pilot constantly adjusts the course of a plane's flight so it actually arrives at its goal – its planned destination.

A clown on a unicycle on a tightrope has to constantly adjust his or her balance.

We ourselves are living a balancing act on the unicycle of our body-mind, on the tightrope of our life! We need to constantly make adjustments so we keep our energy at its optimal frequency range. And resonating with our Point of Choice helps us maintain our balance so we live our best.

AN INPUT OF COHERENT ENERGY

The third truth is that all positive change depends on an input of coherent energy – whether that coherent energy comes from the love of a wise being, listening to music that touches us, wearing a particular color or sitting in a quiet spot and tuning in to 'the still quiet voice within'.

For thousands of years humans have shared and passed on their knowledge of how to maintain balance of body, emotions and mind – healing modalities that input coherent energy that make all good things possible.

"Coherence," writes author James L. Oschman in his foreword to QUANTUM CHANGE MADE EASY, "is a major concept in new physics. Coherence occurs when an astronomical number of subatomic particles move into sync with each other in their pulsation – they become aligned and part of an orchestral whole. Coherence is more than just a few particles resonating with each other and pulsing together – our whole system becomes aligned and undergoes a quantum leap to a higher energy state."

In Resonance Repatterning we call this input of coherent energy an Energizing Option. An Energizing Option is a thought, word or action that inputs a specific frequency – a coherent pulsation – that brings the frequencies of our body, emotions and mind back into sync with their optimal range of frequencies.

As a result of doing an Energizing Option, we resonate with our best. We may experience this in-sync state as a sense of lightness as if a burden has been lifted; or as relief from pain or freedom from the problem that was upsetting us; or perhaps life feels more ordered and meaningful – once more an adventure to be lived rather than a stress or chore to be endured.

Dr. Emoto's well-known photographs show how the disordered patterns of polluted water become brilliant crystalline patterns when positive words like 'love' and 'thank you' are written on the vial of water. The input of coherent energy provided by the words 'love' and 'thank you' is sufficient to bring the out-of-sync frequencies of the polluted water back into sync or resonance with their optimal state of order, clarity and purity.

Every negative mind state, every upset, is simply a word to denote our lack of resonance with its opposite or positive quality – our natural state, our "best." When we input coherent energy we too come back into sync with our 'clarity' and 'purity'.

New Physics and how many Energizing Options we need to do

New Physics tells us that living beings are a **non-linear system**. This means we may need only a small input of energy, at the right time and place, for a positive response to occur throughout our whole body-mind system. One Energizing Option that inputs coherent energy is often enough to shift our resonance (once we have identified the change in resonance we need at this moment in time).

Machines, on the other hand, are **linear systems.** This means that a large input of energy is required to get a significant response. For example, it takes a huge input of energy to get a rocket off the ground. Sometimes we may feel like a linear system that needs a huge amount of energy to get us moving in a new and positive direction. But however resistant we may feel to making a positive change, we are non-linear: a tiny input of the right energy at the right time can do the job!

We are a non-linear system: this means that even doing an Energizing Option on ourselves daily or when we feel off track – despondent, overwhelmed, angry, distracted, afraid or when we have negative thoughts churning repetitively in our head – is enough to bring about a beneficial change physically, emotionally and mentally.

However, doing one or two Energizing Options doesn't automatically bring self-healing of all physical and mental symptoms. For deeper changes we may need to identify and transform the unconscious patterns we resonate with that are causing our body-mind distortions. After transforming unconscious patterns, we often find ourselves ready to incorporate positive life-style changes for a more energized life.

We are wired for wellness.
We are wired to live at our optimal frequency range.
The Point of Choice is our decision
to use the Energizing Options
so we resonate with our optimal frequency range.
The positive change in our thinking
and the way we relate and act
bring us the joy and vitality of a spiral up life.

A SYSTEM THAT WORKS

If we want positive change in ourselves, our life and our relationships, there are truths we can live to bring this about. To summarize:

- **Truth #1 Resonance** We need to change what we resonate with. This truth is not about changing the other person! Our life is a projection of the mental state and attitudes we ourselves resonate with.
- **Truth #2 Point of Choice** We need to resonate with making our Point of Choice to be and do something different and positive, to spiral up to our optimal frequency range – to be our best at this moment in time.

- **Truth #3 An Input of Coherent Energy** We need an energy input to synchronize our frequencies with what is energizing, light-giving and life-giving – called in Resonance Repatterning the Energizing Options.
- **Truth #4 A System that Works** We need a system that enables us to free ourselves from the non-coherent spiral down range of frequencies and enables us to return once more to our natural spiral up state of optimal coherence.

  Such a system enables us to maintain our spiral up way of being more and more consistently. When we drop into a spiral down state, we don't have to stay there: we know what to do to spiral up to our best frequency range once more.

Many years ago I was teaching a seminar in the Fundamentals of Resonance Repatterning. One of the students sat by herself at the back of the room. She didn't talk, she didn't smile and there was nothing I could do in the seminar or in the breaks to draw her out. She made it clear she wanted to be left alone. Towards the end of the day I talked about the power of an Energizing Option called the Zip-Ups, which strengthens a core channel in Acupuncture known as the Conception Vessel. I explained that if you move your fingers up the midline of your body every time you hear de-energizing words or see de-energizing images, this will help you maintain your spiral up state of energy, rather than lose your energy when seeing or hearing what is negative. I then demonstrated on the students how negative thoughts, words and sights literally de-energize the brain and body and how positive thoughts, words and sights energize the brain and body.

The next day the withdrawn woman arrived anything but withdrawn: full of energy, she almost danced into the room. She sat in the front row, smiling and happy. When I asked her what had happened, she said she wanted to wait for the whole group to arrive so she could tell everyone.

She shared with the group that although she was thirty-eight, she still lived with her parents because she couldn't work – she not only had chronic insomnia, but her body was wracked with pain: every joint and muscle hurt, day and night.

At the end of the first day of the seminar, she decided to experiment with doing the Zip-Ups we had talked about. She told us that she had never heard a single positive word from her mother or father: every word they spoke was negative. She spent the whole evening doing Zip-Ups in response to every negative word that came out of their mouth.

In the morning she woke up thinking that something was wrong. Suddenly she realized that she had slept for eight hours: no insomnia for the first time she could remember. But then something else felt wrong. And she became aware that for the first time in six years she was free of all pain. She looked at us and said, "I'm so happy I could dance in front of all of you right now!"

Anything is possible:

- This woman realized that she needed to change her resonance with her parents' negativity
- She made her Point of Choice to do something different
- She went into action with the Zip-Ups Energizing Option – free of fear, hesitation and doubt

As a result she moved into sync with the positive – her own best frequency range that she was ready for at that moment. And in one evening, symptoms of many years' standing disappeared.

Of course, we don't know the end of the story. Did the change last? Was she able to maintain her new-found coherence?

After living with so much negativity all her life, she would most likely be greatly helped by a system that would support her in transforming her resonance with unconscious beliefs, feelings, compensations and survival trauma patterns in response to her neglect/abuse experiences.

These unconscious patterns are directly associated with her symptoms of pain and insomnia and her inability to become independent of her parents at age thirty-eight.

If this woman only needs one Energizing Option for her frequencies to move back into sync with their optimal spiral up range, she will be able to maintain her new state of well-being and happiness. But if one Energizing Option is not enough for her to maintain her resonance with her own personal best frequency range, she has the choice to do some work on transforming her patterns of negative resonance.

Searching for a system that works

As a licensed practitioner of the Five Element system of Acupuncture and as a student, practitioner and teacher of numerous alternative healthcare systems, I spent more than thirty years asking questions about what allows people to self-heal (to identify and transform what comes in the way of their resonating with their best frequency range).

My questions constantly pushed me to my growing edge to find answers; and the answers led me to develop my own personal 'system that works' – **The Resonance Repatterning® System** (originally called Holographic Repatterning). Since 1990 this system has been successfully applied with my own clients, then with students who in their turn became practitioners or teachers of Resonance Repatterning. In this way Resonance Repatterning has quietly spread by word of mouth to more than 15,000 people around the world.

How does the Resonance Repatterning® System work

- We use the muscle checking technique (Applied Kinesiology) to first identify all the out-of-sync frequencies (the beliefs, feelings, perceptions, projections, earlier unmet needs, unconscious patterns etc.) underlying any problem – past or present – that is causing a de-energized spiral down state.

- We then use the universal list of Spiral Up Energizing Options. With muscle checking we are able to identify the precise Option for bringing the frequencies identified in the session back into sync with what is energizing and the client's 'best'.

- In addition to the Spiral Up Options, we use the four other Keys of the Resonance Repatterning System: Orientation, Problems into Opportunities, Intention for a New Possibility and one of over a hundred Repatterning processes – any of which may be needed to help us self-heal our old unconscious patterns, whether personal, family or generational.

- In addition, we often need to do certain Positive Actions *p.245* to detoxify and/or rebuild our body-mind system, to anchor new neural pathways in the body and brain for the positive patterns we want to integrate or to move us towards the healthy life-style changes we are ready for.

There are many systems that may help us transform our patterns and past shocks. As we are drawn to the system we resonate with, our resonance takes us beyond "this is the best" or "this is the only thing worth doing." There is no competition between one system or another, or one Energizing Option or another.

The ultimate "system that works" is spiritual. When we feel spiritually connected to the Divine power within, we automatically spiral up to our best no matter how hard the circumstances of our life may be: we aren't knocked off balance by the ups and downs of life; we understand that everything has a purpose and a lesson for us; and we live in a state of acceptance, joy and gratitude.

But besides our soul, we also have a mind, feelings and a physical body. If we have a toothache, we go to a dentist! Whether we follow a spiritual path or not, having something practical we can do to change a negative state of mind and feelings is reassuring, empowering and boosts our self-confidence that we really can help ourselves.

In the Resonance Repatterning® System we believe we can make the Point of Choice in any situation to align our energy with our optimal frequency range – to spiral up to be our best. When our energy is in sync with what is positive, we become coherent and manifest coherence in every sphere of our life.

- When our body-mind system is coherent (in sync with our optimal frequency range), all our trillions of parts function perfectly as one harmonious whole – expressing spirit through our mind and emotions and the vehicle of our body. Like an orchestra that consists of many individual instruments, each with its own notes and rhythms that together create the magic of music, so with us, when we are in sync, we spiral up to create the magic of a meaningful life.
- The flow of energy that sustains life (the field of energy that Einstein talks about) moves easily through a coherent system. This means that every

coherent choice we make, no matter how small it may be, has more power in it than we realize.

- James L. Oschman writes in his foreword to QUANTUM CHANGE MADE EASY, "When atoms and molecules are energized, they can vibrate in unison and emit coherent energy such as that produced by a laser." The coherence of a laser gives lasers focused power. In contrast, an electric light bulb emits non-coherent energy that is diffused and weak and tends to burn out. Most of us are more like 60-watt light bulbs in the process of burning out, rather than the powerful laser beam that is our potential.
- In every situation, we can choose to stay in our spiral down state and burn out, quickly or slowly, like an old light bulb; or we can use the four truths we've talked about here to become coherent, powerful and focused.
- **When we are coherent, when we resonate with our optimal frequency range, positive change becomes possible. And this transformation can happen in a few seconds, minutes, hours or over the years of our life. It's not the speed of positive change that matters; it's the journey towards being our best and radiating our light that counts.**

Nearly two thousand years ago Plotinus wrote,
"Let the body think of the Spirit as streaming, pouring, rushing and shining into it from all sides."
This is our potential:
to spiral up for more streaming and shining: to radiate our light.

The poet Ezra Pound writes, "The book should be a ball of light in one's hand." This is the aim of SPIRAL UP! – to help all of us bring more light into our lives.

Chloe Faith Wordsworth
June 20, 2014
Scottsdale, Arizona

WAYS TO USE SPIRAL UP

HOW TO USE THE ENERGIZING OPTIONS IF YOU HAVE NOT STUDIED RESONANCE REPATTERNING®

1. **Scan the Index of Energizing Options** ***pp.9–12 / blue pages*** and **choose the one** that you feel will help you in the situation you are in. All Energizing Options input coherent energy; whichever one you choose, it will help! Follow your **gut feeling** as to the details you feel you need when doing an Option. **Of course, if you know muscle checking, you will follow the (mcs) prompts.**

2. Also **scan** ***pp.3–8 / gold pages*** – **Ways to Use Spiral Up.** Choose whichever of the *ways* you feel will be most helpful for you in the situation you are in, follow the directions, and then do an Energizing Option to bring your frequencies back into sync with their optimal range.

3. **Trust your gut feelings:** In an interesting experiment of computer generated pictures – negative and neutral – Heartmath researchers proved that the body responds a few seconds before the computer had selected the picture! On some level, we know more than we realize. *See the documentary* I am.

All Spiral Up Options are positive. As you use them, you will soon discover how they energize, calm and clear the brain of negative or repetitive ways of thinking; how they balance the energy of your body, emotions and mind, stimulate your energy field when you are sluggish or confused and bring calmness when you feel overwhelmed, hyperactive, upset, angry, fearful or depressed.

WAYS TO USE SPIRAL UP

1. **FEELING A LITTLE OFF?**
   What To Do:
   Scan the list of *Energizing Options pp.9–12 / blue pages* and do whichever ones you feel drawn to. Every Option inputs energy that aims to help you feel better from within yourself.

2. **You are stuck in a problem? Ask yourself, "WHAT DO I WANT INSTEAD?"**
   What To Do:
   - Ask yourself, "What do I want instead of (*name your problem*)?"
   - Say aloud, "Instead of (*name the problem*) I (*name what you want to do or feel that is positive*)."
   - Look at the list of Energizing Options. Which one will help you resonate with what you want, instead of resonating with your problem?
   - Do the Energizing Option. Now close your eyes and notice what's changed.

3. **You've spiraled down. Now you have a POINT OF CHOICE: stay where you are or spiral up?**
   Positive change and self-healing always begin when we commit to something better. This is called our Point of Choice.
   - The Point of Choice makes us receptive to what New Physics calls the field of limitless energy – a field of infinite possibilities.
   - Making the Point of Choice helps us adjust our balance on the tightrope of life.
   - The Point of Choice helps us to live in sync with our higher consciousness – the basis for all well-being, positive change and self-healing.

What To Do:

- For any problem you are facing, ask yourself "What do I want instead?"
- Be clear about what you want to do and how you want to be right now.
- Now make your Point of Choice statement: "Yes, I want, choose and am ready for/to (*name what you want instead of your problem / what you want to do / how you want to be that is positive*)".
- Look at the list of Energizing Options. Which one stands out for you that you imagine will help you resonate with your Point of Choice?
- Do the Energizing Option. Close your eyes and notice how you feel. Now go into action, no matter how small it may be, for what you want.

4. WANT TO SAVE YOUR DAY?

Disorganized and losing your confidence? Feeling tired or frazzled? Stress is getting the better of you? Getting reactive, irritated, angry, upset, scared, anxious?

What To Do:

- Ask yourself, "What do I need that would help me most right now?" (Confidence? Focus? To relax? To calm down? To trust in God?)
- Look at the list of Energizing Options. Which one stands out for you that will help you resonate with the quality you need?
- Do the Energizing Option while being aware of the quality you need that will help you most right now. Then close your eyes and notice how you feel.

5. NEGATIVE FEELINGS that keep you trapped in your problem

What To Do:

- Name your problem and notice any tension in your body.
- Name two negative feelings that come up for you when you think of your problem. Say them: "I feel (*name the negative feelings*)."

- Look at the list of Energizing Options. Which one do you feel will change your resonance with the negative feelings and your problem?
- Do the Energizing Option. Now close your eyes. How do you feel?

6. **THREE NEGATIVE ATTITUDES that hurt you, your relationships and your life**
   - **Blame, criticism, anger** Are you complaining about your situation and blaming and criticizing someone else, or others?
   - **Helpless, hopeless, victimized** Do you feel, "It's hopeless....I've been betrayed, let down....There's nothing I can do....I'm helpless....Why don't people help me the way I help them?" You want someone/something to save you, help you – even if it is winning the lotto!
   - **Savior pattern** Do you feel it's your job to save the day, to make everything okay for everyone? – "I'll do it, even though I'm exhausted."

   What To Do:
   - **For blame and criticism** Say aloud: "I build a positive relationship with (*name person you are criticizing*) that is free of blame, and is based on our strengths. I lovingly and with respect communicate about actions I find difficult, and then I let go."
   - **For feeling victimized** Say aloud: "I take responsibility for the situation I am in. I accept it as it is and I go into positive action for what is right."
   - **For feeling it's your responsibility to make everything alright** Say aloud: "I help (*name person / others*) in whatever way is appropriate, while also meeting my own needs. I communicate my needs clearly and lovingly."
   - Look at the list of Energizing Options. Which one do you imagine will help you resonate with the attitude you need for showing up in a positive, strong and confident way in your life?
   - Do the Energizing Option. Close your eyes. What feels different?

7. Why is ACCEPTANCE essential for healing, positive change and survival?

People who survive disasters like airplane crashes in remote regions of the world are those who accept what is, and then go into positive action.

Acceptance gives you the energy you need for handling any difficulty. Resistance blocks the flow of your energy and makes self-healing and positive action hard or impossible.

When in pain, sick, in an accident or you are facing a stressful situation, remember to accept.

What To Do:

- Say aloud: "I accept the present challenging situation free of resistance (regrets / fear / blame / anger). Thank you."
- Now look at the list of Energizing Options. Which one stands out for you that you imagine will help you to resonate with acceptance?
- Do the Energizing Option. Close your eyes and notice how you feel.

8. When LIFE IS TOO MUCH and you can't handle anything more

What To Do:

- Ask yourself, "What weakness in myself is involved?"
- Ask yourself, "What positive quality do I have that will give me the strength to overcome my weakness and deal with this situation positively?"
- Look at the list of Energizing Options. Which one stands out for you that you imagine will help you resonate with the strengths you need?
- Do the Energizing Option. Notice what's changed.

9. The DIAMOND OF INTENTION: manifesting what's best

The significance of creating positive intentions or goals and going into action is that intention + action make us receptive to the field of limitless energy and grace.

There are four sides to every intention – the Diamond – that you need to resonate with:

1. Ask, "What do I want to **do** or **be** (today/this week) that is positive?"
2. What **pleasurable feeling** will this give me?
3. What **action** do I need to take, no matter how small the action is?
4. **Visualize the action and intention** as already manifested.

What To Do:

- Look at the list of Energizing Options. Which one stands out for you that you imagine will help you resonate with the four sides of your Diamond Intention?

- Do the Energizing Option after saying your intention or goal aloud, as though you have already achieved it; be aware of the pleasurable feeling and visualize your successful action. After completing the Energizing Option, close your eyes and notice how you feel.

- Go into positive action towards manifesting your intention, however small the action may be.

10. Spiral Up OUT OF NEGATIVE BELIEFS

We have thousands of unconscious negative beliefs in response to our past that keep us repeating difficult relationship patterns and life situations. Negative beliefs create stress, make us acidic and distort our light.

What To Do:

- Look at the shortlist of 12 negative beliefs. Which one do you imagine you resonate with in your present situation?

- Look at the list of Energizing Options. Which one do you imagine will shift your resonance with your negative belief and your spiral down state? Do the Energizing Option. Close your eyes and notice how you feel.

Negative Beliefs

1. My (fear • anger • *name other*) stops me from receiving the love I long for.
2. (I have no control • I am out of control) .
3. I am powerless to say (No to what is **not** right • Yes to what **is** right) for me.
4. (I don't deserve to be happy • I can't laugh • Life is heavy).
5. (I am alone • I don't belong).
6. (I am inadequate • I am worthless).
7. Life is (threatening • confusing • overwhelming • stressful).
8. I blame myself for what happened.
9. I am a failure.
10. I (deny • ignore • distrust) my feelings and my inner knowing.
11. I am stupid.
12. (No one is attracted to me • People don't like me).

11. Resonate with POSITIVE BELIEFS and spiral up!

- Look at the short list of 12 positive beliefs. Which one do you **need** to resonate with that will help you in your present situation?

- Look at the list of Energizing Options. Which one stands out for you that you imagine will help you resonate with your positive belief and help you spiral up to be your best? Do the Energizing Option. How do you feel?

1. (I am lovable • I open my heart to receive love).
2. (I have so much to give • I make a positive ding in the universe).
3. I enjoy laughter and lightness.
4. I am confident and capable.
5. I am different from my (mother • father • past painful experiences).
6. I am innocent.
7. I relax and enjoy life as an adventure.
8. (Life is safe • My life has meaning • I find my purpose in life).
9. I love and accept myself and others.
10. I am fully alive.
11. I am intelligent, creative and I go into action to achieve what I want.
12. Eating healthy food brings me pleasure, energy and health.

INDEX OF 127 ENERGIZING OPTIONS
TO BE YOUR BEST RIGHT NOW

(mcs) {A–G} for the section needed and then for the numbered item you need.

A. PROCESS OPTIONS 13–27

1. Orientation: Energizing and Soothing Options 15
2. Pause for Centering 16
3. Integration Process for Completions 17
4. Stature of Power and Creativity 20
5. Heart Entrainment 22
6. 24-Hour Time Clock 23
7. Energy Constriction Release (ECR) PROCESS GUIDE *p.21*
8. Diffusion Process PROCESS GUIDE *p.23*
9. Fusion Process PROCESS GUIDE *p.27*

B. SOUND OPTIONS 27–73

1. Haaa Sound for Heart Connection 30
2. Laughing Breath 30
3. Toning 32
4. Gobbledygook 33
5. Appreciation 34
6. Harmonic Overtones 35
7. Clapping 38
8. Humming 38
9. Tuning Forks 39
   - Frequencies of the Om, Naturals, Sharps and Planetary Tuning Forks 40
   - How to use the Tuning Forks 40
   - Information on and intentions for the Planetary Tuning Forks 45
10. Creative Self-Expression 51
11. Developmental Needs Affirmations 55
12. Quantum Healing Codes™ 59
13. Intervals 61

14. Ayurvedic Sounds for the Chakra Energy Centers 63
15. Meridian Consonant Sounds 65
16. Five Element Sounds 69
17. Pentatonic Modes 69

C. COLOR AND LIGHT OPTIONS 75–106

1. Infinity 8s for Absorbing Photons (light) 78
2. Visualizing a Color 79
3. Empowering Memories 80
4. Peripheral Soft Focus Vision 81
5. Palming 82
6. Flower Pattern Cards / Geometric Pattern Cards 83
7. ColorYourWorld Glasses and Color Qualities Chart 86
8. ColorYourWorld Torch and Dinshah Indications Chart 93
9. Circles in the Three Dimensions 101
10. Tracing 102
11. Cleansing the Energy Field with the Seven Colors plus Overtones 103
12. Silk Scarves for the Chakra Energy Centers 104
13. Silk Scarves for the Five Elements 105

D. MOVEMENT OPTIONS 107–161

1. SNS Body Shake-Out 110
2. Free Movement 111
3. Brain-Integrating Cross Crawls 112
4. Yawning and Stretching 113
5. Fountain of Youth Neck Release 114
6. Open Heart Gesture 114
7. Calming Cross-Overs 115
8. Nodding Your Head Yes 116
9. Water 116
10 Chi Kung Bounce, Holding and Energy Circulation 120
11. Diaphragm Anxiety Release 122
12. Shoulder Blade Release 123
13. Katsugen 124
14. Shoulder Joint Opening 126

15. Hip U's, Hula and the Polarity Pyramid 127
16. The Power of Rhythm 129
    - Rumba Rhythm 129
    - Waltz Rhythm 130
17. The Six Fundamental Movements 131
18. Foundation Position for a Stabilized Spine 137
19. Somatic Movements 138
    - Movements to release the Protective-Startle brain-body posture 139
    - Movements to release the Landau brain-body posture 140
    - Movements to release the Trauma brain-body posture 141
20. Makko-ho and the Power of Stretching 142
21. Spinning the Five Platonic Solids 146
22. Spinning 147
23. Chakra Movements with the Silk Scarves 148
24. Lion Pose 153
25. Chi Kung Arm Stretches 154
26. Five Element Movements with Sounds 155
27. Dancing the Five Elements 160

E. BREATH OPTIONS **163–185**

1. Slow Gentle Breathing 167
2. Left Nostril Breath – *anulom-viloma* 168
3. Breath for Mental Tension – *bhramari* 168
4. Calming Breath 169
5. Vitality Breath 170
6. Oxygen Breath 171
7. Control Pause Breath for Stabilizing CO_2 172
8. Throat Breathing 173
9. Control Pause with Creating a Space 173
10. Control Pause with Thymus Tap 174
11. Cleansing Breath 175
12. Pelvic Energizer Breath 175
13. Steam Engine Breath 176
14. Dolphin Breath 177
15. Cellular Breath 177

16. Rainbow Breath 178
17. Sacral Breathing 179
18. Lymphatic Purifying Breath 179
19. Tan T'ien Breath 181
20. Orbital Breath 181
21. Circulation Breath 182
22. Masculine Energy Breath 183
23. Feminine Energy Breath 184
24. Continuous Breath 184
25. Focusing Breath 185
26. Breathing Patterns for the Chakras 185
27. Five Element Breaths 187

F. ENERGY CONTACT OPTIONS **189–232**

1. Brain-Activating Points 191
2. Thymus Tap 192
3. Tongue on the Roof of Your Mouth 192
4. Memory/Listening Ear Massage 193
5. Zip-Ups 194
6. Pulling Your Fingers 195
7. Harmonizing Contact 196
8. Yin Balancing Points 197
9. Yang Balancing Points 198
10. Jin Shin Jyutsu® – The 26 Safety Energy Locks 199
11. Cranial Contacts 223
12. SNS Balancing 227
13. PNS Balancing 228
14. Polarity Contacts *See spiralup127.com for Polarity demonstration*
15. Meridian Massage 228
16. Mu Acupuncture Points 230

G. 18 ESSENTIAL OIL OPTIONS **233–241**

A.
PROCESS OPTIONS

These are step-by-step processes, rather than one Energizing Option alone.

For instance, a woman who had experienced a traumatic marriage and divorce needed the Integration Process for Completions. The practitioner went through each step of the Process in turn. And rather than do this Option for a couple of minutes, as one does on finishing a project or at the end of the day, she spent about forty-five minutes doing this Process Option with the client. By the time they finished, the woman's attitude toward herself and her ex-husband had already begun to shift. Like many clients, she said "I feel light – finally something has been lifted from me."

As processes, each of these Options have a certain number of steps. Follow each step of the Process in the order given.

Process Options are helpful to do

- When you are upset
- When you need to center yourself
- When you need to have a completion or closure on a situation or relationship so you can move forward into new beginnings with more creativity and energy
- When you need to stand in your power
- When you need to let go of your pain and open your heart to love
- When you need to diffuse negativity from your mind, or fuse a positive state into your body-mind field

THE FOUR OVALS FOR EACH OPTION

1. **Muscle check self (mcs) or use your felt sense for the Energizing Option you need**

2. **Read the introduction to the Energizing Option**
   Demo the 'How To' if doing with someone else, or use the video download if needed

3. **Do the Energizing Option**
   - Observe that you are doing it correctly
   - Breathe
   - **(mcs) / felt sense:** This is complete?
   - **(mcs) / felt sense:** Another Option is needed?

4. **After completing the Option**
   - Take a pause to integrate the positive change
   - Recheck your **felt sense:**
     a. Do you feel more relaxed?
     b. Are you breathing more easily?
     c. Do you notice any other positive change?
   - *RR Practitioners recheck *[cr] statements*

1. ORIENTATION: Energizing and Soothing Options

Any of the following Options help when you feel disoriented, upset, out of sorts and need to orient yourself in the direction that nurtures your body-mind and reconnects you to love.

a. (mcs) An energizing Option is needed? (mcs) {1–10}.
Go to the page listed for the energizing Option and follow the directions

1. Toning 32
2. SNS Body Shake-Out 110
3. Free Movement 111
4. Brain-Integrating Cross Crawls 112
5. Water 116
6. Left Nostril Breath 168
7. Brain Activating Points 191
8. Memory/Listening Ear Massage 193
9. Zip-Ups 194
10. Pulling Your Fingers 195

b. (mcs) A soothing Option is needed? (mcs) {1–10}. *Go to the page listed for the soothing Option and follow the directions*

1. Pause for Centering 16
2. Haaa Sound for Heart Connection 30
3. Open Heart Gesture 114
4. Calming Cross-Overs 115
5. Nodding Your Head Yes 116
6. Katsugen 124
7. Breath for Mental Tension 168
8. Thymus Tap 192
9. Tongue on the Roof of Your Mouth 192
10. Harmonizing Contact 196

2. PAUSE FOR CENTERING

This is one of the most powerful ways to center yourself:

- Use the Pause for Centering when you are beginning any new phase of your day.
- Remember to do even a shortened version when you feel upset or disoriented.
- In an argument you can say, "Let's take a pause" or "I need a pause," and start to breathe and relax.
- If you are feeling rushed or overwhelmed, take a pause.
- If a friend is upset, say "Let's slow down and take a pause and breathe."
- This is a wonderful Option to do in a group situation before beginning a meeting or session: just talk through the steps.
- In family situations, practice these steps so when feelings are charged someone can say, "We need to take a pause and breathe."

How To:

Read the following slowly, with a pause at the end of each phrase. Soon you will remember the steps without needing to read them: breathe, relax, connect to your heart.

Eyes
- Close your eyes.

Breath
- Breathe slowly and gently through your nose. As you breathe in, your ribs and belly expand. As you breathe out, relax your ribs and pull your belly inward and upward. Do this gentle breathing until it flows easily and naturally. *Pause*

Relaxation
- Now as you exhale, relax your face, eyes and jaw... Now relax your neck, shoulders and arms... Exhale slowly and relax your chest and upper back... Breathe out and

relax your belly and middle back... Relax your hips and lower back... Let go of the tension in your thighs... Relax your thighs even more deeply... Finally let this relaxation flow through your knees to your feet. Feel your feet grounded on the earth. Feel yourself energized and supported by the earth beneath your feet. *Pause*

Heart

- Once you are relaxed, you can bring your awareness to the center of your chest. Breathe in unconditional love and breathe out unconditional love. Feel your heart's magnetic field expand to include the people who are with you... your family... someone you have a special love for... the people you work with... someone who is a challenge for you... those who are suffering, and the world. *Allow for some silence*

Connection

- When you feel ready you can open your eyes. Look around the space you are in and feel comfortable and relaxed. If you are doing the Pause for Centering with others, make relaxed eye contact and feel supported by their loving presence. You may want to share one or two words that describe how you are feeling, now that you have returned to your center of balance within yourself.

3. INTEGRATION PROCESS FOR COMPLETIONS

- Closure allows you to have completion – for each phase of your day and in your relationships – so you can transition to a new beginning with more energy.
- The Integration Process for Completions helps you let go of regrets and keeps your heart open to love.
- You can do the Integration Process in a few seconds at any time: while sitting at your desk, after completing a project or at the end of a meeting.

- It is good to take a few minutes with your family or your partner at the end of your day to integrate your day and feel complete.
- You can spend half an hour or more talking through this Integration Process with someone who needs help letting go of a painful relationship or a memory or experience that still feels incomplete.
- The Integration Process for Completions can be used at the end of any therapeutic session, a Resonance Repatterning session or at the end of a seminar to provide a relaxing closure.

How To:
Be aware of what you want to complete while doing the Integration Process: the end of a meeting, or day, or relationship, etc. Then read the following slowly and gently, with a pause after each phrase.

Eyes

- Close your eyes.

Breath

- Begin to breathe slowly and gently through your nose. As you breathe in, expand your ribs and belly. As you breathe out, relax your ribs and pull your belly inward and upward.

Relaxation

- As you breathe out, relax – starting with your eyes, mouth and jaw. Slowly move down your body, relaxing your neck and shoulders... your arms and hands... your chest, belly and hips... your upper, middle and lower back... your thighs, lower legs and feet. Scan each part of your body and relax any residual tension you may still be holding. *Pause*

Heart

- Bring your awareness to your heart. Receive love as you breathe in... and as you breathe out expand your love to those you are close to... to everyone in your group... and to the world. *Pause*
- When you are ready, open your eyes. Take your time.

Appreciation

- Ask (*yourself or the person you are doing the Integration Process with*), "What do you appreciate about (*name the project, the person, yourself, etc. – whatever or whoever is involved with this Integration for Completions*)? What positive feelings do you have?"

Regrets

- Now get in touch with any regrets that may have been activated. Accessing your regrets can help you learn the lesson of the regret, and expressing your regret in a few words, even to yourself, often begins to generate understanding, forgiveness and love. As a result of accessing and naming your regrets, you are able to let go of the tension and stress your regrets create and orient yourself to love once more.

  It is important to remember that regrets don't need to be 'fixed'. You don't need to come up with a solution when people share their regrets (or you name your regret). Listen with love and nod your head gently as they name their regret. Even this can open the space for self-healing.

  After sharing your regrets, take a breath and relax with a slow haaa sound. Now ask (*yourself or the person you are doing the Integration Process with*), "What is the higher learning of your regrets? *After naming the learning to yourself, close your eyes.* Breathe the learning into your heart, and breathe out the regret. Say "I (*name the learning*); I appreciate my new learning; I no longer need my regret. I let go of it and open my heart."

Movement

- Life is energy in motion. At the end of the Integration Process, get up and move: stretch, yawn or dance.

4. STATURE OF POWER AND CREATIVITY

This process is gratefully adapted from Arthur Samuel Joseph's Vocal Power: Harnessing the Power Within. See References

- Arthur Samuel Joseph writes about the power of our voice, which broadcasts everything about ourselves to the world.
- In Sharry Edward's work, she discovered that physical, emotional and mental symptoms of distress occur when certain frequencies in the voice are missing, Once the missing frequencies in the voice are regained, symptoms usually self-correct.
- The Stature of Power and Creativity is about the power of our voice: standing in our truth; speaking who we are. When we stop speaking what is in our heart, when we stop living from our essence, we lose certain frequencies in our voice. Our voice becomes thin, losing its natural resonance, and we are unaware that our physical symptoms, emotional upsets and negative thinking have something to do with our voice and the frequency qualities it has lost.

It is wonderful to have someone talk you through the following 9 steps. However, once you have learned the 9-step sequence, you can close your eyes and go through each of the 9 steps in your mind, whether before giving a presentation, taking an exam or even when standing in line at the bank! Observe, both within yourself and around you, the positive change that occurs when you stand in your Stature of Power.

How To:

1. **Come into your stature of power** Sit or stand in a position of "I feel extraordinary about myself and everyone around me." As you say these words to yourself, notice your smile. Also observe the uplift of your spine; feel your feet grounded to earth, about a foot apart; be aware of a gentle pull upwards from the crown of your head. With your thumb and middle finger underneath your collar bone, gently lift your upper chest half an inch and feel a subtle lift of your upper back and chest.

2. **Your contribution** Ask yourself, "What do I contribute or bring to life that I am happy about? What positive qualities do I want to embody?" In your mind answer, "I bring (__). I embody (__)."

3. **Gratitude and surrender** In your mind say, 'Thank you' to Source – thank you to the power that is greater than our ego-self and gives us the strength to face any difficulty or challenge; 'thank you' to the power that makes all good things possible.

4. **Love** In your mind say, 'Love and let go'. Let go of everything that is not love – the fears, doubts, negative attitudes, lack of forgiveness, anger – and become receptive to the grace of being the best that you already are.

5. **Breath** Take a deep-in-your-body loving breath – allow this vibration of life, your own breath, to expand and energize you.

6. **Arc your breath like a rainbow** As you exhale through your mouth, feel your energy arcing up and *out from your mouth* into the room and beyond the room to include the whole world – when you speak, sing or give a presentation, feel your voice arcing up and out to include each person right to the back of the room. When you breathe *in through your nose*, feel your recharged energy filling you. Continue to breathe out and in – arcing your energy up and out and feeling your recharged energy returning to you.

7. **Attention to details** Whatever you are wanting to do, or are doing, whether washing dishes, creating a work of art, running or speed-walking, be totally in the present moment, paying attention to the details of how you are standing or moving, your thoughts and feelings, the quality of your voice. Also be aware of those you are with and the details of how you connect with them.

8. **Take your time** Mentally ask yourself, 'What is the right pacing for me at this time in terms of what I am doing or want to do with my time?' Your body, emotions and mind will stretch time, slowing it down or speeding it up, when you pace yourself in a way that is right for you. There is no rush. Slow down. Let things happen in their own right timing.

9. **Be conscious of your higher self** Be conscious of who you truly are, your essence that is beyond your body, emotions and mind – your pure consciousness that is beyond time and the present life circumstances you are experiencing or the past pain your have gone through. *Pause.* Take a deep breath and breathe out with a gentle haaa sound.

5. HEART ENTRAINMENT

- This powerful Energizing Option supports deep bonding, safety and trust between partners, friends and even those who are a challenge for us.

- The complete Heart Entrainment Option is taught in the TRANSFORMING CHAKRA PATTERNS seminar. The following Heart Entrainment is a shortened version that is wonderful to do with a partner, friend or your child – *on condition that the other person is in the mood for it and loves doing it with you. If you start laughing while doing the Heart Entrainment, relax and enjoy a good laugh before closing your eyes and synchronizing your breathing once more.*

How To:

- Sit opposite your partner and slightly to your right, so your thighs are parallel with theirs, rather than your knees touching as when you sit directly opposite. Make sure your thighs are not touching.

- You are now close enough to place your left hand on your partner's upper chest, below the throat, over the thymus gland. Make sure you are relaxed and free of strain.

- Your partner places his/her left hand on **your** upper chest, below the throat, over your thymus gland.
- Both of you place your right hand on your own chest, over the other's left hand. *When doing this with a woman, make sure the hand contact is above the breast area, just below the collar bone and the throat.*
- Close your eyes and breathe slowly *in unison*. When you inhale, stretch your spine upwards from your belly. When you exhale, feel your belly pulling in and your spine bending and relaxing slightly.
- Now as you inhale and stretch your spine, receive love from the other person; as you exhale and relax, send love to the other person. Feel your heart's magnetic field expanding each time you breathe out.
- When either of you feels complete, after a few minutes or more, very slowly take your right hand away, but keep your eyes closed. Sit and relax with your eyes closed. Feel the loving heart connection between yourself and the other person.
- When ready, open your eyes, allowing the love of your heart to flow through your eyes. See the other person and the world through loving eyes.

6. 24-HOUR TIME CLOCK

- When you feel upset, tired, depressed, etc. at a particular time of day, the problem may lie in your Meridian system.
- Each two-hour period of the twenty-four hour day is associated with one of the twelve Meridians of Chinese Acupuncture. During this two-hour period, each Meridian has a boost of energy. If the Meridian is weak, this extra boost may be too much – like a non-functioning surge protector that cannot protect your computer when there is a sudden surge of electricity. As a result, we may have distress symptoms related to the high-energy Meridian during its two-hour extra surge period.

- ◎ When each Meridian has a boost of energy, at its two-hour high-energy time, its opposite a.m./p.m. Meridian is at its low-energy time. If a Meridian is already weak, then at its low-energy time it has even less energy available to it. As a result, distress symptoms related to the low-energy Meridian may surface during this two-hour period of depletion.

How To:

- Look at the Time Clock chart *p.25* and observe the high- and low-energy Meridians for the time of day when your distress symptoms appear.
- Muscle check, or use your felt sense, whether the Mu point for the high-energy Meridian is needed or the low-energy Meridian (or both). *See Mu Point Charts pp.67–68*
- (**mcs**) whether to make a finger contact, or use the ColorYourWorld Torch or a Tuning Fork on that Mu point. While contacting the point, do the consonant sound for the Meridian Mu point that is needed.

If you have not attended the TRANSFORMING THE FIVE ELEMENT AND MERIDIAN seminar, you can also choose to substitute any other Option you feel you need to support the high-energy and/or low-energy Meridian(s), rather than use the Mu points.

If you feel you need the full Time Clock Repatterning,
see ResonanceRepatterning.net > Sessions > Find a Practitioner

THE 24-HOUR TIME CYCLE CHART

The am/pm high-energy time for each Meridian				**Consonant Sound**
The am/pm low-energy time for each Meridian				
Fire	**I**	**Heart**	**11am–1pm**	**S / Z**
Wood	*vii*	*Gall Bladder*	*11pm–1am*	
Fire	**II**	**Small Intestine**	**1pm–3pm**	**F / V**
Wood	*viii*	*Liver*	*1am–3am*	
Water	**III**	**Bladder**	**3pm–5pm**	**W**
Metal	*ix*	*Lung*	*3am–5am*	
Water	**IV**	**Kidney**	**5pm–7pm**	**K / G**
Metal	*x*	*Large Intestine*	*5am–7am*	
Fire	**V**	**Heart Protector**	**7pm–9pm**	**SH / CH / J**
Earth	*xi*	*Stomach*	*7am–9am*	
Fire	**VI**	**Triple Heater**	**9pm–11pm**	**RRR**
Earth	*xii*	*Spleen*	*9am–11am*	
Wood	**VII**	**Gall Bladder**	**11pm–1am**	**Y**
Fire	*i*	*Heart*	*11am–1pm*	
Wood	**VIII**	**Liver**	**1am–3am**	**TH**
Fire	*ii*	*Small Intestine*	*1pm–3pm*	
Metal	**IX**	**Lung**	**3am–5am**	**Q**
Water	*iii*	*Bladder*	*3pm–5pm*	
Metal	**X**	**Large Intestine**	**5am–7am**	**M**
Water	*iv*	*Kidney*	*5pm–7pm*	
Earth	**XI**	**Stomach**	**7am–9am**	**P / B**
Fire	*v*	*Heart Protector*	*7pm–9pm*	
Earth	**XII**	**Spleen**	**9am–11am**	**H**
Fire	*vi*	*Triple Heater*	*9pm–11pm*	

7. ENERGY CONSTRICTION RELEASE (ECR)

PROCESS GUIDE *p.21*

- The Energy Constriction Release supports profound self-healing when needs were not met in infancy and childhood and when feelings and sensations were not communicated or honored.
- The ECR Energizing Option needs to be done with a practitioner because our energy originally constricted in an earlier experience when no one was there to give us support. When we most needed it, there was no one available to hear our feelings and respond in the way we needed them to.
- This Energizing Option is taught to participants in the TRANSFORMING PRIMARY PATTERNS seminar; if you feel you need the ECR, you are welcome to receive a Resonance Repatterning session. *See ResonanceRepatterning.net > Sessions > Find a Practitioner*

8. DIFFUSION PROCESS PROCESS GUIDE *p.23*

This Energizing Option is for diffusing or removing negativity, shock or pain as a result of accidents or broken bones – shocks still held in the body-mind energy field.

The Diffusion Process is taught in the TRANSFORMING UNCONSCIOUS PATTERNS seminar. It is best to have the support of a practitioner, although trained practitioners can do the Diffusion Process on themselves. If you feel you need the Diffusion, you are welcome to receive a Resonance Repatterning session. *See ResonanceRepatterning.net > Sessions > Find a Practitioner*

9. FUSION PROCESS PROCESS GUIDE *p.27*

This Energizing Option fuses the positive into the body-mind energy field – a positive belief or state of mind, a positive feeling, even a lost quality (as a result of trauma in childhood, that needs to be retrieved). You may need to fuse in something that was missing in your childhood. The Fusion Process is taught in the TRANSFORMING CHAKRA PATTERNS seminar. It is best having a practitioner talk you through the Fusion. *If you feel you need the Fusion see ResonanceRepatterning.net > Sessions > Find a Practitioner*

B.
SOUND OPTIONS

Spiritual literature of all times and parts of the world talks about the Primal Sound or Word that creates and sustains the whole of creation. Therefore it is no surprise that sound has a special significance: the sound of the voice; the effect of song and harmonic overtones; the impact of words – for our benefit or our detriment.

Sound was used for healing purposes in ancient Egypt and Greece and for thousands of years in China and India. Pythagoras (Greek philosopher, mystic and mathematician in the 6th century BCE) taught his students simple chords and melodies that immediately changed negative behaviors.

In modern times, research shows how sound creates forms and sustains those forms. Swiss scientist Dr. Hans Jenny demonstrated in the early 1900s how sound creates patterns in matter. Placing sand and liquids on a metal plate, he vibrated various sounds through the plate: the inert matter immediately moved into patterns that looked like flowers, sacred geometric forms and rotating galaxies. **What is fascinating about his research is that as he raised the frequency, old patterns broke down into chaos and new, more organized, complex and coherent patterns emerged.**

THE FOUR OVALS FOR EACH OPTION

1. **Muscle check self (mcs)**
   or use your felt sense for the
   Energizing Option you need

2. **Read the introduction to**
   the Energizing Option
   Demo the 'How To' if doing
   with someone else, or use the
   video download if needed

3. **Do the Energizing Option**
   - Observe that you are doing it correctly
   - Breathe
   - **(mcs) / felt sense:** This is complete?
   - **(mcs) / felt sense:** Another Option is needed?

4. **After completing the Option**
   - Take a pause to integrate the positive change
   - Recheck your **felt sense:**
     a. Do you feel more relaxed?
     b. Are you breathing more easily?
     c. Do you notice any other positive change?
   - *RR Practitioners recheck *[cr] statements*

As New Physics is proving, we are vibrational beings, and every atom, cell and organ resonates at its own unique and ideal frequency or sound to maintain balanced life energy.

Sound and creativity

One of my favorite stories, which illustrates the power of the Sound Options, involves a board of directors. They were receptive to Resonance Repatterning and had asked a practitioner to attend their meeting to help them open up to a more creative way of thinking.

After identifying the problem, the practitioner used the muscle checking technique to discover which Energizing Option they needed. It turned out to be a Sound option – Gobbledygook! The last thing she wanted was to teach a group of businessmen to speak in gobbledygook nonsense sounds and rhythms!

Seeing no way around it, she explained that this Energizing Option was about activating the right hemisphere of the brain for new creative choices. The men began speaking in gobbledygook. Within seconds they were all laughing, and in good cheer they got on with their meeting. Some months later she bumped into one of the directors and he said, "Guess what! We now start every meeting with gobbledygook!"

1. HAAA SOUND FOR HEART CONNECTION

- The sound of *haaa* is associated in Chi Kung with the Heart Meridian. It is considered to have a strengthening effect on the physical heart, as well as on the emotional and mental level of the Heart Meridian – helping us reconnect to our loving, joyful, compassionate heart energy.

How To:

- Hold your palms facing up, or one facing up and the other on your heart center, and breathe in through your nose. Now relax and let your breath out slowly through your mouth with a long haaa tone.
- Even better, do the haaa tone while standing in your Stature of Power and Creativity *pp.20–22*
- Again tone the haaa sound on one note as you exhale: relax your mouth and throat, smile each time you tone haaa and project a rainbow arc of sound. Notice how you feel.

2. LAUGHING BREATH

Laughter is one of the great universal healing tools of all times and ages. Kings kept their clowns by their side, and people pay to have comedians make them laugh!

- Laughter produces endorphins of joy that bring relief from pain and boost our immune system.
- Those who laugh together automatically feel bonded.
- Laughter creates relaxation, happiness, heart-opening love and relief from stress.
- It is said that if you can laugh at a problem, you have power over it. No matter how challenging your situation if you can laugh, it loses its power over you.

- There is a centuries-old Japanese saying:

  Laugh three times –
  Once in **praise** (in gratitude for the passing year)
  Once in **promise** (new hope for the coming year)
  Once in **purpose** (to clear the mind and heart so we stay aligned with our life's purpose)

- *At first, doing the How To for the Laughing Breath may feel difficult. As you continue to do it, you will probably experience more joy and humor returning to your life.*

How To:

- While standing, breathe in and lift your arms above your head, looking up and bending slightly backwards; now bend forward, letting out a strong but slow Ha-Ha-Ha, squeezing in your belly with each Ha and bouncing your knees up and down.

- Lift your arms up again as you take another breath and again release the Ha-Ha-Ha's, but more quickly.

- The Ha-Ha-Ha's get faster and faster with each breath, until you, or you and the person you are laughing with, are belly laughing and bouncing up and down, slapping your thighs, pointing at each other (with fingers relaxed), holding your belly and making eye contact.

- Another way to do the Laughing Breath, as is done in many parks in India, is to open your mouth with a Ha-Ha-Ha; Ho-Ho-Ho; He-He-He. Smiling, repeat for a few minutes (or for one hour as they do in India).

3. TONING

Chromatic Tuner and ColorYourWorld Glasses:
see ResonanceRepatterning.net/estore/

Toning is another ancient and powerful Option for spiraling up.

- Dr. Alfred Tomatis discovered that high frequency vocal sounds recharge the brain through direct bone conduction, as well as externally through the ears.
- Toning of notes has been shown in photographs by author Fabien Maman to destroy cancer cells and enhance the vibrancy of healthy red blood cells.
- Toning has a positive effect not only on the physical body, but also on the mind and feelings.

See Further Reading: Fabien Maman, The Tao of Sound; Alfred Tomatis, The Conscious Ear.

How To:

- (**mcs**) {1–12} for the note you need from the chart that follows.
- (**mcs**) (*Client*) needs to tone a particular vowel? (**mcs**) oo/or/ah/eh/ee?
- (**mcs**) The toning needs to vibrate a particular area of the body? (**mcs**) the (base of spine • pelvis • umbilicus • heart • throat • brow • crown)? (**mcs**) (Client) needs to place his/her hand on a particular area of the body? *For instance, a place in pain or any area of the body that needs the toning vibration.* (**mcs**) for details.
- (**mcs**) A visual field is needed? (**mcs**) (Up • Down • Diagonally up left • Diagonally up right • Diagonally down left • Diagonally down right • looking with 180° soft focus) is needed?
- (**mcs**) A color is needed? (**mcs**) The color is the same as the note being toned / the opposite complementary color of the note being toned? (**mcs**) Client needs to wear the ColorYourWorld Glasses for the color / visualize the color?

- Play the note on your chromatic tuner, take a deep breath and tone the note along with whatever else is needed above.

	Note	Color	Its opposite note and color	
1.	C	Red	F#	Green
2.	C#	Red-orange	G	Turquoise
3.	D	Orange	G#	Blue
4.	D#	Orange-yellow	A	Indigo
5.	E	Yellow	A#	Violet
6.	F	Green	B	Magenta
7.	F#	Apple green	C	Red
8.	G	Turquoise	C#	Red-orange
9.	G#	Blue	D	Orange
10.	A	Indigo	D#	Orange-yellow
11.	A#	Violet	E	Yellow
12.	B	Magenta	F	Green

4. GOBBLEDYGOOK

- This humorous Energizing Option has a balancing effect on the brain hemispheres: words activate the left cerebral hemisphere of the brain, whereas creating 'gobbledygook' non-word sounds and rhythms activates the right cerebral hemisphere – associated with relationship, creativity, imagination and feelings.

- Gobbledygook sounds have been known to come up before a business meeting, and always to everyone's surprise the sounds and laughter that follow open up the meeting to creative sharing and focused interest.

How To:

- Gobbledygook can be done with two or more people, although in a self-session you will do gobbledygook alone. If there is a small group, everyone 'talks' to each other in gobbledygook non-words, rhythms and tones.

- In this type of communication it is acceptable for everyone to talk simultaneously or to listen and respond. This Energizing Option is about letting go of inhibitions and having fun creating strange sounds, rhythms and pitches.

5. APPRECIATION

- How often do we criticize and blame ourselves and others? How easily we get upset with those we are close to or those we work with, criticizing them for their weaknesses? And how seldom do we say thank you for the little things our family members, friends, colleagues and others do for us?

- The same applies to ourselves: it is too easy to ignore our positive qualities and strengths; we fail to appreciate who we are and the positive things we do and too often we are overly critical of ourselves.

- Appreciation, when genuinely given, energizes the giver as well as the receiver. It opens a channel for acknowledging others' positive qualities and the many things they are and do that we are grateful for.

- It encourages us to be grateful for the gift of life and to see what is positive in difficult situations – constantly turning our mind in an energizing direction. Appreciation challenges us to ask ourselves 'What is good about this,' rather than focusing on what is 'bad' about ourselves, others, a challenging situation we are in or our life.

How To:

- Be aware of what you appreciate at this moment about (yourself, your gifts and good qualities • what you have done well • someone else and their gifts and good qualities • what someone else has done well • any difficult situation you are in • your life).

- Say aloud, even if you are alone, "I appreciate (__)." (**mcs**) I need to repeat this? (**mcs**) I need to appreciate something else?

6. HARMONIC OVERTONES

Nestor Kornblum's Practical Guide and CD of harmonic overtones and the ColorYourWorld Glasses: see ResonanceRepatterning.net/estore/

Everything in the creation is in a state of vibration – a pulsing wave pattern of sound and color.

- One of the characteristics of vibration is speed; this is known as its frequency. Speed or frequency refers to the number of wave vibrations per second, measured as cycles per second (cps) – also measured as Hertz (Hz). Frequency determines the pitch of the note you sing, tone or play.

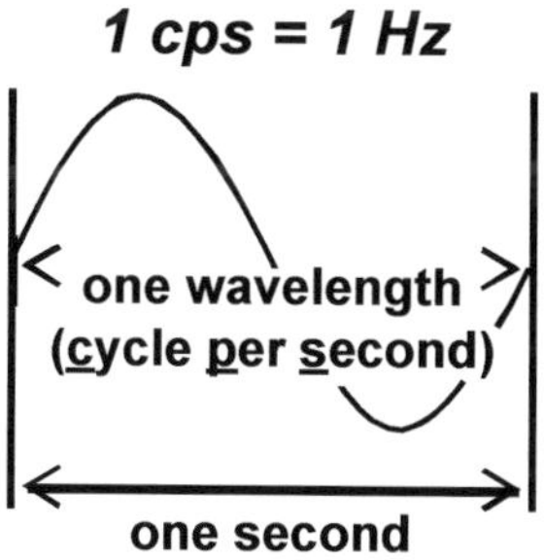

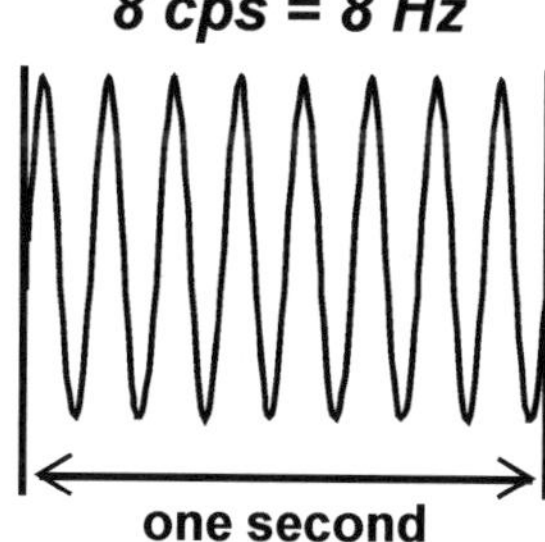

- Another characteristic of vibration is its harmonics. Harmonics – also called overtones – are all the tones that simultaneously sound when a single note is sung or played. A single note is called the fundamental note. Whenever you sing a fundamental note, numerous harmonic tones are simultaneously sounding, although in everyday talking and singing the human ear doesn't hear these harmonic overtones.

- The harmonics you unconsciously emphasize in your speaking and singing are what give your voice its unique quality and resonance, which distinguishes your voice from every other voice in the world. Similarly, the harmonics that are emphasized by each instrument is what distinguishes one instrument from another – a flute from a violin from a piano. Remove the harmonics and you can't distinguish one instrument from another.

- When the voice loses its natural harmonic resonance, this loss is associated with symptoms of disease on the physical, emotional or mental level.

- The human voice has the ability, through harmonic overtoning, to create almost every frequency. This gives the human voice the power to resonate with physical, emotional and mental vibrations that support self-healing.

How To:
Do {a} to learn how to do the harmonic overtones.
Otherwise go to {b} for the details needed while doing the overtones.

a. Learning to do harmonic overtones

- Tone any note and allow your lips to purse as though whistling, and make an 'ooo' sound. Now smile and make an 'eee' sound. Repeat this a few times: ooo–eee.

- Now take a breath and make the ooo–eee sound nasal so it is projected through your nose. Exhale while slowly doing the ooo–eee–ooo–eee nasal sound.

- Gradually lessen the movement of your lips, keeping them almost closed, as you continue to make the ooo–eee nasal sound, allowing the slow back and forward movement of your tongue, rather than your lips, to do the ooo–eee. Move your tongue backward and forward near the roof of your mouth, holding your lips as though whistling.

- Be sure that your tongue moves slowly from the back of your mouth for the ooo sound, and to the front of your mouth, behind your upper teeth, for the eee sound.

- Experiment with your tongue – flattening it out at the back of your mouth and curling it up at the front of your mouth, bringing the tip of your tongue as close as possible to your upper teeth for the eee sound. Your tongue follows the roof of your mouth without actually touching it.
- The movement of your tongue from the back of your mouth to the front of your mouth naturally produces the oo – or – ah – eh – ee vowel sounds that are associated with areas of the body:

oo (as in coo)	pelvic area
or (as in pore)	umbilical area
ah (as in father)	heart area
eh (as in elephant)	throat area
ee (as in see)	center of forehead and head area

b. (mcs) for details needed while doing the harmonic overtones

- (**mcs**) The eyes need to be open / closed / looking in a particular direction: (up / down / left / right / diagonally up left / diagonally up right / diagonally down left /diagonally down right)?
- (**mcs**) The ColorYourWorld Glasses need to be worn? (**mcs**) for details on the color needed in each eye and how long they need to be worn. *Sometimes a few seconds is enough.*
- (**mcs**) Hearing the harmonic overtones done by a professional is needed? (**mcs**) for the track(s) needed from Nestor Kornblum's Practical Guide CD.

7. CLAPPING

- ◎ Clapping breaks up stagnation and clears the air.
- ◎ It can be used close to the body or around a room, especially in corners and near to the floor, to break up stagnant energies.
- ◎ Clapping stimulates the palms of both hands, which are sub-Chakras of the heart. It is interesting that clapping in most parts of the world is an expression of appreciation from the heart.

How To:

- (**mcs**) Clapping is needed in the field around the body?
- (**mcs**) (Client • Practitioner) needs to clap over a particular area? Sometimes the clapping is sharp and sometimes soft – using the finger tips or clapping with the hands cupped, creating a hollow space between them and a different kind of sound.
- (**mcs**) Clapping is needed in a particular area of the room *often in corners* to break up stagnant energy? (**mcs**) to locate the area(s).
- Allow your hands to clap in whatever rhythm you are drawn to.

8. HUMMING

- ◎ Humming vibrates the larynx (voice box), from where the sound is transmitted to the cervical vertebrae of the spine (just behind the larynx).
- ◎ Bones conduct the vibration throughout the body and particularly through the skull bones to the brain, which is recharged by high frequency sound.
- ◎ Children naturally do a lot of humming as they draw, write and play. As adults, we would do well to follow their modeling and hum!

How To:

- Sit on the edge of your chair with a straight spine. Bring your chin in (rather than up) so your voice box is close to your cervical vertebrae.
- Inhale fully. As you exhale with a hum, slowly squeeze your belly inward and upward. If the sound is easy and effortless, you may be able to continue humming for 15–60 seconds without needing to take another breath.
- Gently place the palms of your hands on the back of your neck, various areas of your spine or the top of your head and see if you can feel the subtle vibration created by your humming – easier to feel when humming with a low pitch.

9. TUNING FORKS

Stainless steel tuning forks made in Germany and ColorYourWorld Glasses: see ResonanceRepatterning.net/estore/

- Sound is one of the most powerful Energizing Options for transforming our resonance with negative body-mind patterns. And using a Tuning Fork Option establishes sympathetic resonance with the same frequencies in your own body-mind field.
- You can use a Tuning Fork in various ways: listen to it, move the two tines over particular body areas, place the stem of the fork on a body area, spinal vertebra or Acupuncture point, or you can even place the two tines in water to energize the water with the Tuning Fork frequency.
- You can also use two Tuning Forks together to create various musical intervals. For example, the interval of the 5th – created with two Tuning Forks like, for example, the notes of C and G or E and B, etc. The interval of the 5th is sometimes referred to as the sound of universal harmony that balances the forces of Yin and Yang. *For information on intervals and the significance of each,* *see pp.61–63*

To protect your stainless steel Tuning Forks from damage, tap the Tuning Fork on a hard rubber ball or a rubber doggie bone from a pet shop. Avoid striking the tuning forks against each other or on a metal or other hard surface.

Frequencies of the Om, Naturals, Sharps and Planetary Tuning Forks

Some of the frequencies are associated with energy centers in the body; other frequencies are associated with the planets, calculated mathematically by Swiss mathematician Hans Cousto.

OM
cps
136.10

NATURALS (natural notes)			
note		cps	energy center
1.	C	130.81	Earth – Base of Spine
2.	D	146.83	Water – Pelvis
3.	E	164.81	Fire – Solar Plexus
4.	F	174.61	Air – Heart
5.	G	196.00	Ether – Throat
6.	A	220.00	Brow
7.	B	246.94	Crown

SHARPS (sharp notes)		
note		cps
1.	C#	138.59
2.	D#	155.56
3.	F#	185.00
4.	G#	207.65
5.	A#	233.08

PLANETARY		
planet		cps
1.	Sun	126.22
2.	Pluto	140.25
3.	Mercury	141.27
4.	Mars	144.72
5.	Saturn	147.85
6.	Jupiter	183.58
7.	Earth	194.71
8.	Uranus	207.44
9.	Moon	210.42
10.	Neptune	211.44
11.	Venus	221.23

How To:

- (**mcs**) {1–4} for the Tuning Fork(s) needed.
    1. The **Om** frequency tuning fork is needed?
    2. A **Naturals** frequency Tuning Fork is needed? (**mcs**) (C • D • E • F • G • A • B)
    3. A **Sharps** frequency Tuning Fork is needed? (**mcs**) (C# • D#• F# • G# • A#)
    4. A **Planetary** frequency Tuning Fork and its Intention is needed? (**mcs**) {1–11} *pp.45–51 for information on each Planetary Tuning Fork and its Intention.*
        1. Sun *p.45*
        2. Pluto *p.45*
        3. Mercury *p.46*
        4. Mars *p.46*
        5. Saturn *p.47*
        6. Jupiter *p.47*
        7. Earth *p.48*
        8. Uranus *p.48*
        9. Moon *p.49*
        10. Neptune *p.49*
        11. Venus *p.50*

- (**mcs**) A color is needed with the Tuning Fork? (**mcs**) Wearing the ColorYourWorld Glasses / Visualizing a color is needed? (**mcs**) for details from the color-sound charts. *Info pp.64, 97–100, 106*

- Options for using the Tuning Fork(s)
  (**mcs**) {1–5}. *If a Planetary Tuning Fork is needed, repeat the Planetary Intention as the Tuning Fork is vibrated.*
    1. **Hearing the Tuning Fork(s)**
       (**mcs**) for details on whether to hold the fork(s) still, a few inches from the left and/or right ear, to make circular movements or to move a fork over the head from one ear to the other ear.

       How To: Strike the fork on one of its two tines and place the tines a few inches from the ear.

2. **Energy point**
   (**mcs**) The Tuning Fork is needed over/on:
   - an energy center on the front of the body and/or the back of the body? (**mcs**) for details. *Info p.64*
   - a Jin Shin safety energy lock? *Chart p.201; info pp.202–219*
   - a cranial bone? *Info pp.223–227*
   - a Meridian point? *See the Mu Point chart pp.67–68 or if a student of Resonance Repatterning see* FIVE ELEMENT AND MERIDIAN *book or* INNER CULTIVATION THROUGH THE TWELVE MERIDIANS
   - Over an area of pain

   How To: Strike the fork on one of its two tines and place the stem of the fork on the body point or the area where needed. Or move the two tines over the area in circles (clockwise is energizing; counterclockwise breaks up old patterns).

3. **The spine**
   (**mcs**) A Tuning Fork is needed (on a vertebra • to the right side of the spine • to the left side of the spine). You can touch the spinal area or use the diagram of the spine *p.44* and (**mcs**) for exactly where the Tuning Fork needs to be placed.

   How To: Strike the fork and place the stem on or over the spinal area. Or you can move the two tines above the spinal area. (**mcs**) Another vertebra/area is needed?

4. **In the field**
   - (**mcs**) The Tuning Fork needs to be (held still • moved in the front • moved over the back • over a particular area) in the body's field? *Usually about three inches from the body* (**mcs**) We need to move the Fork Vertically / Horizontally / in circular movements?

5. **Tuning Fork in water**
   Wash the Tuning Fork – *colloidal silver or grapefruit seed extract diluted in water is natural and free of toxins.*

   How To:

   - Strike the tuning fork on one of its two tines and place the tips of the two tines in a glass of pure water. *Structured or filtered, rather than tap water is preferable*
   - (**mcs**) How many times to vibrate the water, before drinking it.

DIAGRAM OF THE SPINE

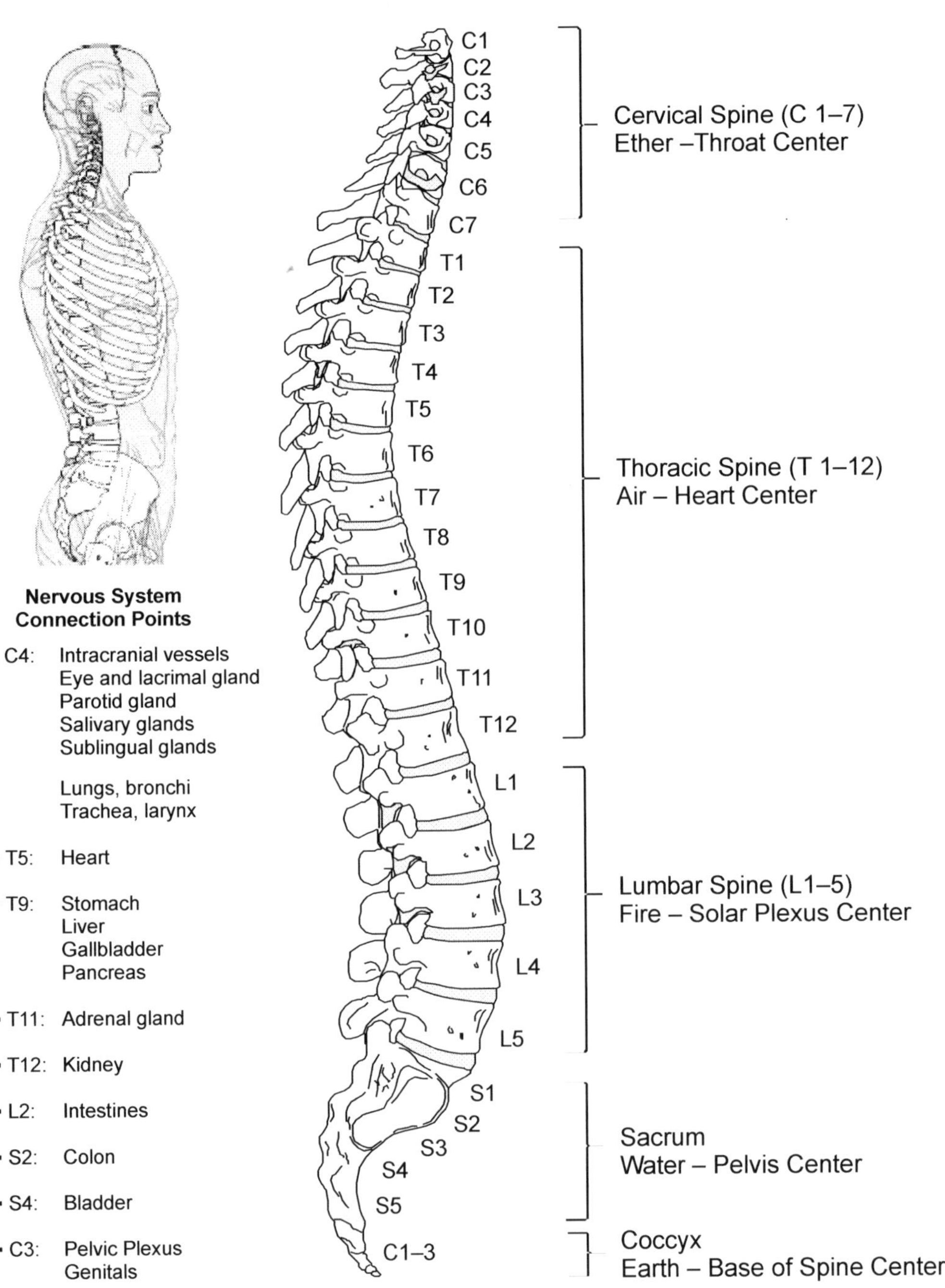
C1
C2
C3
C4
C5
C6
C7
T1
T2
T3
T4
T5
T6
T7
T8
T9
T10
T11
T12
L1
L2
L3
L4
L5
S1
S2
S3
S4
S5
C1–3
Cervical Spine (C 1–7)
Ether –Throat Center
Thoracic Spine (T 1–12)
Air – Heart Center
Lumbar Spine (L1–5)
Fire – Solar Plexus Center
Sacrum
Water – Pelvis Center
Coccyx
Earth – Base of Spine Center
Nervous System
Connection Points
▪ C4: Intracranial vessels
Eye and lacrimal gland
Parotid gland
Salivary glands
Sublingual glands
Lungs, bronchi
Trachea, larynx
▪ T5: Heart
▪ T9: Stomach
Liver
Gallbladder
Pancreas
▪ T11: Adrenal gland
▪ T12: Kidney
▪ L2: Intestines
▪ S2: Colon
▪ S4: Bladder
▪ C3: Pelvic Plexus
Genitals

INFORMATION AND INTENTIONS FOR THE PLANETARY TUNING FORKS

1. **SUN TUNING FORK** *126.22 cps*

The Sun is the energy of light, warmth and life for the earth and all that grows and lives. The Sun is associated with the heart, solar plexus and circulation.

Use the Sun frequency Tuning Fork when you need:

- to feel bright, radiant, joyful
- to bring what is hidden to the light of day
- to radiate warmth and love
- to move in the world with confidence

Intention: I am radiant, charismatic, confident and positive.

2. **PLUTO TUNING FORK** *140.25 cps*

Pluto corresponds to deep change in society's awareness. Pluto rules all that is below the surface – the unconscious – and brings what is hidden to the light of day. Its message is transformation realized through inner awareness and by releasing the darkness of negative or painful experiences. Pluto is associated with the sexual organs.

Use the Pluto frequency Tuning Fork when you need:

- to be empowered
- to go to the depth for inner awareness and self-transformation
- to be engaged in self-mastery through love

Intention: I find the jewel in the dark cave of my painful experiences.

3. MERCURY TUNING FORK *141.27 cps*

Mercury represents intelligence, commerce, exchange, communication and solutions. Mercury is associated with respiratory organs, skin, shoulders, digestion, arms, hands, blood vessels and the nervous system.

Use the Mercury frequency Tuning Fork when you need:

- to be organized
- to communicate effectively and with ease
- to be bright, adaptable and quick-thinking

Intention: I am intelligent and quick and I communicate with ease

4. MARS TUNING FORK *144.71 cps*

Mars represents self-defense, the speed of action, the vital assertive masculine energy of success through effort. Mars is associated with the head, eyes and male sexual organs.

Use the Mars frequency Tuning Fork when you need:

- to be independent
- to be assertive and set boundaries
- to be self-motivated
- to be active and energetic

Intention: I am physically strong, energetic and motivated.

5. SATURN TUNING FORK *147.27*

Saturn represents the human life-cycle on earth, our ambition, disappointments, frustrations, lessons to be learned and the gaining of wisdom. Saturn is associated with the bones, hair, nails, spine and skull.

Use the Saturn frequency Tuning Fork when you need:

- to create more structure in your life
- to be disciplined, precise and hard-working
- to be responsible, honest, wise and to be respected
- to move into a leadership position and overcome weaknesses
- To handle difficult life circumstances with strength

Intention: I use life's lessons for my greater good. I have a healthy awareness of my limitations.

6. JUPITER TUNING FORK *183.58 cps*

Jupiter represents expansiveness, enthusiasm, knowledge, honor, opportunity, fortune and inheritance. Jupiter is associated with the higher mind, religion, teaching, law and travel. The Jupiter frequency provides new opportunities and possibilities. Jupiter is associated with the hips and thighs.

Use the Jupiter frequency Tuning Fork when you need:

- to grow, expand and be successful
- to see the big picture and be receptive to new opportunities
- to be positive and make the most of every situation, however challenging it may be
- to stand for what is true and right
- to awaken the mind to higher spiritual principles

Intention: I hold truth as my highest value and I am successful.

7. **EARTH TUNING FORK** *194.71 cps*

Earth relates to being grounded, to endings, closure, times of integration and recycling into new beginnings with more awareness. The Earth is associated with the body as a whole.

Use the Earth frequency Tuning Fork when you need:

- to be practical, stable, secure, grounded
- to be energized living on the earth
- to integrate new learning and move forward into the next phase with confidence and stamina for the long haul
- to be abundant and generous

Intention: I am stable and secure; I am energized by the earth's magnetic forces. My needs are met.

8. **URANUS TUNING FORK** *207.44 cps*

Uranus symbolizes stepping out of old tracks and creating unexpected new beginnings. Often ahead of its time, Uranus is associated with the flow of information and what is unusual, as well as with all sudden, unexpected events. Its frequency has an electric effect. Uranus is associated with the nervous system, electrical brain impulses and the ankles.

Use the Uranus frequency Tuning Fork when you need:

- to be free and independent
- to be original and unique and break away from old patterns and belief systems
- to intuit future possibilities

Intention: I am a free spirit bound by none; I am before my time, holding a unique vision of future possibilities.

9. MOON TUNING FORK *210.42 cps*

The Moon is associated with the imagination, feelings, instincts and humanitarianism. It represents the charisma of the feminine, reflecting the light of the feminine to all. As the feminine element, it correlates to the home and the emotions. The Moon is associated with the breast/chest, female sexual organs and body fluids: blood, water, lymph.

Use the Moon frequency Tuning Fork when you need:

- to access feelings, instinctual and intuitive knowing
- to be in touch with the feminine and the natural cycles of life
- to nurture yourself and others
- to cleanse your body and emotions of toxicity

Intention: I acknowledge and express my feelings and needs; I am in touch with my instincts and my intuitive knowing.

10. NEPTUNE TUNING FORK *211.44 cps*

Neptune is the archetype of the ocean, the unconscious, spirituality, healing, transcendence and the dissolution of mind and matter. When the Neptune frequency of the unconscious is non-coherent, there may be a lack clarity, chaotic emotional reactions and self-deception. Neptune is associated with the adrenals and feet.

Use the Neptune frequency Tuning Fork when you need:

- to connect to the healing energies within
- to transcend the confusion and chaos of your mind and strive to live your spiritual ideals in action
- to live the truth and rise above camouflage and deception

Intention: I am in touch with my intuition and my healing capabilities. I speak the truth; I live the truth of my ideals.

11. VENUS TUNING FORK *221.23 cps*

Venus is associated with beauty, harmony and refinement. Venus also represents time, wealth, power, art, feminine sensuality and the enjoyment of the five senses. The Venus frequency holds the world together in families, tribes and society. Venus is associated with the neck and kidneys.

Use the Venus frequency Tuning Fork when you need:

- to create beauty and harmony
- to be in touch with the feminine and your sensuality
- to use charm and beauty to inspire others
- to support family unity and the well-being of the community

Intention: I recognize the beauty within each person, regardless of outer appearances. I nurture the family and all communities.

10. CREATIVE SELF-EXPRESSION

(**mcs**) {1–2} for the Sound Menu or Thymus Life Energy Menu needed.

1. **Sound Menu**

Every word and sound we create carries its own frequency and harmonic pattern that affects us and others. Sound vibrates our bones, enlivens healthy cells and – as illustrated by Fabien Maman's photographs – can even destroy cancer cells.
See Further Reading: Fabien Maman, The Tao of Sound

Supplies you may personally need to collect:

- CDs of songs, musicals and lullabies you love
- Any instrument you are drawn to: a drum, xylophone, wooden flute, didgeridoo, Tibetan bells, Tibetan bowls
- A favorite poetry book

How To:

(**mcs**) {1–8} for the sound needed.

1. **Humming** *vibrates the bones*
2. **Singing** (**mcs**) for the song needed
3. **Drumming** *If no drum is available, drum on a chair, table, book or on your own legs or body. This is lots of fun to do as a family or in any group!*
4. **Playing a musical instrument** (**mcs**) from any instrument you have available: xylophone / piano / wooden flute / Tibetan bells / Tibetan bowls / other. Enjoy playing freely without reading music or thinking.
5. **Didgeridoo** (**mcs**) whether for yourself / other. If for another, (**mcs**) whether to play the didgeridoo with the end placed in front of various body areas (heart, feet, knees, etc.).

6. **Gobbledygook** words, rhythms and sounds that have no meaning, and yet communicate with others via the right cerebral hemisphere. *Sound Spiral Up Energizing Option #4 p.33*

7. **Creating rhythms** with your voice; imagine your voice is a drum and use it to create different drum rhythms.

8. **Poetry** Hear it and/or speak it aloud. When speaking poetry aloud, allow yourself to elongate words and phrases in an exaggerated way; change tones, articulate words in different ways; play with singing certain words and phrases. Have fun with being creative in expressing frequencies in the form of poetic words.

2. **Thymus Life Energy Options**

The thymus gland is closely associated with the heart and the immune system. The Thymus Life Energy Options may be needed for boosting the heart or immune system. Creative self-expression involves opening our heart and coming from our heart. The Thymus Life Energy Options aim to increase our heart's magnetic field, which in turn supports our creative self-expression from our heart.

How To:

(**mcs**) {1–13} for the Thymus Life Energy Option needed.

1. **Thymus Tap** Tapping over the thymus has an activating effect on the immune system and a relaxing effect on your heart, so we come from our heart in our create self-expression. *Energy Contact Options #2 p.192*

2. **Tongue on the Roof of Your Mouth** (front/middle/back) *Energy Contact Options #3 p.192*

3. **Classical music** (**mcs**) for the classical music you need to listen to that strengthens your thymus and activates your right-brain creativity.

4. **Dancing or Free Movement / Katsugen** *Movement Options #2, 13, #16, #23, #26, #27*

5. **Walking** involves moving your arms and legs in a cross-crawl motion, which integrates the left and right brain hemispheres with the heart – especially when we walk in slow motion. *Movement Options #17 p.131*

6. **Open Heart Gesture** opens the heart, which is essential for creative self-expression. *Movement Options #6 p.114*

7. **Smiling** activates endorphins of joy. It is difficult if not impossible to be depressed when you smile, and smiling makes you receptive to the flow of creativity.
   - Smile, with all your teeth showing and your lips turned up, for two to five minutes and observe how you feel. Breathe and relax your eyes and face as you smile!

   - As a positive action, experiment with smiling for at least one hour (more difficult than you think!).

   - Pinching the zygomatic smile muscles above the corners of your mouth also strengthens your thymus.

8. **Tadasana** brings a lot of energy to the heart-thymus area.
   - Clasp your hands and stretch them overhead, palms facing the ceiling, come onto your toes; hold your breath; exhale and slowly release your hands, allowing your arms to float down on either side of your body.

   - Now keep your feet flat on the floor and again clasp your hands and bring them above your head. Bend to the right and then to the left. Return to the center and exhale as you release your hands, allowing your arms to float down on either side of your body.

9. **Nodding Your Head Yes** is a Yes to life, your strengths and to your creative essence. When you nod your head Yes, it immediately begins to shift your thinking in a more positive direction.

10. **Aromatherapy** activates the limbic emotional brain, allowing for the expression of coherent feelings in creative self-expression. *Essential Oils Spiral Up Options pp.237.*

11. **Sunlight** recharges your body, brain and energy field and invigorates the expression of your light through the vehicle of your creative self-expression. If possible, go out into the sun. With eyes closed, move your head from side to side while allowing the full spectrum light to revitalize every part of your brain, body and energy field. As a Positive Action it is good to be in the sun for at least ten to twenty minutes, even on a cloudy day. Expose as much of your skin as possible to the sun's healing rays.

12. **Repeat the following words:** love, trust, courage, faith, thank you. Repeating any or all of these words boosts the immune system by strengthening the thymus and bringing your frequencies into sync, which helps you express yourself creatively.

13. **A Homing Thought**
    - A Homing Thought is a thought of a beautiful place, or a special person in your life, that brings you peace and joy.
    - A Homing Thought may also be an ideal or goal that inspires you.
    - A Homing Thought brings you back to your center, reconnecting you to what is most important and supporting you in expressing yourself creatively in every part of your life.
    - Visualizing your Homing Thought place, person, ideal or goal when under stress, often brings you the inner strength to handle the challenges you are facing.

11. DEVELOPMENTAL NEEDS AFFIRMATIONS

- Jean Illsley Clark describes six segments of time and stages of growth from infancy through adolescence, with characteristic needs, tasks, and helpful and unhelpful behaviors. With her permission, I have borrowed from and adapted her ideas to create affirmations for each stage. I have also added a seventh stage of growth – interdependence, the adult stage – and have created developmental affirmations for this stage too.

- In Resonance Repatterning we use the Muscle Checking Technique to identify which parental message was not given or which life need was not met at a specific developmental stage of growth. We then support the client to resolve the absence of the positive parental message (frequency) by hearing it and resonating with the positive message for the age when it was needed. Use your felt sense to choose the parental message if you do not yet know how to muscle check for it.

- Resonating with the positive parental message in the present creates new neural connections in the brain, producing life-enhancing biochemicals and feelings of pleasure.

See Further Reading: Jean Illsley Clark, Growing Up Again

How To:

- (**mcs**) {1–7} for the age and for the specific parental message or need.
- (**mcs**) I need to represent the (mother • father) saying the parental message? If not, the practitioner simply says the affirmation gently and lovingly. In a self-session, you yourself can represent your own mother or father saying the parental message to your child aspect at the age needed.
- (**mcs**) *(Client's)* eyes need to be open / closed? *If open, practitioner looks into the client's left or right eye while lovingly saying the statement. Use muscle checking to determine the eye that will activate new neural pathways in the heart and brain. In a self-session, you can use a mirror.*
- (**mcs**) for the number of times to repeat the parental message. *Usually one or two times is sufficient.*

- (**mcs**) (*Client*) needs to wear the ColorYourWorld Glasses to enhance hearing and integrating the parental message? (**mcs**) for details on the color for each eye.

1. **Being: 0–6 months** (**mcs**) {1–8}
   1. I'm glad you are alive.
   2. You belong here.
   3. What you need is important to me.
   4. I'm glad you are you.
   5. You can grow at your own pace.
   6. You can feel all of your feelings.
   7. I love you and I care for you willingly.
   8. *Other:* What would you have loved your (mother • father) to say to you at this age? (**mcs**) Need to list more?

2. **Doing: 6–18 months** (**mcs**) {1–9}
   1. You can explore and experiment and I will support and protect you.
   2. You can use all your senses when you explore; it's fine for you to touch what you explore.
   3. You can do things as many times as you need to and take your time.
   4. You can know what you know.
   5. You can be interested in everything.
   6. I like to watch you initiate, grow and learn.
   7. I love you when you are active and when you are quiet.
   8. I enjoy taking care of you, and taking care of my own needs.
   9. *Other:* What would you have loved your (mother • father) to say to you at this age? (**mcs**) Need to list more?

3. **Thinking: 18 months–3 years** (**mcs**) {1–8}
   1. I'm glad you are starting to think for yourself.
   2. It's okay for you to be angry and I won't let you hurt yourself or others.
   3. You can say 'no' and push and test limits as much as you need to.
   4. You can learn to think for yourself and I will think for myself.
   5. You can think and feel at the same time.

6. You can know what you need and also ask for help.
7. You can become separate from me and I am here for you, loving you.
8. *Other:* What would you have loved your (mother • father) to say to you at this age? (**mcs**) Need to list more?

4. **Identity and power: 3–6 years** (**mcs**) {1–10}
   1. You can explore who you are and find out who other people are.
   2. You can be powerful and ask for help at the same time.
   3. You can try out different ways of being powerful, with love and joy.
   4. You can discover the results of your behavior.
   5. All of your feelings are okay with me.
   6. You can learn what is pretend and what is real.
   7. I love who you are.
   8. You can do what is right for you and be loved.
   9. You can ask for help when you feel unsafe.
   10. *Other:* What would you have loved your (mother • father) to say to you at this age? (**mcs**) Need to list more?

5. **Structure: 6–12 years** (**mcs**) {1–8}
   1. You can trust your intuition to help you decide what to do.
   2. You can think before you say 'yes' or 'no' and learn from your mistakes.
   3. You can find a way of doing what works for you.
   4. You can learn the rules that help you live with others.
   5. You can think for yourself and get help instead of staying in distress.
   6. You can learn when and how to disagree.
   7. (I love you even when we differ • I love growing with you).
   8. *Other:* What would you have loved your (mother • father) to say to you at this age? (**mcs**) Need to list more?

6. **Identity, sexuality and separation: Adolescence** (**mcs**) {1–9}
   1. You can know who you are and learn and practice skills for independence.
   2. You can learn the difference between friendship and sex, and be responsible for your actions.
   3. You can develop your own interests, relationships and causes.

4. You can learn to use what you know in new ways.
5. You can grow in your maleness/ femaleness and know that we are here for you when you need us.
6. I look forward to knowing you as an adult.
7. My love is always with you. I trust you to ask for my support.
8. You can be independent and also protect yourself and be protected.
9. *Other:* What would you have loved your (mother • father) to say to you at this age? (**mcs**) Need to list more?

7. **Interdependence: Adult years** (**mcs**) {1–16}
   1. Your needs are important.
   2. You can be uniquely yourself and honor the uniqueness of others.
   3. You can be independent and interdependent.
   4. Through the years you can expand your commitments to include your personal growth, your spiritual practice, your career, your family, your friends, your community and humankind.
   5. You can be responsible for your contribution to each of your commitments.
   6. You can be creative, competent, productive and joyful.
   7. You can trust your inner wisdom.
   8. You can say your hellos and goodbyes to people, roles, dreams and decisions.
   9. You can finish each part of your journey and look forward to the next part.
   10. Your love matures and expands as you continue to grow and learn.
   11. You are lovable at every age.
   12. You are perfect at every stage in your journey.
   13. You can let go and start again with ease and trust.
   14. You can find pleasure and fulfilment in whatever work you choose to do.
   15. You can achieve your best while being honest and of service to others.
   16. *Other:* What would you have loved your (mother • father) to say to you at this age? (**mcs**) Need to list more?

12. QUANTUM HEALING CODES™

Quantum Healing Codes booklet and CD: see ResonanceRepatterning.net/estore/

- All matter, writes Stephen Linsteadt in his *Quantum Healing Codes* booklet, owes its existence to vibrating frequencies. Frequencies govern all the molecular and biochemical processes of our body, as well as our thoughts and emotions.

- Quantum Healing Codes™ are based on the idea that there is a geometric pattern behind all matter. Geometric shapes and forms – based on coherent frequency patterns – are the building blocks of our physical existence.

- The ancient Solfeggio scale of six musical notes, on which Quantum Healing Codes is based, was discovered by Dr. Joseph Puleo. Over 2,500 years ago Pythagoras knew the mathematical and geometric significance of the frequencies of these six notes; and even today these same frequencies are used. For instance, the frequency of 528 is the exact frequency used by genetic engineers throughout the world to repair DNA.

- The Quantum Healing Codes CD provides specific frequency sounds made by the human voice, for both individual notes and intervals as well as the tri-tone interval, which brings a sense of inner quietness and contemplation.

- Discordant frequencies, which still hold the imprint of painful earlier experiences, can be harmonized by Energizing Options such as the Quantum Healing Codes, using either the consonant frequencies to strengthen positive patterns or dissonant frequencies to break up painful memory imprints.

- Quantum Healing Codes is often used in the Negative Thoughts Repatterning and the Diffusion Process for breaking up dissonant patterns. This Option can also be used to strengthen coherent patterns, which is why it is often used in the Fusion Process Energizing Option.

- The CD of specific frequency notes and intervals comes with the revised edition of the booklet by Stephen Linsteadt that explains the dissonant notes, the consonant notes, the extraordinary tri-tone interval and the notes in relation to sacred geometry, as well as how to use these frequency sounds and intervals.

How To:

- See Quantum Healing Codes™ booklet.
- (**mcs**) for the Quantum Healing Code™ needed:
    - **a specific note** associated with the Chakra energy centers (track #1–6)
    - **a consonant interval**: 3rd for a sense of hope (track #12 and #19; Minor 3rd, track #16) / 4th for feelings of serenity, clarity and light (track #8 and #20) / 5th to cancel out any disturbing vibration in the field and bring a sense of power and being centered (Track #13) / Minor 6th for its soothing quality (track #9 and #18) / the octave for completeness and oneness (track #11 and #15).
    - **a dissonant interval to break up discordant patterns**: (track No. 7, 10, 11, 14, 21).
    - **the tri-tone for inner quietness and to be in touch with the Divinity** (track #17).
- (**mcs**) ColorYourWorld Glasses are needed? (**mcs**) for which color in which eye and for how long. *Only a few seconds may be needed.*
- (**mcs**) A visual field / Eye movements are needed?

  Visual field (**mcs**) (Up • Down • Left • Right • Diagonally up left • Diagonally up right • Diagonally down left • Diagonally down right • Looking with 180° soft focus) is needed?

  Eye movement (**mcs**) (Up-down • Left-right • Diagonally up left to diagonally down right • Diagonally up right to diagonally down left • Clockwise or counterclockwise circles)?

- (**mcs**) A contact is needed over (an area of tension • a past broken bone • a site of injury and pain • a site where surgery was involved • other)?
- Play the CD track while you periodically (**mcs**) This is complete? *Only a few seconds may be needed.*

13. INTERVALS

Chromatic Tuner and ColorYourWorld Glasses: see ResonanceRepatterning.net/estore/

- An interval is the space between two notes. When two notes are sung or played simultaneously, the interval between the two notes balances the energy of our body-mind system.
- **The 2nd** interval initiates movement, it provides a sense of difference and separation. You may need it when there is a certain tension within you or in your life that drives you to seek resolution.
- **The 3rd** interval activates feelings of strength, lightness, joy and love.
- **The 4th** interval is awakening and startling and creates a tension that seeks harmony and resolution. Through resolution it has the potential to bring serenity, clarity, openness and light.
- **The 5th** interval is associated with expansion, joy and creativity. It activates a wide movement of Chi energy and has a relaxing effect; it cancels out disturbing vibrations in the field, allowing you to feel centered and empowered.
- **The 6th** interval brings sweetness, softness and opening. It is light and free of stimulation and tension. *Most lullabies use this interval.*
- **The 7th** interval creates an extreme but healthy tension calling for resolution through growth, unity and a higher state of consciousness.
- **The 8th** interval of the octave creates resolution and stability, a sense of oneness and completeness. It is associated with resolution, stillness, peace and transformation.

How To:
Do {a–e} in sequence. Without knowing the Muscle Checking Technique, simply use your intuitive knowing to get the details you need.

a. (**mcs**) {1–8} for the interval needed and whether its minor or major aspect is needed. Write down the number of half-tones for the interval needed:

2.	Minor 2nd	1 half-tone
	Major 2nd	2 half-tones
3.	Minor 3rd	3 half-tones
	Major 3rd	4 half-tones
4.	4th	5 half-tones
	Augmented 4th	6 half-tones
5.	5th	7 half-tones
	Augmented 5th	8 half-tones
6.	Minor 6th	8 half-tones
	Major 6th	9 half-tones
7.	Minor 7th	10 half-tones
	Major 7th	11 half-tones
8.	Octave	12 half-tones

b. (**mcs**) for the lower or fundamental note of this interval:

C	C#	D	D#	E	F	F#	G	G#	A	A#	B

c. To get the second note of the interval, put your finger on the fundamental note you muscle checked was needed *{b}*, and count the number of half-tones for the interval needed *{a}*, starting with the note after the fundamental note.

- Remember, the fundamental note is the lower note and the second note creates the higher note, that when sung together make the interval. *For example, let's say you need an interval of a 5th and the lower fundamental note is D#. There are 7 half-tones in a 5th, so you put one finger on D# and then, starting with the note of E, move to the right and count up the musical scale for 7 more notes to A#. Toning the lower note of D# and the higher note of A# together creates the interval of a 5th.*

d. (**mcs**) for who needs to tone the lower, fundamental note and who needs to tone the higher interval note. In a self-session you may need to use the Chromatic Tuner for the second note or ask a friend or family member to tone your interval with you.

e. (**mcs**) The ColorYourWorld Glasses / Visualizing a color is needed? (**mcs**) for details on which color, or go to the chart of notes with their corresponding colors. *Info pp.64, 97–100, 106*

14. AYURVEDIC SOUNDS for the Chakra Energy Centers

Chromatic Tuner; Silk Scarves for the Chakras; ColorYourWorld Glasses: see ResonanceRepatterning.net/estore/

- In the Indian system of Ayurveda – which means 'sacred knowledge about life'– particular sounds are traditionally associated with each of the Chakra energy centers.
- Dr. Mishra, who brought these Ayurvedic sounds to the attention of many in the United States, suggests that people free-flow with the sound, using any variation of the consonants and the vowel – for instance the LAM sound *the 'a' sound is expressed as in 'father'* may be toned as L, LA, LAM, LAAAM, LA-MMM.
- You can explore using any pitch you are drawn to or use the note that traditionally corresponds to the Chakra energy center. For example, on the chart that follows, notice that the Earth Chakra corresponds to the

sound LAM, and the note traditionally associated with the Earth Chakra is the note of C, which is said to correspond to the color red and to three particular areas of the body known as the Earth triad.

How To:

- **Chakra sound** (**mcs**) for which chakra sound is needed {1–7} *below.*
- **Color** (**mcs**) ColorYourWorld Glasses / Silk Scarf for the Chakra sound is needed? (**mcs**) for details.
- **Note** (**mcs**) The note of the Chakra / Other Chakra note is needed? (**mcs**) for details.

Chakra	Sound	Color	Note	Chakra Triads		
				(+)	(ø)	(−)
1. Earth Coccyx	LAM	Red	C	Neck	Knees	Colon
2. Water Pelvis	VAM	Orange	D	Chest	Pelvis	Feet
3. Fire Solar Plexus	RAM	Yellow	E	Head, Eyes	Solar Plexus	Thighs
4. Air Heart	YAM	Green	F	Shoulders	Kidneys, Colon	Ankles
5. Ether Throat	HAM	Blue	G		Joints	
6. Brow	OM	Indigo	A			
7. Crown	High-pitched humming	White, Violet	B			

- **Contact** A Polarity contact with two hands is needed on any two of the three (Chakra triad) areas of the body associated with the Chakra sound? (**mcs**) for details. *For example: you may need to contact your forehead and belly area for the Fire Solar Plexus Chakra, while doing the sound of Ram and wearing the yellow ColorYourWorld Glasses.*

15. MERIDIAN CONSONANT SOUNDS

ColorYourWorld Torch (maglight, holder, clear quartz crystal and thirteen Dinshah mini color filters): see ResonanceRepatterning.net/estore/

Dr. John Diamond used Applied Kinesiology (muscle checking) and his personal research to identify the consonant sounds that correspond to each of the twelve Meridians of Chinese Acupuncture. He discovered that contacting a Meridian Mu Point and repeating its consonant sound has an overall strengthening effect on the Meridian. *The roman numerals before each Meridian are traditionally used in Acupuncture to denote that particular Meridian.*

How To:

- (**mcs**) {1–14} *p.66* for the consonant sound of one of the twelve Meridians, or one of the two 'Extraordinary Vessels' – the Conception Vessel (CV) or Governor Vessel (GV).
- (**mcs**) The ColorYourWorld Torch/Tuning Fork/Finger Contact is needed on the Mu Point? (**mcs**) for details on which color, which Fork or which finger *usually the middle or index finger.*
- The client says the Consonant Sound while the practitioner contacts the Mu Point *pp.67–68* with the ColorYourWorld Torch or Tuning Fork. *If a finger contact is used, the client holds the Mu point on themselves, with instruction from the practitioner.*
- *If you do not have the CYW Torch or Tuning Forks, you can use a finger contact on the Mu point. The Mu points are taught in the Resonance Repatterning Five Element and Meridian seminar.*

MERIDIAN CONSONANT SOUNDS

	Consonant Sound	Meridian	Element	Function
1.	S / Z	I Heart	Fire	The Supreme Controller who rules through love
2.	F / V	II Small Intestine	Fire	The Sorter of what is rich
3.	W	III Bladder	Water	The Container
4.	K / G	IV Kidney	Water	The Provider of power and vital energy
5.	SH / CH / J	V Heart Protector	Fire	The Protector, trust in intimate relationships
6.	R	VI Triple Heater	Fire	The Harmonizer and Regulator of temperature
7.	Y	VII Gall Bladder	Wood	The Decision Maker
8.	TH	VIII Liver	Wood	The Planner
9.	Q	IX Lung	Metal	Divine connection and inspiration
10.	M	X Colon	Metal	Supports letting go
11.	P / B	XI Stomach	Earth	The Nurturer; generous giving
12.	H	XII Spleen	Earth	The Transporter of nurturance to where needed
13.	L	CV Conception Vessel	An Extraordinary Vessel	Reservoir of Yin energy
14.	T / D / N	GV Governor Vessel	An Extraordinary Vessel	Reservoir of Yang energy

MIDLINE MU POINTS

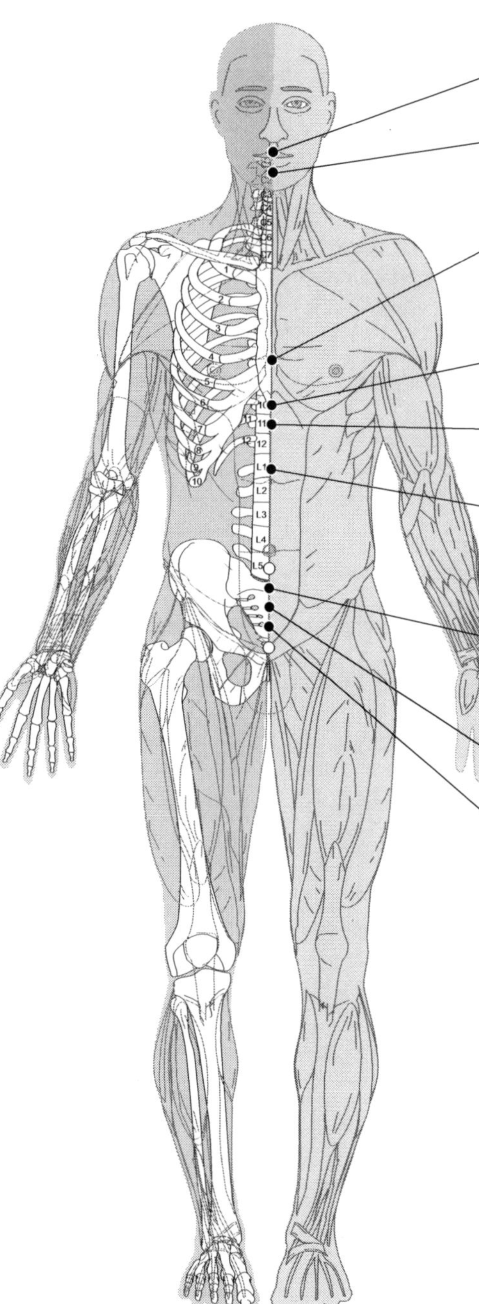

Mu Point for Governor Vessel (T/D/N)
GV 28: Mouth Crossing: *above lip*

Mu Point for Conception Vessel (L)
CV 24: Receiving Fluid: *indent of chin*

Mu Point for upper Triple Heater (Rrrr)
+ Sea of Energy
CV 17: Within the Breast: *on sternum, level with the nipples*

Mu Point for Heart Protector (SH/CH/J)
CV 15: Dovetail: *beneath xiphoid bone*

Mu Point for Heart (S/Z)
CV 14: *in soft tissue below CV 15*

Mu Point for Stomach (P/B)
+ middle Triple Heater (Rrrr)
CV 12: Middle Duct: *half way between sternum and belly button*

Mu Point for lower Triple Heater (Rrrr)
+ Main Center of Energy
CV 5: Stone Gate: *about an inch below the belly button*

Mu Point for Small Intestine (F/V)
CV 4: First Gate: *about an inch above CV 3*

Mu Point for Bladder (W)
CV 3: Utmost Middle: *about an inch above the midline of the top of the pubic bone*

Midline Mu Points

BILATERAL MU POINTS

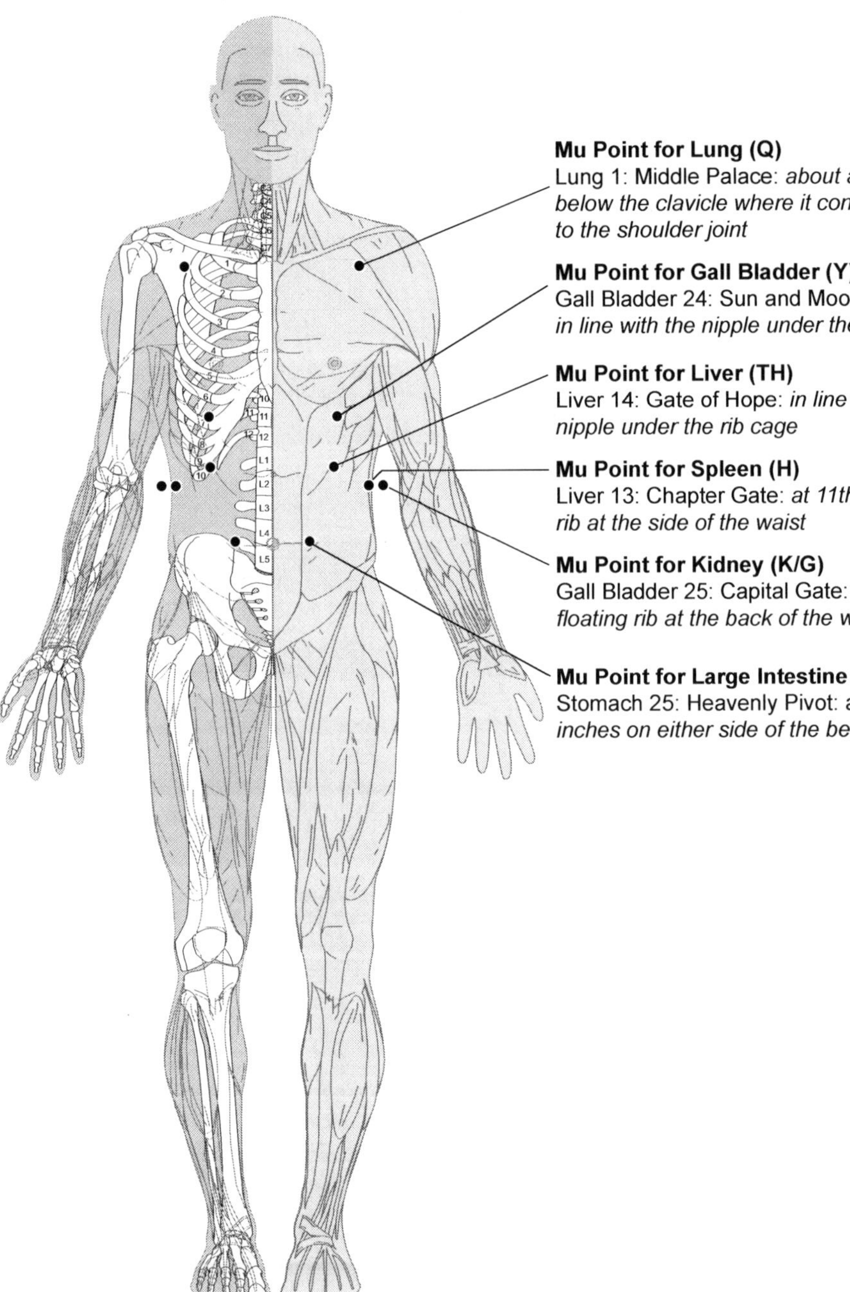

Bilateral Mu Points

16. FIVE ELEMENT SOUNDS

The following Five Element sounds are used in certain schools of Chi Kung to harmonize the five Yin meridians of the Liver, Heart, Spleen, Lung and Kidney.

How To:

- (**mcs**) {1–5} for the Five Element sound you need:

	Element	Sound	Meridian
1.	Wood	SSS	Liver Meridian
2.	Fire	HAAA	Heart Meridian
3.	Earth	WHOO	Spleen Meridian
4.	Metal	HEE	Lung Meridian
5.	Water	SHAE	Kidney Meridian

- Take a deep breath and release the sound in a long-drawn-out tone. After a few repetitions or doing the sound for a minute or two, (**mcs**) This is complete?

17. PENTATONIC MODES

Chromatic Tuner; ColorYourWorld Glasses:
see ResonanceRepatterning.net/estore/

- A pentatonic mode is an ancient scale consisting of five notes, which has both a stimulating and relaxing effect. Each mode has specific intervals (the space between two notes) occurring at a predetermined place in the scale.

- Fascinating research has been done on the Pentatonic Modes: Fabien Maman – author of *The Tao of Sound* and the musician who developed the original theory that the Modes correlate to the seasons associated with the Five Elements of Chinese Acupuncture – discovered that the pentatonic modes have a direct effect on the spine and activate memories.

- Dr. Hans Jenny, who developed Cymatics, vibrated sounds through sand, water and other materials and discovered that it took five notes to create three-dimensional shapes.

- Rudolph Steiner emphasized the importance of the interval of the fifth, which he said is associated with the boundary between the inner 'heavenly' and outer 'worldly' environments and supports the expression of the heavenly in daily life.

- The pentatonic modes often include the interval of the fifth, which is thought to activate creative potential, a sense of expansion and joy, and to stimulate the movement of Chi life energy.

See Further Reading: Fabien Maman, The Tao of Sound

How To:
(**mcs**) {1–5} for the pentatonic mode needed or do the mode for the season you are presently in:

1. Spring pentatonic mode Wood Element
2. Summer pentatonic mode Fire Element
3. Late Summer pentatonic mode Earth Element
4. Autumn pentatonic mode Metal Element
5. Winter pentatonic mode Water Element

- Go to the seasonal mode needed and then (**mcs**) {1–2} for which of the two possible choices for each seasonal mode is needed. Then (**mcs**) {1–12} for its starting note, as shown in the charts that follow. *pp.71–73*

- Write down the notes of your pentatonic scale/mode.

- (**mcs**) for the specific order for toning the notes. You end up with a melody that may use some or all of the five notes in your pentatonic scale, and may repeat certain notes – or may not use certain notes from your pentatonic scale at all. The melody often has a strange ethereal quality to it.

- (**mcs**) *(Client)* needs to wear the ColorYourWorld Glasses while toning or singing the pentatonic melody? (**mcs**) for details on which color in which eye.
- Client listens to the practitioner tone or play the pentatonic melody and then tones the pentatonic melody along with the practitioner.
- *The easiest way to play the mode is with a small keyboard or instrument.*

1. Wood Element

(**mcs**) {1–2}, then (**mcs**) {1–12} for the starting note of the mode. *Write down the notes of the pentatonic mode needed.*

1. Spring pentatonic mode

1.	C	C#	D#	G	G#	C
2.	C#	D	E	G#	A	C#
3.	D	D#	F	A	A#	D
4.	D#	E	F#	A#	B	D#
5.	E	F	G	B	C	E
6.	F	F#	G#	C	C#	F
7.	F#	G	A	C#	D	F#
8.	G	G#	A#	D	D#	G
9.	G#	A	B	D#	E	G#
10.	A	A#	C	E	F	A
11.	A#	B	C#	F	F#	A#
12.	B	C	D	F#	G	B

2. Spring pentatonic mode

1.	C	D	F	G	A	C
2.	C#	D#	F#	G#	A#	C#
3.	D	E	G	A	B	D
4.	D#	F	G#	A#	C	D#
5.	E	F#	A	B	C#	E
6.	F	G	A#	C	D	F
7.	F#	G#	B	C#	D#	F#
8.	G	A	C	D	E	G
9.	G#	A#	C#	D#	F	G#
10.	A	B	D	E	F#	A
11.	A#	C	D#	F	G	A#
12.	B	C#	E	F#	G#	B

2. Fire Element

(**mcs**) {1–2}, then (**mcs**) {1–12} for the starting note of the mode. *Write down the notes of the pentatonic mode needed.*

1. Summer pentatonic mode

1.	C	D	E	G	A	C
2.	C#	D#	F	G#	A#	C#
3.	D	E	F#	A	B	D
4.	D#	F	G	A#	C	D#
5.	E	F#	G#	B	C#	E
6.	F	G	A	C	D	F
7.	F#	G#	A#	C#	D#	F#
8.	G	A	B	D	E	G
9.	G#	A#	C	D#	F	G#
10.	A	B	C#	E	F#	A
11.	A#	C	D	F	G	A#
12.	B	C#	D#	F#	G#	B

2. Summer pentatonic mode

1.	C	D	F	G	B	C
2.	C#	D#	F#	G#	C	C#
3.	D	E	G	A	C#	D
4.	D#	F	G#	A#	D	D#
5.	E	F#	A	B	D#	E
6.	F	G	A#	C	E	F
7.	F#	G#	B	C#	F	F#
8.	G	A	C	D	F#	G
9.	G#	A#	C#	D#	G	G#
10.	A	B	D	E	G#	A
11.	A#	C	D#	F	A	A#
12.	B	C#	E	F#	A#	B

3. Earth Element

(**mcs**) {1–2}, then (**mcs**) {1–12} for the starting note of the mode. *Write down the notes of the pentatonic mode needed.*

1. Late Summer pentatonic mode

1.	C	D#	E	F	G	A#	C
2.	C#	E	F	F#	G#	B	C#
3.	D	F	F#	G	A	C	D
4.	D#	F#	G	G#	A#	C#	D#
5.	E	G	G#	A	B	D	E
6.	F	G#	A	A#	C	D#	F
7.	F#	A	A#	B	C#	E	F#
8.	G	A#	B	C	D	F	G
9.	G#	B	C	C#	D#	F#	G#
10.	A	C	C#	D	E	G	A
11.	A#	C#	D	D#	F	G#	A#
12.	B	D	D#	E	F#	A	B

2. Late Summer pentatonic mode

1.	C	C#	E	F#	A	C
2.	C#	D	F	G	A#	C#
3.	D	D#	F#	G#	B	D
4.	D#	E	G	A	C	D#
5.	E	F	G#	A#	C#	E
6.	F	F#	A	B	D	F
7.	F#	G	A#	C	D#	F#
8.	G	G#	B	C#	E	G
9.	G#	A	C	D	F	G#
10.	A	A#	C#	D#	F#	A
11.	A#	B	D	E	G	A#
12.	B	C	D#	F	G#	B

4. Metal Element

(**mcs**) {1–2}, then (**mcs**) {1–12} for the starting note of the mode. *Write down the notes of the pentatonic mode needed.*

1. Autumn pentatonic mode

1.	**C**	**D#**	**F**	**G#**	**A#**	**C**
2.	**C#**	**E**	**F#**	**A**	**B**	**C#**
3.	**D**	**F**	**G**	**A#**	**C**	**D**
4.	**D#**	**F#**	**G#**	**B**	**C#**	**D#**
5.	**E**	**G**	**A**	**C**	**D**	**E**
6.	**F**	**G#**	**A#**	**C#**	**D#**	**F**
7.	**F#**	**A**	**B**	**D**	**E**	**F#**
8.	**G**	**A#**	**C**	**D#**	**F**	**G**
9.	**G#**	**B**	**C#**	**E**	**F#**	**G#**
10.	**A**	**C**	**D**	**F**	**G**	**A**
11.	**A#**	**C#**	**D#**	**F#**	**G#**	**A#**
12.	**B**	**D**	**E**	**G**	**A**	**B**

2. Autumn pentatonic mode

1.	**C**	**C#**	**F**	**G**	**B**	**C**
2.	**C#**	**D**	**F#**	**G#**	**C**	**C#**
3.	**D**	**D#**	**G**	**A**	**C#**	**D**
4.	**D#**	**E**	**G#**	**A#**	**D**	**D#**
5.	**E**	**F**	**A**	**B**	**D#**	**E**
6.	**F**	**F#**	**A#**	**C**	**E**	**F**
7.	**F#**	**G**	**B**	**C#**	**F**	**F#**
8.	**G**	**G#**	**C**	**D**	**F#**	**G**
9.	**G#**	**A**	**C#**	**D#**	**G**	**G#**
10.	**A**	**A#**	**D**	**E**	**G#**	**A**
11.	**A#**	**B**	**D#**	**F**	**A**	**A#**
12.	**B**	**C**	**E**	**F#**	**A#**	**B**

5. Water Element

(**mcs**) {1–2}, then (**mcs**) {1–12} for the starting note of the mode. *Write down the notes of the pentatonic mode needed.*

1. Winter pentatonic mode

1.	**C**	**C#**	**F**	**G**	**G#**	**C**
2.	**C#**	**D**	**F#**	**G#**	**A**	**C#**
3.	**D**	**D#**	**G**	**A**	**A#**	**D**
4.	**D#**	**E**	**G#**	**A#**	**B**	**D#**
5.	**E**	**F**	**A**	**B**	**C**	**E**
6.	**F**	**F#**	**A#**	**C**	**C#**	**F**
7.	**F#**	**G**	**B**	**C#**	**D**	**F#**
8.	**G**	**G#**	**C**	**D**	**D#**	**G**
9.	**G#**	**A**	**C#**	**D#**	**E**	**G#**
10.	**A**	**A#**	**D**	**E**	**F**	**A**
11.	**A#**	**B**	**D#**	**F**	**F#**	**A#**
12.	**B**	**C**	**E**	**F#**	**G**	**B**

2. Winter pentatonic mode

1.	**C**	**E**	**F#**	**A**	**B**	**C**
2.	**C#**	**F**	**G**	**A#**	**C**	**C#**
3.	**D**	**F#**	**G#**	**B**	**C#**	**D**
4.	**D#**	**G**	**A**	**C**	**D**	**D#**
5.	**E**	**G#**	**A#**	**C#**	**D#**	**E**
6.	**F**	**A**	**B**	**D**	**E**	**F**
7.	**F#**	**A#**	**C**	**D#**	**F**	**F#**
8.	**G**	**B**	**C#**	**E**	**F#**	**G**
9.	**G#**	**C**	**D**	**F**	**G**	**G#**
10.	**A**	**C#**	**D#**	**F#**	**G#**	**A**
11.	**A#**	**D**	**E**	**G**	**A**	**A#**
12.	**B**	**D#**	**F**	**G#**	**A#**	**B**

C.
COLOR AND LIGHT OPTIONS

The new science of photobiology is now proving what the ancients have always known, that we are beings of light. Biophysicists like Fritz-Albert Popp show how light initiates positive reactions in cells. It can repair cellular and DNA damage, often within hours, using faint beams of light, and transmit information instantaneously to every cell in the body.

- Light exists at the core of every cell.
- The functioning of our entire metabolism is dependent on light.
- There are channels of light that in all likelihood correspond to the twelve Meridian channels of Chinese Acupuncture (the research of Professor Kaznachejew and his Russian team).
- Our eyes need to receive more light. Optometrist Dr. Harry Sirota spent more than forty years helping people overcome pain, physical and emotional distress and difficult relationships by prescribing glasses that let in more light to the retina of the eyes and the brain (rather than glasses for 20/20 acuity that many people feel do more harm than good).
- Light, or photons, is one of the major nutrients of our body. Colors – the components of light – are another example of how the Color Energizing Options create positive change.
- It is possible that Acupuncture Meridian points are where we take in and radiate coherent light frequency information. Chloe Wordsworth believes that stimulating or sedating the appropriate Meridian points transforms non-coherent light frequencies (that transmit distorted information to the body-mind) into coherent light frequencies (that transmit coherent, life-giving information to the body and mind).

THE FOUR OVALS FOR EACH OPTION

1. **Muscle check self (mcs)**
or use your felt sense for the
Energizing Option you need

2. **Read the introduction to**
the Energizing Option
Demo the 'How To' if doing
with someone else, or use the
video download if needed

3. **Do the Energizing Option**
   - Observe that you are doing it correctly
   - Breathe
   - **(mcs) / felt sense:** This is complete?
   - **(mcs) / felt sense:** Another Option is needed?

4. **After completing the Option**
   - Take a pause to integrate the positive change
   - Recheck your **felt sense:**
     a. Do you feel more relaxed?
     b. Are you breathing more easily?
     c. Do you notice any other positive change?
   - *RR Practitioners recheck *[cr] statements*

Light and hearing

A Resonance Repatterning practitioner shared a moving story that involved a Color/Light Option. She was doing a session on a ten-year-old boy who couldn't hear without hearing aids. His posture was stooped and his head permanently in a drooped position. When he arrived, he showed no interest in joining the other kids, who had asked him if he wanted to play football with them.

The Resonance Repatterning practitioner had the boy remove his hearing aids and turn his back to her; it was clear that he could hear nothing she said to him. She did a Resonance Repatterning session, using the muscle checking technique to identify the exact unconscious patterns underlying his postural problem and his deafness. To bring these non-coherent patterns back into sync with his optimal frequency range, he needed the color green to be shone into his ears. Using the ColorYourWorld Torch (a flashlight with special combinations of Dinshah color frequency gels and a crystal), she did this Energizing Option with him.

After the session was complete, something dramatic changed: the child's head was now upright and when the practitioner again had the child turn his back to her, so he couldn't lip read, he could hear enough to respond. While she and the mother talked, they suddenly noticed the child was playing football with the other children – another 'first'.

See Further Reading: Dr. Jacob Liberman, Light Medicine of the Future; Dr. John Ott, Health and Light; Darius Dinshah, Let There Be Light; Jack Allanach, Color Me Healing; Chloe Wordsworth, A New Vision.

1. INFINITY 8s FOR ABSORBING PHOTONS (LIGHT)

- Light or photons is one of the major nutrients of our body and brain.
- If we are deficient in light stimulation, we may feel depressed or mentally confused and we may experience physical pain, a lack of well-being or even chronic illness.
- Changing the direction our eyes move to lets in more light to the retina of our eyes and our brain, and may have a powerful healing effect. For example, a woman was seriously depressed; her sister felt instinctively that she needed to constantly remind her to look up so she could take in light, rather than down the way many depressed people do; day by day the depression began to lift.
- When we increase the amount of light we absorb into the brain, the body-mind frequencies become coherent; as a result, we feel happier, more efficient, more loving, less critical, calmer, able to read with more ease, have less pain, and so on.

How To:
It is best to do the Infinity 8s outdoors, but not looking directly at the sun. Feel light (the full spectrum of colors) entering your brain and body through your eyes and even through your closed eyelids.

- Take off your glasses or contact lenses.
- Stand or sit while you move your eyes up an imaginary line in front of you, corresponding to the central midline of your face, and circle them to the left, up the midline and then to the right.
- As you do the Infinity 8s, move your eyes slowly and include the visual fields both above and below the eyes and to the left and right.

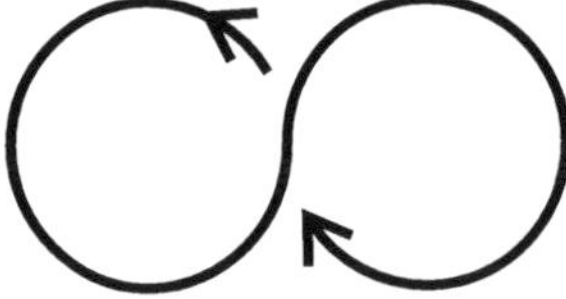

- You can also use the thumb of your right and left hand to make the Infinity 8 circles, making the circles larger – so you move your eyes above your head and down to the chest region as your thumb circles.
- Make sure your eyes are moving, rather than your head.
- Some people feel drawn to do the Infinity 8s by moving their eyes down the midline and then circling them to left and right. This may help break up old vision patterns, but generally we move the eyes up the midline (energizing), and then circle to the left or right.
- (**mcs**) This is complete? If it is, close your eyes and cup your palms gently over your closed eyes, relaxing them into the darkness.

2. VISUALIZING A COLOR

See pp.88–92 for specific information on all thirteen colors.

Each color consists of a particular frequency of light. By visualizing a color, you are bringing its frequency not only to your physical brain and body but also to your emotional and mental bodies.

For people who are in pain or recovering from an accident or operation, sending colors to the area involved may have a healing effect.

- **Green** is associated with balancing, healing and rebuilding muscles and tissues.
- **Yellow** is uplifting, brightening, and is associated with mental stimulation.
- **Red** is associated with warmth and blood circulation, which may be needed if there is coldness, a lack of circulation or during endurance sports.
- **Blue** has been found to relieve itching and has a calming and cooling effect. Blue has also been used for children with dyslexia, helping them read with more ease.

- **Indigo** causes contraction and has been successfully used to stop hemorrhaging.
- **Turquoise** and **pink** are used for anti-wrinkle support.

How To:

- (**mcs**) for the color needed: (red • orange • yellow • green • turquoise • indigo • lavender • purple • magenta • pink • white).
- (**mcs**) for the specific area of the body where the color needs to be visualized: (an area in pain • an area or organ needing light energy • head • face • neck • throat • chest • stomach • pelvis • back • legs • feet • arms/hands • around your body).
- Breathe in the color and as you exhale visualize the color going to the area where it is needed.

3. EMPOWERING MEMORIES

- Happy memories activate endorphins that boost your immune system and bring a sense of well-being.
- The coherent frequencies of happy memories increase the light you radiate and absorb.

How To:

- Close your eyes.
- Think of a happy memory: notice the images and colors; hear the sounds; be aware of the smells and sensations associated with your happy memory; re-live the positive feelings you had in that earlier experience.

- Notice your body's felt sense response to this memory: what do you notice in your belly, spine, heart or other areas? This happy memory is creating coherence in your body-mind energy field; on the physical level it produces a cascade of relaxing neurotransmitters, which is why you may feel energized and optimistic after visualizing a happy memory.

- If possible share your happy memory with someone else, which may increase well-being and coherence for both of you if the person is receptive and 'sees' and feels your happy memory.

4. PERIPHERAL SOFT FOCUS VISION

- Peripheral soft-focus vision activates your Parasympathetic Nervous System (PNS), which, among other functions, allows for relaxation and relationship bonding.

- Soft focus vision gives you a broad global perspective.

- Soft focus vision helps you to be in touch with your feelings.

- When you maintain a soft focus, you are able to see movement, rather than sharp details (helpful when driving or in sports).

How To:

- Remove glasses or contact lenses.

- Look straight ahead while relaxing your eyes so you see 180° around you.

- Bend your elbows so your hands are on either side of your head at eye level. Now move your fingers. While looking straight ahead, see the fingers of both hands moving. Relax your hands by your side and look in different directions while continuing to see 180° all around you.

- Close your eyes and cup your palms over your eyes. Feel your eyes relaxing into the darkness.

5. PALMING

- The optic nerve of the eyes only relaxes when there is no outer light.
- Palming has been used to help numerous eye conditions, including near blindness.
- In addition to many physical benefits, palming has a deeply relaxing effect mentally and emotionally.

How To:
Palming can be done while repeating positive words out loud or in the mind. Words such as 'love', 'thank you', 'faith', 'trust' and naming all the things you are grateful for. Such words stimulate the thymus gland and boost the immune system.

Another option is to alternately palm and then allow sunlight to enter your eyes **through your closed lids.** This alternating light and dark is thought to stimulate the pineal gland. **If outside, lift your palms to face the sun, before placing them over your closed eyes.**

- Cup the right palm over the right eye, with the right fingers resting diagonally across the left side of your forehead.
- Cup the left palm over the left eye, with the left fingers resting diagonally across the right side of your forehead (on top of the right fingers or with the right fingers on top of the left).
- Make sure no light is entering your eyes; now close your eyes. Let them relax deeply into the velvety darkness.
- (**mcs**) Alternate light and dark stimulation is needed? If this is needed, keep your eyes closed and periodically remove the palms from your closed eyes and allow light to enter through your **closed** lids. Then cup your palms over your eyes again, allowing your eyes to relax deeply into the darkness once more. Repeat the alternating light/dark stimulation.

- (**mcs**) Positive words to increase the heart's magnetic field are needed? (**mcs**) for the words needed: (thank you • love • trust • faith • acceptance • gratitude for something). (**mcs**) The words need to be repeated gently (out loud • in the mind)?

- (**mcs**) Palming is complete? If it is, keep your eyes closed as you break the palming contact. When ready, slowly open your eyes, blinking gently, and let in the brightness and beauty of life that surrounds you.

6. FLOWER Pattern Cards / GEOMETRIC Pattern Cards

Flower Pattern Cards; Geometric Pattern Cards:
see ResonanceRepatterning.net/estore/

- Flowers are said to be the language of the heart.

- Each flower vibrates at a high frequency that is associated with its shape (a manifestation of sacred geometry), its essential oil fragrance, taste, texture and color.

- Although each flower's unique frequency note is not audible to the human ear, its frequency as color, shape and fragrance is an Energizing Option that creates coherence and a sense of pleasure and well-being.

- **The Flower Pattern cards** shift our perspective as we see light and shadow, color and shape, depth and texture. Focusing on the flower pattern activates the right brain of imagination, feeling, creativity and global vision.

- **Geometric patterns** represent the basic patterns or building blocks of the creation. When energy vibrates, its movement creates patterns that are universal – intricate patterns such as those seen in the movement of water, cloud shapes and galaxies. A major shape found in nature is the spiral that creates a vortex. Vortices are found in water (they enliven water), and in air, the growth patterns of plants, the spiral of our DNA, as well as in tornados and hurricanes.

- Viktor Schauberger, one of the most knowledgeable researchers on water and its vortices, describes **outwardly expanding motion** from the center of the vortex to the periphery – centrifugal motion – as being explosive, dispersing and destructive, taking more energy than it generates and leading to disorder and decay. Schauberger also talks about the inwardly **in-winding motion** from the periphery to the center – centripetal motion – that is constructive and energy-generating, leading to more order and coherence.
- The vortex contains and gathers energy that sustains life and it disperses what needs to be broken down – the eternal cycle of order and disorder, construction and destruction, life and death.

How To:
Using the Flower/Geometric Pattern Cards, we can feel their energizing effect as each frequency pattern of the geometric shape creates coherence in its own unique way.

- (**mcs**) for which **flower/geometric pattern is needed**; or you can pick whichever card you are drawn to, or randomly pick from the pack.
- (**mcs**) There is an **optimal distance** for holding the pattern from the eyes? (**mcs**) for details.
- (**mcs**) The pattern needs to be **held in a particular visual field?** (Up • Down • Left • Right • Diagonally up left • Diagonally up right • Diagonally down left • Diagonally down right • Straight ahead)?
- (**mcs**) The pattern needs to be **moved slowly** (up-down • left-right • diagonally • in circles • an X • Infinity 8s)?
- (**mcs**) The **eyes need to move from near to far**, to whatever they are drawn to on the card?
- (**mcs**) The **eyes need to trace the shapes**, in whatever way they want? *Use your nose to trace shapes*
- If you have a spiral geometric card, be aware that **tracing the spiral** from the outside to the center generates energy and order, and tracing the spiral from the center to the periphery has a dispersing effect – helpful when you need to disperse negative thoughts, etc. You can (**mcs**) whether to trace the spiral both inward and outward, or in one direction only.
- (**mcs**) **A message from the pattern** is needed? Ask, "If this flower / geometric pattern had a positive message for you, what do you imagine it would be?" *Pause for silence*

7. ColorYourWorld GLASSES

ColorYourWorld Glasses: see ResonanceRepatterning.net/estore/

- The ColorYourWorld Glasses provide you with frames and thirteen sets of roscolene filters that have been combined to create a specific frequency of scarlet, red, orange, yellow, lime, green, turquoise, blue, purple, indigo, violet, magenta and pink. These color frequencies are the same as those used by Dr. Dinshah P. Ghadiali, MD, in his many years of helping people self-heal through color and light.

- It is essential that we absorb the colors of the spectrum in the correct quantity and quality needed for health and well-being.

- Negative beliefs, feelings and attitudes distort or inhibit the absorption of particular color wavelengths (or the lack of a particular color wavelength may manifest as negative beliefs and feelings).

- If we are unable to absorb a specific frequency, we are also unable to radiate that frequency. This lack of radiant color in our energy field impacts our energy level, our emotional well-being, our thinking, and how others relate to us and we to them.

- Each color frequency is traditionally associated with a psychological effect as well as a physical effect. *The colors and their associated qualities pp.88–92; The Dinshah indications for each color pp.97–100.*

- The awareness that light frequencies influence our brain and body helps us understand why wearing tinted glasses is not a good idea: the person wearing them is stuck with one color all day and every day – and it's often a color that does not create a Spiral Up effect!

- As you use the ColorYourWorld Glasses you will discover for yourself the effect they have on your mood, attitude and thoughts, and their ability to help you absorb new information.

See Further Reading: Darius Dinshah, Let There Be Light.

How To:
When wearing the CYW Glasses, periodically (**mcs**) This Energizing Option is complete? *Sometimes a specific frequency may only be needed for a few seconds.*

If you have not yet learned how to muscle check, stay conscious of your **felt sense** so you 'know' inside yourself when you are complete with a particular color frequency, which at the most are worn for five-ten minutes, but usually only for a minute or two. With this information in mind, remove your CYW Glasses when wearing them feels complete.

Muscle checking facilitates identifying the exact color you need in each or both eyes. If you are not muscle checking for a color, be aware that sometimes you may need the complementary color to the color you are drawn to.

- (**mcs**) A color frequency needs to be assimilated through the (right • left • both) eye(s)? *You may need one color for one eye and another color for the other eye; or one color for one eye with no color for the other eye; or the same color for both eyes.*
- (**mcs**) for the color(s) needed {1–13}. *Info pp.88–92 and pp.97–100*

  1. Scarlet
  2. Red
  3. Orange
  4. Yellow
  5. Lime
  6. Green
  7. Turquoise
  8. Blue
  9. Indigo
  10. Violet
  11. Purple
  12. Magenta
  13. Pink

- (**mcs**) (*Client*) needs to allow his/her eyes to move (in whatever direction they choose • in a specific direction)? (**mcs**) for details.
- (**mcs**) *(Client)* needs to express whatever (feelings • images • memories) come to mind while wearing the CYW Glasses? (**mcs**) *(Client)* needs to say more?

- If it is possible to go outside, (**mcs**) *(Client)* needs to do the following sunning exercises while wearing the CYW Glasses: (**mcs**) *(Client)* needs to swing the (head • whole body in a semi-circle movement) from side to side while looking (above the sun • below the sun) through the colored lenses?

THE QUALITIES ASSOCIATED WITH THE COLORS

	Color	Physical Associations	Vitamin-Gemstone Association	Associated Physical Benefits	Associated Psychological Attributes
1.	Scarlet	• Kidneys • Adrenals • Heart • Sexual organs	Vitamin E Garnet	• Diuretic • Assists in the birth process	• Stimulating • Strengthening • Aphrodisiac • Helpful in impotency and sexual apathy
2.	Red	• Spine • Legs • Feet • Large intestines	Vitamin B Garnet	• Brings problems to the surface • Builds liver and blood cells • Stimulates the senses • Dissipates radiation • Anemia	• Courage • Stimulation • Strength • Grounding • Stamina

THE QUALITIES ASSOCIATED WITH THE COLORS

	Color	Physical Associations	Vitamin-Gemstone Association	Associated Physical Benefits	Associated Psychological Attributes
3.	Orange	• Spleen • Lungs • Hips • Sacrum • Lower back • Reproductive organs • Thyroid	Vitamin B Tiger's eye	• Strengthens bones, teeth, hair • Releases muscle spasms (calcium / silicon element) • Lifts prolapsed organs • Stimulates respiration • Decongestant	• Confidence • Expansiveness • Self-assurance • Releases inhibitions • Peacefulness • Resilience
4.	Yellow	• Brain • Solar Plexus • Lymphatic system • Pancreas • Stomach • Liver • Gall Bladder	Vitamin A Citrine	• Aids digestion • Builds nerves and muscles • Expels parasites • Laxative • Activates cranial nerves • Stimulates brain and cervical spinal cord for movement	• Optimistic • Joyful • Playful • Inventive • Original • Adventurous • Spirited • Versatile • Mental ability
5.	Lime	• Brain • Digestive system • Lymphatic system	Vitamin C Citrine	• Builds the thymus and strengthens the immune system • Builds bones • Master cleanser of body (phosphorus content) • Strengthens eyes and bones • Disinfectant	• Persistence • Accuracy • Tidiness

THE QUALITIES ASSOCIATED WITH THE COLORS

	Color	Physical Associations	Vitamin-Gemstone Association	Associated Physical Benefits	Associated Psychological Attributes
6.	Green	• Chest • Heart • Pituitary • Head • Spine • Blood • Lungs	Chlorophyll Emerald Green Jade	• Destroys bacteria • Prevents decay • Rebuilds muscles and tissues • Activates pituitary • Cleanses the system • Balanced cell growth	• Peace • Balance • Relaxation • Emotional calm • Regeneration • Rejuvenation
7.	Turquoise	• Thymus • Brain • Skin • Nervous system	Zinc Turquoise	• Dissipates pain • Tones muscles and skin • Alleviates headaches • Restores vitality	• Tranquility • Resourcefulness • Refreshing • Restoration
8.	Blue	• Skin • Thyroid • Nervous system • Head • Throat • Vocal area • Bronchials	Vitamin B Sapphire Topaz Lapis	• Builds vitality • Soothes irritation and itching • Increases perspiration • Fights infection • Helps in laryngitis • Soothes nerves	• Peace • Contentment • Tenderness • Direction • Confidence • Clarity • Communication

THE QUALITIES ASSOCIATED WITH THE COLORS

	Color	Physical Associations	Vitamin-Gemstone Association	Associated Physical Benefits	Associated Psychological Attributes
9.	Indigo	• Pituitary • Nose • Ears • Left eye • Circulation • Parathyroid • Skin • Nervous system	Vitamin K Diamond	• Causes contraction • Arrests discharges • Slows hemorrhages • Shrinks tumors • Purifies the blood • Relieves convulsions • Tightens and firms muscles and skin	• Inspiration • Power • Protection • Purpose • Introspection • Dispels fear
10.	Violet	• Crown • Cerebral cortex • Right eye • Pineal • Brain • Spleen • Lymphatic system	Vitamin D Amethyst	• Strengthens immune system • Nourishes the brain • Purifies	• Change • Transformation • Accelerated vibration • Inspiration • Expands creative thinking and intuition
11.	Purple	• Neo-cortex • Head • Nervous system • Blood cells • Heart • Kidneys • Adrenals	Bromine Amethyst	• Controls fever • Helps in high blood pressure • Induces sleep • Stimulates circulation in the veins • Calms emotions • Dilates blood vessels • Relieves pain	• Creativity • Synthesis

THE QUALITIES ASSOCIATED WITH THE COLORS

	Color	Physical Associations	Vitamin-Gemstone Association	Associated Physical Benefits	Associated Psychological Attributes
12.	Magenta	• Etheric body • Heart • Nervous system • Kidneys • Adrenals	Vitamin E	• Strengthens and balances the energy field • Regulates the heart, blood pressure, adrenals • Improves circulation • Helps in bronchial ailments and fevers	• Compassion • Mental and emotional balance • Love • Acceptance
13.	Pink	• Heart • Skin • Nervous system	Rose quartz	• Soothes the skin • Anti-wrinkle properties • Lifts the spirits • Aids in circulation	• Sensitivity • Love • Refinement • Delight • Joy • Calming

8. ColorYourWorld TORCH

ColorYourWorld Torch; red LED light; Near Infrared Red light (NIR): see ResonanceRepatterning.net/estore/

- The CYW Torch box set includes a quartz crystal on a silver base for amplifying and transmitting the color frequency; thirteen Roscolene color gels; and the maglight with its 'holder' for the crystal and gels.

- The color gels for the CYW Torch have been combined to create the specific color frequencies recommended by the Dinshah Health Society. Each color, with its own frequency, is transmitted through the light of the CYW Torch, amplified by a quartz crystal. (A rose quartz crystal can also be used.)

- Geometric symbols, which include the Sanskrit Chakra symbols, the five Platonic solids and the Flower of Life, can be placed in the 'holder' attached to the CYW Torch, to be used along with the colors and the quartz crystal.

- **Research on light** Through the science of photobiology, German biophysicist Fritz-Albert Popp and Russian researchers have discovered that light can initiate or stop reactions at the cellular level, and genetic cellular damage can be repaired, sometimes within hours, by faint beams of light.

- We literally communicate through light: optical fiber telecommunications networks transmit data through impulses of light. For instance, a single beam of light, smaller than a human hair, can carry 200,000 telephone conversations simultaneously! In other words, light carries information. It is like tuning our radio to a particular frequency that gives us the 'information' of a specific radio program. Similarly, our trillions of cells – which at their core emit light, says Popp – are constantly receiving and communicating information, through light, for the millions of per-second cellular responses that make our life possible.

- What is even more fascinating about Popp's research is that light emitted from cells can be coherent or non-coherent. This means that non-coherent light carries distorted information to the body-mind field; and coherent light carries coherent life-giving information. **From this point of view we can see that disease, pain, emotional reactiveness, mental upsets, depression, relationship problems, negative habits, attitudes and addictions, can be viewed as the outcome of non-coherent or distorted light information.**

- The purpose of the CYW Torch – whether it is used on Acupuncture points, Jin Shin Jyutsu Safety Energy Locks, the spine, cranial bones, over a place of pain or over the seven energy centers or Chakras – is to help correct distorted light information that may be causing our physical, emotional and mental non-coherence.

- By introducing the color light frequencies, it may help our cells to emit coherent light and transmit life-giving information to our body-mind field.

- The ideal is always to re-establish the natural balance of the body-mind for its optimal functioning. Since we are a non-linear living system, it may take only a very small input of light to have a significant and positive outcome for our body and mind.

- The use of color is becoming more and more widely accepted, thanks to the pioneering research and experience of contemporary and earlier generations of scientists and explorers. Over the last 150 years people like Goethe, Rudolph Steiner, Edwin Babbit, Dinshah Ghadiali, Spitler, Fritz-Albert Popp, Peter Mandel, John Ott, Jacob Liberman, Harry Sirota and others have proven the effectiveness and power of light – not to talk of past pioneers: Hippocrates, the father of modern medicine, who two thousand years ago used color for healing in ancient Greece; and Ayurvedic medicine, which has used color for thousands of years.

- Modern research is now discovering that shining a Near Infrared Red (NIR) light intra-nasally (in the nose) has given people significant improvement in their Alzheimer's condition. Melatonin levels and mental test scores have improved with the near infrared red light. In

China researchers treated 43 patients with Parkinson's disease for ten days at thirty minutes per day. 26 of the 43 patients had significant improvement. Stroke victims and patients with traumatic brain injury, depression, migraines, allergies, skin problems and insomnia are other conditions, among numerous others, that have been helped.

How To:

- If using the red LED light (said to boost the immune system and has been used for back pain and blood pressure problems) or the NIR red light, you clip it in the nose and use each day for up to twenty-five minutes. There are no side effects. It needs to be used daily as a Positive Action for more serious conditions or until results are experienced.

- For the CYW Torch (**mcs**) {1–13} for the color needed from the chart. *pp.97–100*

- *If you do not have the geometric symbols, simply use the quartz crystal and color gels that come with the CYW Torch.* (**mcs**) A (Sanskrit Chakra symbol • Platonic solid symbol • Flower of Life symbol) is needed? (**mcs**) for details.

- (**mcs**) {1–3}.

  1. **The light needs to be focused on one of the following:**
     - on an Acupuncture point *Mu Points pp.67–68 or use the* FIVE ELEMENT AND MERIDIAN *and* INNER CULTIVATION *books for those who have attended these seminars*

     - on a Jin Shin safety energy lock *p.201*

     - on a cranial bone *p.223*

     - on a vertebra *p.44*

     - over a front/back Chakra area *Info* CHAKRA *book*

     - in the energy field? (**mcs**) for details on where and what kind of movement

2. **The light needs to be shone on one of the following:**
   - into the mouth
   - into the nose (You may need the NIR red light, which has been used in China for stroke, neurological disorders, Alzheimer's, Parkinson's, migraines and pain.)
   - into the ears {left • right}
   - on an ear reflex Acupuncture point (**mcs**) for details on where
   - on a foot or hand reflex point (**mcs**) for details on where
   - on a face reflex point? (**mcs**) for details on where

3. **(*Client*) needs to look at the light** (*NOT* the LED or NIR lights) with the (left • right • both) eye(s)? Cup the palm over whichever eye does not need the color and simultaneously move the CYW Torch in one of the following ways: (**mcs**) for details.
   - in the Circles in the Three Dimensions *#9 p.101*
   - in a visual field: up-down / left-right / diagonally from down left to up right / diagonally from down right to up left / spiraling from the periphery to the center both clockwise and counterclockwise (breaks up non-coherent patterns) • spiraling from the center to the periphery both clockwise and counterclockwise (energizing).

DINSHAH INDICATIONS FOR THE 12 COLORS/LIGHT

1.	**Scarlet**	• Dinshah uses this color as a kidney and adrenal stimulant when shone over the kidneys. • A general stimulant. • Raises blood pressure by constricting the blood vessels, increasing heart rate and stimulating activity of the kidneys and adrenals. • Stimulates the reproductive system, menstrual function and sexual desire when deficient. • Scarlet is generally used only for a short time.
2.	**Red**	• Red is the color of the Earth Coccyx Energy center and is associated with grounding, stamina and the will to live. • Because it has the longest wavelength, red is able to penetrate the skin and stimulate blood circulation, for which this color is well known. • The red color causes detoxification through the skin and is used to counter burns and x-ray burns. • Red stimulates vitality in the heart, lungs and muscles. • It excites activity when there is sluggishness or a lack of motivation. • It is often used for skin problems, eczema and frostbite, as well as for coughs, asthma and laryngitis.

3.	**Orange**	• Orange is the color of the Water Pelvis Energy center and is associated with confidence, expansiveness, resilience and creativity. • Orange relieves muscle spasms and tension. • It stimulates the mammary glands for milk production. • It stimulates the appetite for those suffering from underweight. • It is used in cases of fear (alternate with blue), depression, pessimism and for people who wake up in a bad mood. • Orange has been used successfully in cases of arteriosclerosis and heart problems (alternating orange and blue). • Dinshah uses orange to correct bone softness, build the lungs and to stimulate respiration and the thyroid.
4.	**Yellow**	• Yellow is the color of the Fire Solar Plexus Energy center and is associated with intelligence, focus, clarity, power, vitality, warmth and self-confidence. • The color yellow helps concentration and stimulates the brain (writing on yellow paper also helps stimulate the brain). • Yellow is the color of the sun energy with its stimulating effect and ability to uplift the spirits. Used for depression and sadness. • Yellow is used for detoxification of the liver and lymphatic system; especially helpful for combatting colds and flu. • Dinshah uses yellow to energize muscles and support the motor nervous system; to stimulate the digestion and pancreas; to increase bowel movements and expel worms.
5.	**Lime (lemon)**	• Dinshah uses lime for dissolving blood clots. • Helps expel mucus and fluids from the lungs. • Bone builder, by phosphorus effect. • Brain and thyroid stimulant.

6.	**Green**	• Green is the color of the Air Heart Energy center and is associated with cleansing, healing, calming and balancing. • Green supports the regeneration of muscles and tissues. This color relaxes and is revitalizing when exhausted. • Green helps reduce swellings, balance the immune system, regulate the lymph system, eliminate bronchial catarrh and balance the body-mind in cases of chronic disease, tumors, cysts, ulcers, eye diseases and diabetes. The color green is said to control histamine release and to stimulate the pituitary. • Green is soothing and brings a sense of contentment. • Green alternated with blue is effective for joint inflammation. It is also a germicide, bactericide, antiseptic and disinfectant.
7.	**Turquoise**	• Turquoise calms the brain (used on the front and back of the head). • Skin tonic (wrinkles). • Used for rebuilding burned skin.
8.	**Blue**	• Blue is the color of the Ether Throat Energy center and is associated with peace, relaxation and contentment. Blue is soothing, calming and cooling: it is used in all cases of heat, fever, hyperactivity and itching. It is a natural sedative. • Blue is associated with the endocrine system and the pituitary gland and is excellent to use when under stress. As a pineal stimulant, it builds vitality. • It is used for infections and allergies, and because it is anti-bacterial it is said to reduce or eliminate infection when shone on infected areas of the body; it is also used for eliminating warts. Alternating blue with green is used for joint inflammation. • Blue is excellent in cases of hyperactivity, insomnia, hemorrhaging, impotence, frigidity, menopause. • Blue regulates contraction of muscles, ligaments and tissues.

9.	**Indigo**	• Indigo is a mixture of blue and violet and is the color of the Brow Energy center. • It is associated with inspiration, vision, intuition and clear perception. • Indigo has a contractive effect: good for hemorrhaging.
10.	**Violet**	• Violet is the color of the Crown Energy center and is associated with intuition, spirituality and inner stillness. • According to Dinshah, violet is a spleen builder and stimulant, it tranquilizes the nervous system, promotes production of white blood cells (leukocytes) and decreases muscular activity.
11.	**Purple**	• Dinshah uses purple as a kidney and adrenal depressant for its calming effect when they are over-active. • Decreases sensitivity to pain; induces relaxation and sleep. • Lowers blood pressure by dilating blood vessels, reduces heart rate (when used over the left and right side of the chest) and slows down the activity of the kidneys and adrenals. • Lowers body temperature; controls fever. • Balances sexual desire when excessive. • Helpful in dry coughing (no production of phlegm).
12.	**Magenta**	• Balances the emotions and strengthens the energy field. • Helpful for the kidneys, adrenals and the reproductive system.
13.	**Pink/rose**	*Additional to the basic 12 Dinshah colors* • Pink is associated with unconditional love. • Pink has a calming effect in cases of anger and violence. • Indicated when a client needs to see life through 'rose-colored glasses' to shift a negative, critical attitude.

9. CIRCLES IN THE THREE DIMENSIONS

- This Energizing Option encourages the eyes to move near-far and in circles to release eye muscle tension.
- The movement of the eyes stimulates the input of light/photons to the retina (the back of the eyeball), which are transmitted to the brain-body system as electrical impulses of light.
- This movement of the eyes is significant in view of modern research showing that light may be one of the major nutrients of the body-mind system.

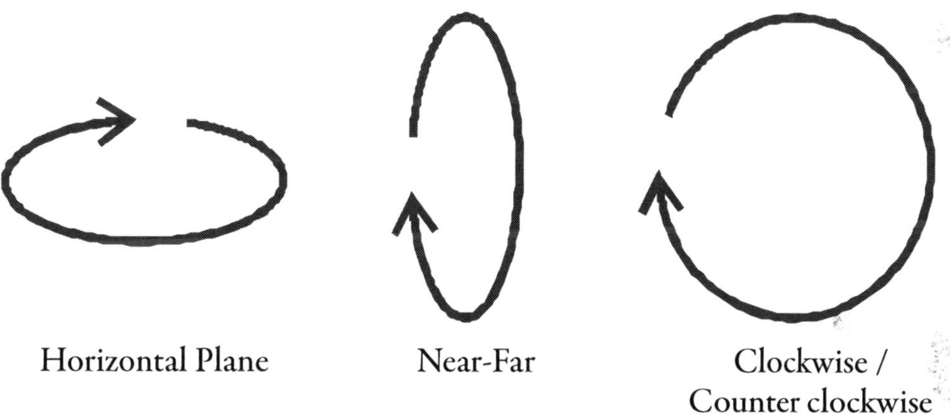

Horizontal Plane   Near-Far   Clockwise / Counter clockwise

How To:

- If you have the ColorYourWorld Torch you can (**mcs**) for the color needed, and then circle the Torch in the three dimensions. *It is easier having someone else do these circles for you.* Relax your eyes and follow the crystal color. *Do not use the LED or NIR red lights for this.*
- If you have the CYW Glasses, but no CYW Torch, you can (**mcs**) for the color needed in one/other/both eyes as you circle in the three dimensions with your thumb.
- If doing the circling with your thumb instead of the CYW Torch, stretch your arm in front of you with your thumb pointing up and your elbow a

little bent. Bring your thumb in front of your nose so you can easily see the 'smile' lines of the 1st joint.

Begin moving your thumb slowly in a big circle on a horizontal plane, as though tracing the edge of a large plate. Move your eyes only, rather than your head.

Breathe and focus on the smile lines of your thumb joint. After circling a few times, change the direction.

- Now bring your thumb in front of your nose and move it in a circle away from you and then toward your nose again in a near-far plane. Breathe and focus on the lines of your thumb joint. After circling a few times, change the direction.

- Finally, bring your thumb to a 12 noon position above your head and circle your thumb in a clockwise direction. Breathe and focus on the lines of your thumb joint. After circling a few times, circle your thumb in a counterclockwise direction.

- End with some palming: cup both palms over your eyes with the fingers relaxed diagonally across your forehead. Breathe and relax into the darkness.

10. TRACING

- Tracing stimulates the tiny saccadic movements of the eyes, which are essential for attracting photons of light into the eyes.

- It has been said that if the saccadic movements stopped, we would be blind within three minutes!

How To:
With your nose, trace the edges of objects both large and small, as well as shadows, colors, pictures and the shapes of people's faces. Connect one shape to another as you trace.

11. CLEANSING THE ENERGY FIELD with the Seven Colors plus Overtones

Nestor Kornblum's Harmonic Overtone CD and booklet:
see ResonanceRepatterning.net/estore/

- Each Chakra energy center is traditionally associated with a color: red, orange, yellow, green, blue, indigo, violet and white, as in the colors of the rainbow.

- The colors of the Chakras can be 'seen' in the energy field around the body by those who have a broader range of color frequency vision; there are also special cameras that are able to photograph these colors in the etheric field.

- If there are distortions from non-coherent light frequencies – caused by life-depleting beliefs, attitudes, mental stress, emotional reactivity or physical problems – these blocks are seen in the energy field as dark areas where there is an absence of light/color, or as a dulling of the colors.

- Cleansing the energy field with the seven colors while doing the harmonic overtones, helps to balance the energy field colors. Try doing this Energizing Option when you feel tired, depleted or exhausted. See if it helps you.

How To:

- (**mcs**) for the **color(s)** needed (red • orange • yellow • green • blue • indigo • violet • white). *White is the color of purification. As white contains within it all the colors of the spectrum, it is said to bring balance to the whole body-mind field.*

- (**mcs**) for the **direction** in which the client needs to sweep:
  - **a. In front:** from the top of the head to the feet
  - **b. In back:** from the feet to the top of the head
  - **c. In front:** from the feet to the top of the head
  - **d. In back:** from the top of the head to the feet

- (**mcs**) for the number of times you need to repeat each *{a–d}* color sweeping. *Usually one to three times is sufficient*

- Have the palms of your hands facing your head / feet within about six-twelve inches from your body. Imagine the (*name color*) light radiating from your palms. Relax and breathe.
- When holding your hands at your head or feet, imagine the color light flowing throughout your body.
- Now, as you do the harmonic overtones, or listen to the harmonic overtoning, sweep your hands slowly down or up your body. Pause in front of the Chakra energy center associated with your color, or over any place where you have pain or discomfort. Feel the color-light moving into this area bringing relaxation from tension and healing. Imagine the color-light and sound, regenerating every cell and organ of your body and brain and bringing emotional and mental balance.
- As you sweep the color-light, be aware of some of the major qualities associated with the color. *Info pp.88–92 It is good to memorize some of these basic qualities and indications before you begin; in this way you think/say the appropriate qualities while you or your client does the sweeping and toning.*
- On completing the sweeping of one color, (**mcs**) or ask yourself, another color is needed?

12. SILK SCARVES FOR THE CHAKRA ENERGY CENTERS

The nine Silk Scarves for the Chakra Energy Centers, including the five needed for the Five Elements of Chinese Acupuncture: see ResonanceRepatternng.net/estore/

- The Chakras are reservoirs of energy that make all physical, emotional and mental functioning possible.
- Each Chakra is traditionally associated with a color and we can use these colors to harmonize our Chakras.

How To:

- (**mcs**) {1–7} for the color needed for balancing its associated Chakra Energy Center.
- (**mcs**) Client needs to (place the scarf around the neck • place it on or around a particular area of the body • move with the scarf). (**mcs**) Music needed?

	Color	Energy Center
1.	Red	Earth: Base of Spine Coccyx
2.	Orange	Water: Pelvis
3.	Yellow	Fire: Solar Plexus
4.	Green	Air: Heart
5.	Blue	Ether: Throat
6.	Indigo	Brow
7.	Violet	Crown

13. SILK SCARVES FOR THE FIVE ELEMENTS

The nine Silk Scarves for the Chakra Energy Centers, including the five needed for the Five Elements of Chinese Acupuncture: see ResonanceRepatternng.net/estore/

- The five Elements of Chinese Acupuncture (Wood, Fire, Earth, Metal and Water) are a map of universal frequency patterns. Everything in the creation – including mental and emotional states, physical organs, sounds, tastes and colors – resonates with one of these five Elements.
- If you have an excess or deficiency in any Element, it will show up as a symptom of distress – either in your life, your relationships or in your physical, emotional and mental state.

- The colors associated with the Elements can help restore balance and harmony to your Five Elements (and the twelve Meridians that correlate with the Elements) through the use of the silk scarves, the ColorYourWorld Glasses, the ColorYourWorld Torch, and even the colors of the clothes you wear.

How To:

- (**mcs**) {1–5} for the Element needed and its color from the chart *p.106*.
- (**mcs**) for what to do with the color scarf: (Move with it: (**mcs**) for music needed • Have it in the room where you can see it • Wrap self up in it *children tend to love this* • Place it over any area of pain or discomfort • Cover the meridian organ associated with the Element).

	Element	Color	Associated Meridian	Associated Emotion
1.	Wood	Green	Liver Meridian Gall Bladder Meridian	Excess / Suppression of Anger
2.	Fire	Red	Heart Meridian Small Intestine Meridian Heart Protector Meridian Triple Heater Meridian	Excess / Lack of Joy
3.	Earth	Yellow	Spleen Meridian Stomach Meridian	Excess / Lack of Empathy or Sympathy
4.	Metal	White	Lung Meridian Large Intestine Meridian	Excess / Lack of Grief
5.	Water	Blue	Kidney Meridian Bladder Meridian	Excess / Lack of Fear

D.
MOVEMENT OPTIONS

Life is energy in motion. If we want life, we must move. As Peter Egosque, developer of the Egosque Method, says:, "We don't move enough to maintain our health."

Children, whose energies are vibrating optimally, are full of vitality and movement; old people, whose energies are vibrating less than optimally, have diminished vitality and move slowly or with difficulty and pain.

As we age or experience pain and mental-emotional upsets, we tend to avoid moving, not realizing that correct movement will release pain and rejuvenate our energy and health. A sedentary lifestyle always leads to diminished energy, obesity and sickness.

Even when we are mentally and emotionally 'sedentary', this lack of movement stops us from moving forward confidently in our life. We are no longer open-minded to new possibilities for being fully engaged in life – a sign that our mental and emotional frequencies have spiraled down.

Movement activates the spiral structure of our bones, muscles and ligaments for growth and strength. It integrates our brain hemispheres, relieves anxiety and stress, stimulates our blood and lymph circulation. It produces endorphins of joy that boost our immune system and leads to relaxation, human connection and joy.

THE FOUR OVALS FOR EACH OPTION

1. **Muscle check self (mcs) or use your felt sense for the Energizing Option you need**

2. **Read the introduction to the Energizing Option**
   Demo the 'How To' if doing with someone else, or use the video download if needed

3. **Do the Energizing Option**
   - Observe that you are doing it correctly
   - Breathe
   - (**mcs**) / **felt sense:** This is complete?
   - (**mcs**) / **felt sense:** Another Option is needed?

4. **After completing the Option**
   - Take a pause to integrate the positive change
   - Recheck your **felt sense:**
     a. Do you feel more relaxed?
     b. Are you breathing more easily?
     c. Do you notice any other positive change?
   - *RR Practitioners recheck *[cr] statements*

Movement and self-healing

There is a tendency to remember dramatic Resonance Repatterning cases, which is natural because the strong emotional charge associated with them makes these sessions stand out in our memory. The following story, to illustrate the power of movement, is no exception.

In a Resonance Repatterning seminar I taught Movement Option #10 – the Chi Kung Bounce, Holding and Energy Circulation. I also shared what a Chi Kung Master had said about this Option: that if you do the Chi Kung Holding every day for forty minutes and then circulate the energy, you will never be sick a day in your life, and you can heal yourself of any problem.

Some of the students had a friend who was scheduled for surgery to remove fibroids from her ovaries. The students told her about this Movement Option and, motivated by her desire to avoid the surgery, she started doing the Chi Kung Bounce and Holding every day for forty minutes, followed by the four circulation movements. Within a few days she could feel heat from her palms, and her belly area became warm. By the end of two weeks she knew without a doubt that the fibroids were gone. When she insisted on a check-up before the surgery, they discovered what she already knew – there were no fibroids.

How movement improves our health and level of energy

- Movement stimulates the production of **endorphins,** which bring a sense of joy, well-being and a feeling of uplift. Even moving our arms and legs freely and energetically as we walk or run will uplift our spirits as a result of the endorphins that are activated.

- Movement automatically stimulates our **breathing**, which brings **oxygen** to every cell – the brain and eyes need more oxygen to function than any other organ in the body. Breathing also carries away toxic gases.

- When walking and swinging both our arms freely – one arm swinging in unison with its opposite leg – this natural cross-crawl movement integrates our **brain hemispheres** so we access a higher state of intelligence and creativity.

- Movement is the primary way to keep **lymph** moving. Lymph removes blood proteins and toxic material from around each of our millions of cells; when our lymph system is unable to function – for instance in cases of severe shock – it can lead to death.

- Movement activates **blood circulation** so nutrients are carried to every cell and metabolic acid wastes and gases are carried away for elimination.

- Movement disperses adrenaline and cortisol – activated by our **fight-flight stress responses.** If not dispersed through movement, adrenaline and cortisol are deposited in muscles and joints and these acid deposits cause stiffening of muscles, tendons and joints, or even arthritis.

- Movement keeps the **joints** open and the **tendons and muscles** relaxed and toned, so we maintain our flexibility and our muscle mass, free ourselves from pain, encourage the full flow of energy and blood circulation and maintain our youthful vitality into old age.

- Movement stimulates the flow of **Chi life energy** throughout our body-mind system so we feel on top of the world.

The following movements offer a universal range of ways to keep our energy balanced and flowing. In relation to any problem that we **don't** want to resonate with, or any intention that we **do** want to resonate with, we can shift our resonance through one or more of the Movement Options.

If you have not yet learned the muscle checking technique to identify which Movement Option is best for you, simply listen to your felt sense – how your body and feelings respond when you look at the Movement Options list. You already 'know' what you need. Trust yourself.

1. SNS BODY SHAKE-OUT

- The Sympathetic Nervous System or SNS Body Shake-Out releases residual tension from the body-emotions-mind system, helping you recharge and re-energize yourself.

- After a shock, stress or upset, it is essential that you release any excess energy your sympathetic nervous system mobilized for handling the stress.

- After an animal goes on the alert for danger, it automatically releases any excess SNS energy (not already discharged in running away or fighting) by rolling, running, shaking or trembling. Similarly, the Body Shake-Out is one way for you to quickly release stress (adrenaline and cortisol) from your system.

How To:

- Start by shaking out your wrists, the way children do – vigorously.

- Now shake your wrists and elbows vigorously... Add your shoulders into the shaking.

- Now include your neck in the shake-out, as well as your wrists, elbows and shoulders.

- Shake out your chest and hips. Bounce and move your knees. Shake out your ankles and finally shake your whole body!

- Complete the SNS Body Shake-Out by bending forward from the hips and shaking out your jaw, shoulders and arms. Let your mouth hang open and even relax and shake out your tongue! Slowly straighten from the hips. Take a breath, relax, smile and sigh out slowly.

2. FREE MOVEMENT

- Movement is an expression of Life. Find any excuse to move: stretch and dance as often as possible during the day to integrate your brain hemispheres and produce endorphins of pleasure that boost your immune system.

- Endorphins have a close association with memory, so movement done during any learning process helps you remember with pleasure what you have learned.

- Remember what one 95-year-old lady said when she was asked what she did to stay so youthful and active: "I dance and sing all day!"

How To:

- Choose music you love. *See Resources for a few CD suggestions*
- You can have your eyes open or closed.
- Allow every part of your body to move spontaneously and freely, as an expression and celebration of the powerful being you are. Experiment with new ways of moving your shoulders, arms, ribs, hips, knees, ankles and toes. Sing along as you move.

3. BRAIN-INTEGRATING CROSS CRAWLS

This movement (used in different healing and educational systems for learning and body coordination) simultaneously activates the left and right hemispheres of your brain.

Brain-Integrating Cross Crawls is excellent to do:

- when your thinking is unclear or confused
- when communication is difficult
- when you need to increase your learning capacity, memory retention or quick thinking.
- for athletes, dancers and actors, Brain-Integrating Cross Crawls are particularly important for high-level body coordination and memorizing lines, steps and movements, especially in stressful conditions.

See Further Reading: Paul Dennison, Brain Gyms

How To:

- Lift one knee and tap it with the opposite hand. Let that knee drop and lift the other knee and tap it with the opposite hand. (Make sure you are not lifting and moving **the same** arm and leg as many people find themselves doing in the beginning. Observe what you are doing and make sure you are moving **the opposite** arm and leg.)

- Do the movements rhythmically, moving your shoulder towards its opposite hip. Swing your arms across the midline of your body as you move. Feel your upper and lower ribs moving too in a counter-rotation.

- Experiment with slowing the movement down, like a Tai Chi dance, slowly bending the knee of each standing leg once you land on that side.

- You can experiment with variations in the Cross Crawl, as long as you move the opposite arm and leg together: with bent knee and lifting the foot behind you, tap the foot with the opposite hand.

- Continue this rhythmic movement until you (**mcs**) This is complete?

4. YAWNING AND STRETCHING

- ◎ Yawning and stretching release tension, especially in the jaw, mouth and eyes.

- ◎ Yawning and stretching also release excess sympathetic nervous system energy (and adrenaline and cortisol), which is mobilized for handling daily stresses.

- ◎ As yawning recharges our energy, ideally we need to yawn and stretch constantly throughout the day, not just when we wake up in the morning.

How To:

- Stretch every part of your body, especially your spine, arms, hands, fingers and feet.

- Yawn with your mouth wide open to release jaw and eye tension.

- Allow yourself to make uninhibited, pleasurable yawning noises!

5. FOUNTAIN OF YOUTH NECK RELEASE

- The Fountain of Youth Neck Release, a Chi Kung movement from China, is said to be the fountain of youth because it aligns your cervical vertebra. This alignment supports the flow of nerve impulses and increases the flow of Chi life energy between your brain and body.

How To:

- Inhale while you slowly raise your shoulders towards your ears and lift your face to the sky.
- Exhale as you slowly lower your shoulders and bring your face to its normal horizontal position. Now bring your chin in slightly, creating traction in the back of your neck. Hold for a few seconds and then relax before repeating the Fountain of Youth a few times.
- Make sure you bring your chin in, rather than down towards your chest. Also make sure your head is back, aligned with your spine, rather than jutting forward, which happens when our upper chest collapses. With your fingers under your clavicle bones, lift your upper chest about a quarter of an inch; notice how your head automatically moves backwards into its proper alignment.

6. OPEN HEART GESTURE

- This position represents the mudra or hand position of unconditional love.
- Doing the Open-Heart Gesture has an energizing and strengthening effect on you as well as anyone present.
- In the face of potential violence, several Resonance Repatterning practitioners went into the Open-Heart Gesture, which seemed to calm the assailant so that no harm was done.

How To:

- Stand or sit with your palms open by your sides, facing upwards. In public you can inconspicuously do this Open Heart Gesture at any time.
- You can also lift your arms, holding your palms open in front of you. If you feel like moving, do so while holding your palms up and open.

7. CALMING CROSS-OVERS

- The Calming Cross-Overs position releases emotional and environmental stress and integrates both hemispheres of your brain.
- It is a wonderful position to do while lying in bed at night before sleep or in the morning in preparation for getting up and starting a new day; or when you return home after a day of work.
- Your children may want to do the Calming Cross-Overs whenever they feel upset, worried, stressed, and especially before taking a test. Teachers who have taught children the Calming Cross-Overs say that it works magic with behavioral problems.
- At the end of a day the Calming Cross-Overs clears the day's stresses and strains. Try it during an argument and watch how things calm down!

How To:

- Cross one ankle over the other. (It doesn't seem to matter which ankle you place over the other.)
- Place your hands in front of you, with **the backs of your hands** touching.
- Still with your hands back to back, place one wrist on top of the other so your palms now face each other. Palms facing, interlock your fingers. Bring the two clasped hands down and in a half circle towards your chest so your interlocked hands rest on your chest, and your elbows are relaxed against your ribs.

- Place your tongue on the roof of your mouth, close your eyes and breathe slowly. Relax deeply and feel the layers of tension letting go. Often within fifteen seconds you will feel a profound sense of release.

- The final part of the Calming Cross-Overs is to uncross both your ankles and wrists and place your fingertips together. Allow your fingertips and hands to move in any way they are drawn to: up-down, left-right and out-and-in. These movements have a synchronizing effect on your brain areas: upper and lower brain areas, the left and right brain hemispheres and the front and back brain areas.

8. NODDING YOUR HEAD YES

- This powerful yet simple Energizing Option strengthens your thymus gland, which is associated with your immune system.

- Nodding your head Yes also lets people see that you have heard them. A man who was having trouble with his teenage son went home after attending the EMPOWERING YOURSELF WITH RESONANCE REPATTERNING seminar, and gently nodded his head when his son spoke to him. After two days his son said, "Dad, you've really changed since that seminar. You are communicating so much better!"

- Nodding your head Yes, associated with the quality of empathy in Chinese Five Element Acupuncture, has a calming and grounding effect on you as well as the person you are talking to. It is particularly calming to nod your head slowly when someone is angry or upset, especially if your eyes are relaxed and loving.

- When you feel off-balance you may inadvertently shake your head No. Change it to a Yes and notice how you immediately feel more centered.

9. WATER

Conduction of electricity

Water is a medium for a different kind of movement: conducting electrical impulses throughout the body, which makes movement possible. Every cell is filled with and surrounded by water – ideally 60% inside our cells and 40% held in the fluids outside our cells (in the blood and the lymph fluid that bathe every cell).

Cell dehydration

Dr. F. Batmanghelidj has proven that many chronic illnesses are directly related to cell dehydration and can be corrected through drinking pure water. Pangman and Evans state that the 60:40 ratio of water inside and outside our ten trillion cells supports optimal functioning of all our organs. When this ratio is not maintained and total body water diminishes or water inside the cells decreases, illness results.

The reality of bottled water

The Environmental Working Group analyzed the company websites of 170 varieties of bottled water:

- Only one brand supplied purification and contamination information.
- Nine out of ten top-selling water companies refused to disclose where their water comes from.
- 32% did not disclose information on treatment or purity of the water.
- Only three bottled water products received good ratings by the researchers.
- 40% of bottled water is regular tap water.
- 38 low-level contaminants were found in bottled water.
- Ten tested brands contained disinfectant by-products, caffeine, Tylenol, Nitrate, Arsenic, industrial chemicals, and of course Fluoride.

Fluoride

Fluoride – an industrial waste product – was originally put in tap water to prevent tooth decay. However, numerous studies with fluoride and non-fluoride communities indicate that fluoride does not prevent decay in teeth. (The fifty billion dollars spent on the treatment of cavities each year supports the fact that fluoride is not the answer to decaying teeth!)

In the meantime, the general public is being medicated without its consent. Fluoride is a trace element, and we only need minute amounts in its natural form (found in food); we do not need synthetic fluoride in our toothpaste and water supply.

Scientist Dr. Paul Connett in his book *The Case Against Fluoride,* discusses the hundreds of peer-reviewed studies proving that fluoride has been scientifically linked to:

- arthritis and bone fractures
- increases in infertility and sperm damage
- increase in lead absorption
- lowered IQ
- lowered thyroid function
- bone cancer
- inactivation of thirty-two enzymes
- dementia
- fluorosis of the teeth

So why is the government paying to have this waste product put in our water?

What To Do:

- A whole-house CNS water structuring unit (no filters or changeable parts) delivers structured water to kitchen, bathroom and all water appliances in the house. Structured water contains vortices that gather energy and bring life to water. Third-party laboratory tests show that ordinary tap water cannot be distinguished from pure spring water when it is filtered through one of the CNS water structuring units. In addition, structured water is rich in hydrogen – the key to cellular energy – which means that potentially water could turn out to be a potent force in our self-healing process.

- A whole house or counter top certified water filter that removes chlorine by-products, fluoride, lead, arsenic and other toxins, is essential.
- A seven-minute shower exposes you (through your lungs and skin absorption) to more toxins than drinking a gallon of unfiltered tap water. A shower filter that guarantees removal of toxins, chlorine, fluoride, lead and other toxins, and protects your lungs from airborne water contaminants, is another important healthcare insurance.
- Always store your water in glass bottles. Cancer-causing PFOAs, flame retardant chemicals and BPA, which mimics the female hormone estrogen, leach into the water from plastic bottles. If you leave a plastic bottle of water in your car, heat increases the amount of chemicals that leach out of the plastic!
- **Your need for water may not necessarily register as thirst so it is important to drink pure, (structured and filtered) water regularly: 8 glasses per day in normal circumstances. Drink more often if you work-out, live in a hot dry climate or are going through a stressful situation. Dr. Batmanghelidj recommends two glasses on rising, two glasses before bed, and one or two glasses half an hour before meals.**

See Resources: Your Body's Many Cries for Water by F. Batmanghelidj; Dancing with Water by M.J. Pangman and Melanie Evans for both structuring and creating hydrogen-rich water; see cnswater.com for information on structured water and CNS units; The Water Prescription for Health, Vitality and Rejuvenation by Christopher Vasey.

How To:

- If water is needed as an Energizing Option, drink a little pure water, holding it in your mouth before swallowing it.
- During a Resonance Repatterning session, a client may need water as deep stresses are released and new coherent life patterns are created.
- You can also (**mcs**) how much pure water you need to drink daily as a Positive Action. If you eat a lot of fruit and drink fresh organic vegetable

juices, you may find your need for water is less. Organic fruit and vegetables are the ultimate in terms of structured water and the minerals, enzymes and vitamins they contain.

10. CHI KUNG BOUNCE, HOLDING AND ENERGY CIRCULATION

- The Chi Kung Bounce is energizing so is good to do whenever you feel tired or low in energy.
- The Holding position builds your vital force, needed for regenerating the body when pain or problem areas have created a devitalized state.
- Once you have built up an energy charge with the Holding position, you can do the Circulation movements to circulate your energy throughout your body-mind energy field. *See spiralup127.com for the video download of all Spiral Up Energizing Options, including this one.*

How To:
Chi Kung Bounce

- Make sure your toes are pointing forward. Turning your toes out depletes your energy.
- Start to bounce only your knees. The rest of your body relaxes and bounces in response to your knees. If you relax your chin as you bounce you will hear your teeth clicking together, which stimulates your brain. Relax your arms so you can feel your wrists, elbows and shoulders bouncing. Relax your chest and belly. Let everything bounce!

Chi Kung Holding

- After bouncing for about a minute, slowly bring your palms so they are facing your belly area, about 6–12 inches away. Your fingers are relaxed and your hands are slanted upwards as though supporting a ball of air. Your wrists and fingers are soft and flexible, not rigid; relax your thumbs. Your knees are flexed and your toes are still pointing forward. Breathe rhythmically. Relax into stillness to build the vital energy that is needed for all self-healing.

Chi Kung Energy Circulation 1 - 2 - 3 - 4

- **Circulation (1)**
  This particular movement activates circulation in your legs – good for swollen legs and ankles, stagnant lymph in the legs and varicose veins – and stimulates the movement of energy from the pelvis, where stagnation may cause pelvic issues or congestion in the legs. If you feel spaced out or not fully present, Circulation (1) is excellent as it helps you to ground yourself to the earth, especially if you do it while standing barefoot on the earth.

Stand with your feet shoulder-width apart with your toes pointing forward.

Have your hands flexed with your palms facing the floor on either side of your hips.

As you exhale, bend your knees a little and press your palms down towards the floor.

As you inhale, straighten your legs slightly, and your fingers and hands relax as you lift your wrists up – just a few inches.

Repeat the downward pressing movement and upward lifting relaxation of your wrists a few times or until you feel complete.

- **Circulation (2)**
  With your arms at shoulder height on either side of your body, elbows slightly bent and your palms facing the floor, exhale as you slowly press your palms down to waist height.

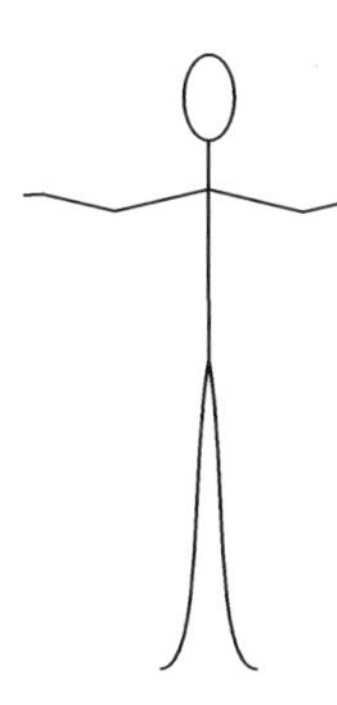

Very slowly turn your palms up, inhaling as you lift your palms and arms to shoulder height.

Again, **slowly** turn your palms down and press towards the floor once more.

Do the movements as slowly as possible and with focus. Repeat a few times until you feel complete.

- **Circulation** (3)
  Bring your hands to the top of your chest about an inch away from your body – your elbows are bent and your arms and hands are parallel to the floor with your palms facing down.

  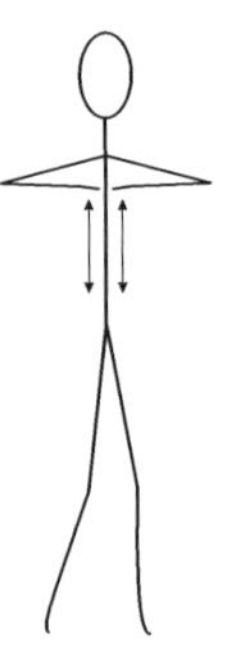

  Press your palms downwards to your lower belly; then **slowly** turn your palms up and let your palms float up to the top of your chest once more.

  Again, **slowly** turn your palms down and press the palms downward. Repeat a few times until you feel complete.

- **Circulation** (4)
  Bring the backs of your hands together in front of your belly.

  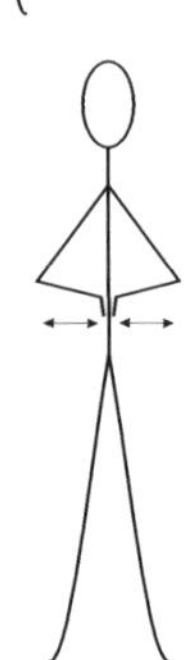

  Inhale and move your palms out to the sides of your waist.

  Turn your palms slowly so they face each other and as you exhale 'press' the ball of energy between your hands until your hands are about 6"/15cm apart in front of your belly.

  Repeat a few times until you feel complete.

11. DIAPHRAGM ANXIETY RELEASE

- A tight diaphragm stops you from breathing freely, which can create an imbalance in the oxygen/carbon dioxide ratio needed for energy and health.
- A constricted diaphragm is associated with anxiety, hiccups and a lack of energy.
- If your diaphragm is tight, it may cause top/bottom 'splits'. As a consequence, you may feel disconnected from your lower body (the waist down), or from your upper body (the waist up), or you may have weight issues in your upper or lower body or at your waist.
- Diaphragm tension always leads to a feeling of not being fully energized.

How To:

- Slightly bend forward. Place your fingertips under your rib cage. (You can rest the back of your wrists on your upper thighs so you have leverage to press your fingers higher under your ribs as the diaphragm relaxes, but avoid bending too far over or causing pain.)

- Press your fingers under your ribs. Take a deep breath and exhale, making a powerful *Ha!* sound by strongly squeezing in your belly. This *Ha!* pushes your fingers out from under your ribs. Relax after the *Ha!* and without inhaling press your fingers under your ribs and massage as deeply as you can.

- Again, press under your ribs, take a breath and once more let out a powerful *Ha!* on the exhale. Without inhaling, press your fingers under your ribs as high as you can and massage.

- Repeat a few times until you muscle check or feel it is complete.

- Stand up, relax and take a deep breath, expanding your ribs fully. Exhale with a slow gentle haaa.

12. SHOULDER BLADE RELEASE

Dr. Randolph Stone, who developed Polarity Therapy, observed that people with heart problems have extremely tight shoulder blades. When we walk, ideally we need to swing our arms from our shoulder blades: the shoulder blades should alternate between moving away from the spine and towards the spine with every step and forward-backward arm swing.

How To:

- Stand with your feet wide apart. Place the palms of your hands together behind your back. Now clasp your fingers so your palms face upwards (rather than turned down toward the floor).

- While standing, inhale and lift your arms straight up behind you as high as is comfortable for you. Feel your shoulder blades coming together and your chest opening up. As you exhale, relax your arms down behind you, feeling your shoulder blades releasing and your chest relaxing. 
- Lift your arms up behind you, holding the stretch for two seconds only, and then relax. Repeat a few times.
- Now inhale and lift your arms up behind you and simultaneously bend at the hips – keeping your spine straight as you bend forward, your spine and neck parallel to the floor. 
- Exhale and relax your arms over your head without any force or bouncing. As your shoulder blades release and your spine becomes stronger and more flexible, you will be able to bring your arms a little further over your head. Hold the stretch for a few seconds. It is essential to avoid bouncing or forcing when you do this stretch. If you over-stretch an elastic band it eventually becomes flaccid and loses its natural tone. So we need to avoid over-stretching ourselves. 
- Inhale, hold your breath and slowly straighten up – keeping your spine straight and your arms held up as high as possible behind you. Once standing, exhale and release your hands. Your arms slowly float up in front of your chest and then slowly relax down to your sides.

13. KATSUGEN

- Katsugen was developed by Haruchika Noguchi, a Japanese healer who originally used Katsugen movements for pregnant women to give birth free of pain.

- Katsugen consists of movements that arise naturally and automatically from within. These movements balance and circulate the Chi life energy to support health, vigor, confidence and physical coordination. Noguchi says they encourage the release of physical and emotional toxins, leading to a sense of freedom, fulfillment and well-being.

- Katsugen movements activate and balance the primal life energy as a means for bringing health, stamina and boundless vitality.

See Further Reading: Richard S. Omura, Katsugen – The Gentle Art of Well-being

How To:

- You can do Katsugen with your whole body or, as we sometimes do in Resonance Repatterning, with your hands.

- If using your hands, place your hands, palms up, in front of the body center that you feel needs balancing or recharging (the pelvis, solar plexus, heart, throat, or head) or (**mcs**) which center needs balancing.

- Close your eyes to keep your focus within and relax, breathing slowly. Now allow your hands to move in whatever way they are drawn to, whether in the field or touching the body center: just allow the dance to happen. If there is fear about closing the eyes, try closing them for short moments only.

- If doing Katsugen with your whole body (whether standing or sitting), again, close your eyes, relax and breathe. Allow your whole body to move in any way it wants. The movement comes from within you by itself, rather than from your left hemisphere thinking brain.

- Katsugen can be done in a few minutes or over a period of 30 minutes or more. When complete, the movement automatically comes to a natural ending, or you can consciously decide to end the Katsugen movement; or you can (**mcs**) for when it is complete.

- If this spontaneous movement does not happen, it is possibly because of tension. The following tension releases in preparation may help:

1. As you inhale, bring your bent elbows to shoulder height, on either side of your body, with your hands and forearms facing the opposite wall. As you exhale, bring your shoulder blades together. At the furthest point of the exhale and the tension, suddenly relax everything: arms, breath, head, body. Repeat a few times.

2. Kneel or sit for this preparatory release. Breathe in. As you exhale, twist to the left as though looking over your shoulder toward the base of your spine. At the furthest point of tension, suddenly relax and return to your forward-facing position. Repeat on the other side.

14. SHOULDER JOINT OPENING

- The shoulder joints often become chronically tight. Besides tension, acid deposits can cause arthritis

- Joint tension blocks the full range of motion and inhibits the energy flow of the six Meridians that pass through the chest and shoulder joints (Lung, Heart, Heart Protector, Large Intestine, Small Intestine and Triple Heater Meridians).

How To:

- Bring your left elbow in the air and place the palm of your left hand on the back of your left shoulder.

- Bend your right elbow behind your back, placing the back of your right hand on your spine, only as far up your spine as you can reach **without pain.**

- Touch your left and right fingers, and gradually over time clasp the fingers of your two hands together.

- Repeat with the other side: Bring your right elbow in the air and place the palm of your right hand on the back of your right shoulder. Bend your left elbow behind your back, placing the back of your left hand on your spine, until the fingers of your two hands touch or clasp together.

- **Preparatory release for the Shoulder Joint Opening** (if your shoulder joints are very tight and you can't easily clasp hands behind your back).

  Stand with your feet wide apart, turn your right foot to the right and bend your right knee. Facing right, place your right hand on your right thigh and as you exhale swing your left arm in circles (up in the air in front of you and **circle the arm back**).

  Straighten up and repeat on the other side, turning your left foot to the left, bending your left knee. Facing left, place your left hand on your left thigh and as you exhale swing your right arm in circles (up in the air and **circle it back**).

- You should now be able to touch or clasp your hands behind your back with more ease. If it is difficult, start slowly and persevere.

15. HIP U'S, HULA AND THE POLARITY PYRAMID

- In Polarity Therapy, the hips and pelvis are considered the negative pole to the positive pole of the shoulders.
- Energy tends to stagnate and become blocked in the negative pole, which is perhaps why so many people become constricted in their hips, have sacral misalignments, hip surgeries and pelvic problems (such as prostate troubles, bladder infections and womb prolapses).
- Movement of your pelvis and hips encourages the free flow of energy all the way to your feet, as well as releasing tension in the positive pole of your shoulders.
- Releasing the positive pole of your shoulders similarly stimulates energy flow in your hips.
- Once your hips are feeling flexed and relaxed through the Hip U's and Hula, you can do the Polarity Pyramid to energize your hips and shoulders, release energy blocks in your spine and help move stagnant energy in the pelvis, causing such problems as menstrual cramps and pelvic 'heaviness'.

How To:

- **Hip U's** Stand with your feet at shoulder width apart. Begin to free up your pelvis by bending your knees and moving your hips in a U-shape from the right side, downward and up to the left side, and again down and up to the right. As you do this movement, place your hands in a side-to-side contact over your hip joints. Repeat until you feel complete.
- Repeat the same movements, but this time backwards and forwards. Tip your sacrum back, arching your back slightly, bend your knees and swing the pelvis down and tip it forward and up. As you do this movement place your hands in a front-to-back contact – one hand below your belly button and the other hand on your sacrum in the back. The movements can be quite small. Repeat until you feel complete
- Now with your feet apart and keeping your legs straight, circle with your hips – left, forward, right and back. Your body is attached to the hips and naturally rotates along with your hips.
- **Hula** Keeping your upper body still, do the hula – moving your hips left, forward, right and back, rotating them in a complete circle, visualizing the Hawaiian hula. Put on some good 'hip' music and explore moving, releasing, relaxing, flexing, strengthening and empowering your hips, rotating both clockwise and counterclockwise!
- **Polarity Pyramid** stand with your feet wide apart, knees bent so your thighs are almost parallel to the floor. Place your hands above your knees – thumbs on the inside of your thighs, fingers on the outside. Straighten your arms and then bend your knees as far as you are able (knees are over the ankles, not bent over your feet). With straight arms, bent knees and the buttocks behind you, this creates traction in the whole of your spine and opens up the pelvis. Keep your arms straight (they tend to bend). You can gently rock from side to side, or (with arms still straight), alternately bring one shoulder, and then the other, gently towards its opposite hip.

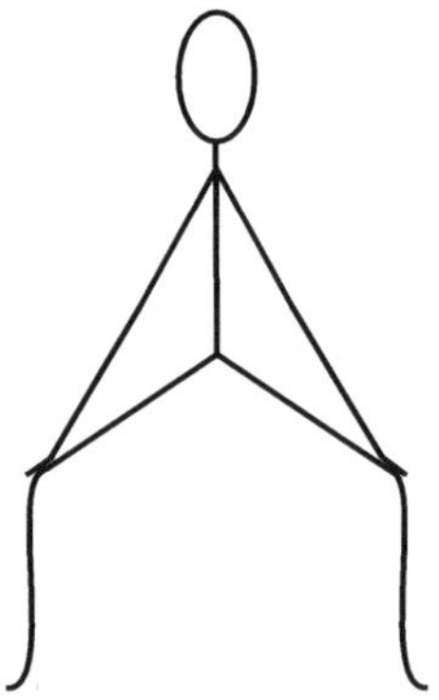

16. THE POWER OF RHYTHM

See Resources for CD suggestions for rumba music.

- Life is energy in motion, or in rhythm. One of the core reasons for all distress or disease is that we are out of rhythm – we have lost the frequency pulsation at which we most optimally vibrate.
- It is no surprise that people in cultures that have a deep connection to their bodies, their feelings, the earth and with each other, dance regularly, if not daily.
- A lady in her mid-90s, who was vital, flexible and ageless, was asked what she did to maintain her youthfulness. She answered that she danced and sang all day long!
- Dance is about rhythm. Rhythmic movements reconnect us to our natural pulsation and to others' natural pulsation – to our body, to our sensations and our feelings of joy.
- Rhythmic movement stimulates neural connections in the brain and body for brain-body coordination and clear thinking, and activates endorphins that boost our immune system and bring a sense of joy and heightened well-being.

Rumba Rhythm
How To:

- The rumba rhythm is a simple 'quick-quick-slooow' rhythm.
- With each quick-quick-slow, change your body weight from one foot to the other. Practice moving round the room – walking, moving sideways, backwards, forwards – always changing your weight completely so your body is directly balanced over the foot you are on. You may want to practice this so you can balance on each foot, slightly lifting the other foot, to check that you really are fully over each foot as you step from one to the other – quick, quick, slow and pause.
- Once you are comfortable with the basic quick-quick-slow, you can now have fun doing the 'quick-quick-slooow' rumba rhythm along with hip

rotation. Step on the 'quick' bringing your body fully over that foot – and rotate your hips in a small half circle behind you. Repeat with the next 'quick': step, body weight over that foot, relax the hip rotating it behind you. On the 'slooow' do the same thing: balance your body fully over the standing foot, and on the 'slow,' elongate the hip rotation, slowing it down. Put on some rumba music and enjoy moving round the room: always fully changing your weight with each step and then rotating your hip.

- Now as you move, slide the inside of your big toe along the floor – never lifting your feet from the floor. You are totally grounded: the toe of the foot you are **not** standing on is always pointed behind you, firmly on the floor. With professional Latin dancers, the buttocks and thigh of their back, non-standing leg, pointed behind them, is so straight and strong that you wouldn't be able to lift that leg off the floor!

- Once your feet have the rhythm and your big toe is sliding on the floor (rather than lifting your foot with each step), explore relaxing your body, arms and head! Freely follow the rhythmic movement of your feet, breathe, allow your arms and head to move with the music and have fun.

Waltz Rhythm

See Resources for CD suggestions for waltz music.

How To:

- The waltz rhythm is about opening the heart. It is a 1-2-3 rhythm: walk, walk, feet together. Ladies start by stepping back with the left foot; gentlemen start by stepping forward with the right foot.

- **Ladies:** On the first beat slide your left toe back. On the second beat slide your right foot in a big step diagonally back (not directly back), coming onto your toes and bringing your left foot next to your right foot. On the third beat relax, bending your knees in preparation for the next step back with your right foot.

- **Gentlemen:** Step forward with your right foot – sliding with your right toe but placing your right heel on the floor. **Beat two**: Slide your left toe in a big step diagonally forward, coming onto your toes and sliding your right foot next to the left foot, and on **beat three** relax and bend your knees, already moving your body and your left toe forward on beat one.

- The emphasis is on the second step or beat – one, **two**, three. On the second step stretch up your body and arms, on the third step bring your feet together, relax and pause, bending your knees in preparation for the next step on the first beat. This is the first basic step of the waltz that can lead to numerous variations and rhythms that make the waltz one of the most beautiful of ballroom dances.

- Now let go of the steps. Feel the one-**two**-three rhythm and move in any way you want with your body and arms. Let your steps become bigger as they keep the 1-2-3 rhythm. Enjoy opening your heart and feeling the rhythm of the beautiful music.

17. THE SIX FUNDAMENTAL MOVEMENTS

- There are six fundamental movements we need to integrate into our daily life if we want vitality, balance, health, good posture and grace into old age.

- Infants and small children quickly master these six movements, which are the basis for all movement. But over time our pains, shocks and traumas manifest as constriction in one or more of these six fundamental movements. As a result we are unable to access each of the six movements naturally, spontaneously and with ease as we walk, run and dance. Our posture now becomes locked in one of the six ways of moving, our energy becomes blocked and moving depletes our energy rather than recharging us with energy.

These six fundamental movements are based on ideas gleaned from Gyrotonics developed by Juliu Horvath; Awareness through Movement developed by Moshe Feldenkrais – plus latin and ballroom dancing!

How To:

Do each of the six movements in sequence.

1. **Extending**

   Sit on the edge of your chair; with feet wide apart and turned out, extend your spine from your feet by pulling in from your belly and narrowing your waist as you gently lift your ribs and upper chest, keeping your shoulder blades together and down. Your chin is in and there is a gentle pull on the crown of the head (or you can extend your head, facing the sky).

   - Some people are stuck in extension or this sway-back position.

2. **Flexing**

   With feet turned in, press your feet to the floor. This tips your pelvis forward, causing you to bend your spine, round your shoulders so your head and neck to move forward (rather than back, aligned with your straight spine).

   - Many people – not just seniors, where it is commonly seen – are stuck in flexion, unable to extend or elongate their spine, neck and head. This flexed posture of rounded shoulders, a caved-in chest and head held forward, is accompanied by tension in the shoulders, rounded shoulders, back and neck stiffness or pain and diminished energy.

   - Repeat the Extension and Flexion movements are few times, always starting with your feet.

3. **Rotating**

   - As we walk or dance, the hips and lower ribs rotate to the left and right, equally on both sides. And the upper ribs and shoulders rotate in the opposite direction to the hips: for example, the left hip rotates backward and the left shoulder moves forward, toward the right standing leg side.

   - When you walk, bring one shoulder towards the opposite hip as you swing that arm forward from your shoulder blade.

- Many people hardly rotate their hips at all when they walk; some not at all. Others are stuck with one hip slightly rotated to the left or right.

How To:

- Sit on a chair with your spine straight – knees and feet about a foot apart.
- Press with your right foot into the floor, which moves your right knee and hip back. Repeat with the left foot. As you press, see the knee moving back a few inches. Relax back to center and repeat a few times
- Now after you press the foot into the floor and the knee moves back a few inches, feel the same side hip rotating, which then rotates your back, and finally your upper back, neck and head. Rotation starts with your feet and moves up your body to your head. Be gentle with yourself. Do less rather than more, as Feldenkrais teachers always insist.
- Release the pressure of your foot on the floor, and your knee, pelvis and spine will unwind in sequence, relaxing back to neutral.
- Repeat on your left side. Observe which side is easier for you.

4. **Translating**
   - Translating our weight means that we change our weight from one foot and side of our body to the other foot and side, constantly moving our center of gravity from side to side with each step we take.
   - With each step, we need to fully place our weight on our standing leg and shift our center of gravity over this leg, while maintaining complete balance. Then we shift our weight, center of gravity and balance to the other leg. When we fail to translate or shift our weight and our center of gravity, we become stuck favoring one foot and side of the body over the other foot and side – commonly seen with people who stand on one leg when they are talking or on the phone, rather than standing on both feet.

- With age, or with people who have had accidents, we may avoid shifting our weight from one foot to the other altogether. Because of our lack of balance, we tend to stay in the middle with no shifting of our weight and center of gravity as we walk. This way of moving leads to a lack of freedom in our movement, a loss of grace and to shuffling our feet – associated with the aged and infirm. Even people in their thirties and forties may stop shifting and balancing their weight easily from side to side, inadvertently de-energizing themselves.

- When sitting at a desk or computer, you may notice that you favor sitting on one sitz bone and tipping your body to that side. We need to be balanced on both sides, both sitz bones and both feet (unless we want to move, in which case we need to translate or shift our weight to one side or the the other before returning to the balanced state once more).

How To:

- Stand with your weight exactly balanced on both feet in neutral. Now slowly move just your right foot to the right, placing your toe and then foot on the floor. As slowly as possible shift your hips and body over your right foot. When your weight is fully on your right foot and side, lift your left foot and balance.

- Now place just your left foot to your left, placing your toe and then foot on the floor. Shift your hips and body so you are exactly balanced on both feet in neutral, and now slowly shift your weight onto your left foot. Lift your right foot and balance.

- Repeat a few times, moving the foot first, then your weight to neutral, and then to left or right.

- Do the movement forward and backward, moving one foot forward, shifting your weight over the front foot, and balance on the front foot. Repeat, taking a step backward.

- Walk around in slow motion, feeling the translating or shifting of your center of gravity as you balance on one foot completely and swing the back leg forward in preparation for the next step. Feel the point at which your weight is exactly balanced on both feet (easier to feel when moving from side to side).

- Sit down and move from side to side, from one sitz bone to the other. Observe if you favor one. Experiment with 'planting' your sitz bones, in full contact with the chair (or floor if sitting on the floor). Feel yourself sitting with complete balance on both sitz bones.

5. **Side-bending**
   - Walking or dancing, the hip of the forward standing leg is slightly lower than the hip of the leg behind, which is slightly higher. As we walk, our hips gently rock up and down like water being tipped from one side of a bowl to the other side.

   - Simultaneously, the rib cage on the forward leg is elongated or the forward hip and shoulder stretch away from each other and the rib cage on the back leg is shortened – the hip and shoulder of the back leg are closer together or a little 'scrunched'. This is side bending. (You may notice that many men walk with a side-bending motion – their shoulders moving side to side in a sailor roll. This is because they are not using their hips and hip rotation to walk.)

How To:

- Stand with your feet about six inches apart with your hands resting by your side. Slide your right hand a few inches down the outside of your right thigh; then your left hand down the left thigh, feeling the hip and shoulder coming to meet each other as you bend to each side.

- With feet together, bend your right knee by coming onto the ball of your right foot; press on the ball of your right foot and rotate your left hip to the left – so your right chest now faces forward and your left leg is straight. Notice that your left hip is now slightly higher than your right hip. The right side of your body is elongated and the left side of your body is shortened or 'scrunched' – in the side bend.

- Now bend your left knee by coming onto the ball of your left foot; press on the ball of your left foot and rotate your right hip to the right. Your left chest faces forward and your right leg is now straight. Notice that your right hip is now slightly higher than your left hip. The left side of your body is elongated and the right side of your body is shortened or 'scrunched' – in the side bend.

- Have fun **gently** repeating these easy hip-rotating side-bending movements. When it begins to feel more natural, swing your arms and tap your right hand to your bent left knee and your left hand to your bent right knee. As you exaggerate the cross-crawl, see if you can feel the gentle counter-rotation of your upper ribs twisting in the opposite direction to your hips. (This movement is the basis for rumba!)

- With every step you take, feel the side-bending, the balanced translation or shifting of your weight, the rotation of your hips and the flexion and extension of your spine. In addition, feel the strong, engaged muscles of your buttocks and thighs in the back leg as you walk forward. Who knew that walking was this complex! **When these five movements are integrated, walking becomes a total energizing exercise for every muscle in the body.**

6. **Spiraling**
   - Spirals are one of the most predominant patterns found in nature – whether in galaxies, hurricanes, tornadoes, sea shells, flowers or the way water moves in streams and meandering rivers.

   - Spirals gather energy as seen in hurricanes; and the vortex or spirals in water maintain its vitality and aliveness. Similarly, spiraling movements of the body can revitalize us physically and mentally.

   - Spiraling from the outside to the center gathers energy, which would be needed if you are feeling depleted or tired.

   - Spiraling from the center to the periphery discharges energy, which may be needed if you are in a negative state of mind.

How To:

- Sit with your knees and feet apart.
- Begin by circling just your pelvis clockwise, extending your spine as you circle forward and flexing your lower spine as you circle back.
- Now circle your belly, lower ribs and mid-body clockwise, extending the belly area and mid-spine on the forward clockwise circling and flexing your belly and mid-spine as you circle back. Feel your lower ribs circling.
- Move the spiral to your upper chest, extending your upper spine and chest on the forward clockwise circling and flexing your shoulder blade area and spine as you circle back.
- Now spiral the pelvis, mid-body and chest, doing the spiral for each body area in sequence, starting in the center and spiraling outward.
- Finally, spiral the pelvis, mid-body and chest, starting the spiral on the outside, the periphery, and spiraling in toward the center.
- You can also experiment doing the spirals clockwise – often used for bringing new life, energy and order – and counterclockwise for dissipating non-coherent energy patterns. We need both. Every kind of movement has an energy purpose.

18. FOUNDATION POSITION FOR A STABILIZED SPINE

- This position for a stabilized spine is one of the positions used in Foundation, developed by Dr. Eric Goodman and Peter Park, who successfully work with world class athletes and people with chronic back pain. Their book and DVD, *Foundation – Redefine Your Core, Conquer Back Pain, and Move with Confidence* is worth using on a daily basis.

How To:

- Stand with your feet about twelve inches apart, knees very slightly bent and knees over your ankles – not bent over your feet. Stick the buttocks out behind you, keeping your weight on your heels. Your spine is now extended. The hands and arms are held straight and slightly behind you, with your palms and thumbs turned up, which opens up your chest and brings your shoulder blades together and down. Hold and breathe slowly three times.

- Still holding this Foundation position, raise your arms on either side of your ears and breathe three or four times. Finally, place your hands on your knees and elongate your back, with a slight arch. Make sure your knees are over your ankles throughout, rather than bending forward over your feet. *To do the complete set of positions, follow the instructions in the 'Foundation' DVD.*

19. SOMATIC MOVEMENTS

- Somatic Movements are the breakthrough contribution of the late Dr. Thomas Hanna – influenced by Awareness through Movement developed by Moshe Feldenkrais, that re-educates the brain and body for new and more coherent options in how we hold and move our body.

- Elmer Green of the Menninger Clinic writes about Hanna's book, "If I could, I would put *Somatics* in the hands of every neurologist, nurse, psychophysiologic therapist and clinical psychologist in the country."

- Somatic movements offer the possibility for maintaining supple, graceful and healthy bodies that resist the aging symptoms of chronic pain, fatigue and back trouble.

- The following movements represent a few of Dr. Hanna's many powerful, self-healing, re-vitalizing movements, adapted for use in Resonance Repatterning, particularly for the Reptilian Limbic Brain Repatterning taught in the Transforming Unconscious Patterns seminar.

See Further Reading: Thomas Hanna, Somatics.

How To:

(**mcs**) {1–3} for the movements to release the Protective-Startle, Landau or Trauma brain-body posture responses.

1. **Movements to release the Protective-Startle brain-body posture** (**mcs**) {a–b} for the one(s) needed and the number of times to repeat (usually 1–5 times).

   The soft spiraling through the front anterior muscles opens up the contracted anterior muscles and retrains the belly area. Do {a and b} in any order, if doing both of them.

   With each movement, say to yourself, 'Tensing my muscles is in my control. Relaxing them is also in my control'. As you slowly relax, experience how relaxation is under your voluntary control.

   a. **Lie on your back with your knees bent and both feet on the floor.**
      - Clasp your hands under your head. Lift up your head and pelvis in a small movement. Lower your head and pelvis to the floor, arching your back and pressing your bent elbows and shoulders onto the floor.
      - This gentle oscillation between the Protective-Startle movement (head and pelvis lifted) and the Landau movement (back arched and pressed to the floor) lengthens posterior muscles and retrains your back.

   b. **Lie on your back with your legs straight.**
      - Slowly, with awareness, slide your right knee up, keeping your knee to the right, close to the floor. Roll the knee up into the center, so your right foot is on the floor, and then move your right knee to the left towards your left foot, keeping your right foot on the floor and allowing your right hip to gently come off the floor. Relax your head to the right, opposite to the direction of your knee.
      - Now relax the right hip down to the floor again and let your head and knee roll back to center. Your right knee now relaxes to the floor on the right, head to the left. Slide your right foot down until both your legs are straight once more and your head relaxes to the center.
      - Repeat with the left side.

2. **Movements to release the Landau ready-for-action brain-body posture**
Do {a–b} in sequence. (**mcs**) for the number of times to repeat (usually 1–5 times).

By three months of age, the baby initiates the Landau ready-for-action reflex with movements that strengthen the back posterior muscles.

Because of constant tension and repetitive over-use and holding, this natural Landau posture response becomes chronically tight and can't relax. The following movements retrain and relax the posterior muscles.

a. **Lie on your stomach with the left side of your face resting on the back of your right hand.**
   - With awareness of your posterior muscles, lift and lower only your **right elbow** a few times. Relax.
   - Now lift and lower only your **head** a few times, looking over your right shoulder as you lift. Relax.
   - Lift and lower your **right arm and head** together a few times. Relax.
   - Lift and lower only your **left straight leg** a few times. Relax.
   - Now lift and lower the **left straight leg and the opposite arm and head** a few times. Relax.
   - Repeat with the other side.

b. **Lie on your back with your knees bent and both feet on the floor.**
   - Clasp your hands under your head. Lift up your head and sacrum in a small movement. Lower your head and pelvis to the floor arching your back and pressing your bent elbows and shoulders onto the floor. This gentle oscillation between the Protective-Startle movement (head and sacrum lifted) and the Landau movement (back arched and pressed to the floor) lengthens posterior muscles and retrains the back.

3. **Movements to release the Trauma brain-body posture**
These spiraling movements release asymmetrical contractions.

There is no force with any of the movements. They are subtle, easy, totally relaxed, free of pushing yourself into a dramatic stretch.

With each movement, say to yourself, 'Tensing my muscles is in my control. Relaxing them is also in my control'. As you slowly relax, experience how tensing and relaxing are under your voluntary control.

(**mcs**) {a–c} for the one(s) needed and the number of times to repeat (usually 1–5 times).

a. **Lie on your back with your legs straight.**
    - Slowly, with awareness, slide your right knee up, keeping your knee to the right, close to the floor. Roll the knee up into the center, so your right foot is on the floor, and then move your right knee to the left towards your left foot, keeping your right foot on the floor and allowing your right hip to gently come off the floor. Relax your head to the right in the opposite direction to your left knee.
    - Now relax the right hip down to the floor again and let your head and knee roll back to center. Your right knee now relaxes to the floor on the right, your head to the left. Slide your right foot down until both your legs are straight once more and your head relaxes to the center.
    - Repeat with the left side.

b. **Lie on your belly.**
    - Bend and slide the right knee up slightly to the right, keeping it on the floor. Lift the right foot, allowing it to rest on your left calf.
    - Now lift the right foot from the left calf and circle it up and out until the right foot rests on the floor to the right – as far as you can go easily, free of any force.

- Straighten the right leg on the floor as you simultaneously bend and slide your left knee up slightly, lift the left foot so it is resting on the right calf, and then circle the left foot up and out, until it rests on the floor to the left – as far as you can go easily, free of any force.

- The result is a gentle, alternate rocking motion between the right and left hip, knee, lower leg and foot.

c. **Lie on your side with your knees bent.**

- Lie on your left side, resting your head on your arm. Lift your head up and down a few times.

- Now slowly lift the **lower** right leg a few times – only lifting the lower leg from the hinge of the knee.

- Slowly lift and lower your head and lower leg simultaneously, lifting the lower leg from hinge of the knee – knees and thighs holding together.

- Repeat with the other side.

20. MAKKO-HO AND THE POWER OF STRETCHING

- The original Makko-Ho stretches were developed in Japan by Haruka Nagai, after his father had a car accident that left him semi-paralyzed. Zen shiatsu master, Shizuto Masunaga, further developed these stretches by integrating them with the Five Elements and twelve Meridians of Chinese Acupuncture.

- Jacques Gauthier, a French Canadian, had a disease that left him in constant pain and he was becoming paralysed. He too did some similar stretching movements and within three weeks his pain was 50% less. Doing the movements every day and many times a day led to him overcoming his chronic and 'incurable' disease. He now walks across Canada and the USA to prove that there is always hope: we can do anything!

- Combining the stretching movements of Makko-Ho with those of Shizuto Masunaga and a few variations I include creates a quick and powerful way to stretch the body, free up the flow of nerve impulses in our often contracted spine and stimulate the energy flow in all twelve of our Meridians.

It is very important to ***avoid*** *all bouncing with these stretches. Whatever you are able to do is your personal best stretch. You don't need to do more. There are some good YouTubes that demonstrate these stretches. The Makko-Ho stretches are done in the following order:*

1. **Lungs and Large Intestine Meridians**
   Stand with your feet a little apart for balance; interlock your two thumbs behind your back, point your index fingers and curl your other three fingers towards your palms.
   - Bend at the hips, bringing your arms in the air behind your back. Hold the stretch and breathe. Inhale and straighten. You can repeat this three times.

2. **Stomach and Spleen Meridians**
   Kneel, sitting on your feet.
   - Place your hands on the floor behind your feet and lift your pelvis toward the ceiling, arching your back gently and bringing your shoulder blades together. Hold and breathe.

   - When complete, relax your head on the floor in front of your knees (the Child Pose).

   The Fish (an additional position for the Stomach and Spleen Meridians)
   If your knees are tight or you have any back problems, it would be wise to avoid doing the Fish altogether.
   - Come into a kneeling position and sit on your heels with your toes bent under. This stretches your feet (can be painful in the beginning). Breathe.

- Now flatten your toes on the mat so you are sitting on your feet.
- Gently try to sit on the floor between your feet. Just this position, with a straight spine, may be sufficient for you. Breathe.
- If you are easily sitting on the floor between your feet, **and you have no knee or back problems,** you can lean back onto one elbow and then the other; finally you may be able to lie down and stretch your arms above your head. *Always stay in touch with your body, avoiding all pushing or forcing, knowing what is enough for you on any given day. Over-stretching an elastic band leads to its collapse; you don't want to over-stretch your muscles and tendons for a similar result.*

3. **Heart and Small Intestines Meridians**
   Sit on the floor with the soles of your feet together.
   - Relax your knees to the floor equally on both sides while bringing the two feet as close to your body as possible.
   - Maintaining a straight spine, bend forward from your hips. Hold and breathe.
   - Move your feet further away from your body, still with the soles together; now you can bend your spine, relaxing your head on your feet, but still free of bouncing! With your thumbs, press into the arch of each foot to stimulate the reflexes to your spine and your Spleen Meridian (good for prolapses; when you feel emotionally collapsed and needing support).

4. **Bladder and Kidney Meridians**
   Sit with both legs together, straight in front of you, toes pointing to the ceiling.
   - With a straight spine and keeping your toes up to the ceiling, bend forward. The tendency is to round your chest and upper back in an attempt to reach your toes. This defeats the purpose of the stretch. Keep a ruler-straight extended spine.

- Even if you are only able to sit up straight with your toes to the ceiling, hold the stretch and breathe. As you inhale, bring your chin in, rather than up, and feel a gentle pull on the crown of your head toward the sky, elongating your spine and neck. As you exhale, relax your hips and feel yourself relaxing a tiny bit forward (as long as your spine is straight). Eventually, with a straight spine and toes up to the ceiling, your chest will be relaxed on your legs. In the meantime, any stretch is good!

5. **Heart Protector and Triple Heater Meridians**
   Sit cross-legged on the floor either with the right foot in front of the left foot or the right foot resting on your left thigh. Cross your arms with the right arm on top of the left arm.
   - Bend forward with your head towards the floor, your crossed-over hands resting on either side of you.

   - Repeat with the left foot in front of the right or resting on the right thigh. Cross your arms with the left arm on top of the right arm.

6. **Liver and Gall Bladder Meridians**
   Sit with your feet as far apart as is comfortable for you.
   - With your spine straight and the five toes on each foot parallel and pointing evenly up to the ceiling, come forward: inhale and elongate your spine, chin in, feeling the gentle pull on the crown of your head; exhale and relax forward from your hips, keeping your spine straight. Breathe while holding the stretch, free of all forcing and bouncing.

   - You can also sit up straight, with your arms above your head. Bend sideways over your right leg, rest your right arm on the floor by the inside of your thigh and knee and curve your left hand over your head towards your right foot. Repeat on the other side, bringing your curved right arm from over your head towards your left foot.

   - Gently bring your legs together and shake out your knees. When ready, come into a kneeling position.

7. **Cat Stretch and Downward Dog**
   - Start by kneeling and sitting on your toes to stretch our your feet and create more flexibility in your toes and arches.
   - Come onto all fours and flex and elongate your spine like a cat. The cat stretch movement doesn't need to be big. Subtle is often more powerful.
   - Come onto your hands and feet with your buttocks in the air for 'Downward Dog'. Flatten your feet on the floor as much as you can, stretch your spine, look at your thighs.

8. **Lie down and relax**
   Lie down with your knees bent: gently rock your knees left and right before straightening them one at a time onto the floor. Breathe, relax and appreciate what you have just done.

21. SPINNING THE FIVE PLATONIC SOLIDS

See ResonanceRepatterning.net/eStore for the platonic solids;
see Thrivemovement.com for a fascinating video on the geometry of life

◉ These ancient geometric shapes – the cube, icosahedron, tetrahedron, octahedron and dodecahedron – are known as the Platonic solids. They form the building blocks of the physical creation.

How To:

- (**mcs**) {1–5} for the Platonic solid needed

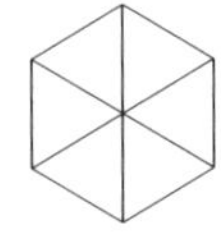

1. **Cube:** This shape, associated with the Earth base of the spine Chakra, may be helpful for grounding, security, providing the will to live and the capacity to manifest ideas and goals in the world of matter.

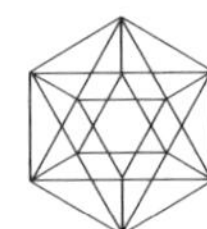

2. **Icosahedron:** This shape, associated with the Water pelvis Chakra, is created from triangles (The male principle of the Fire Chakra) and represents movement, flow and change. It may be helpful when you feel stuck or frozen.

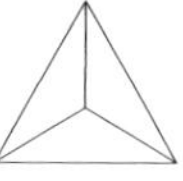

3. **Tetrahedron:** The triangle represents the Divine, the three-in-one of perfect harmony and equilibrium. This shape, associated with the Fire solar plexus Chakra, may be helpful when you need to be ignited by spirit; when you need inner strength and stability.

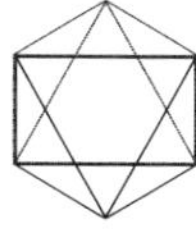

4. **Octahedron:** This shape consists of two pyramids both resting on the same square foundation. The pyramid acts as a lens that focuses the light of spirit into matter. The octahedron, associated with the Air heart Chakra, may be helpful to open your heart to give and receive love, especially when it has closed through pain, trauma and betrayals.

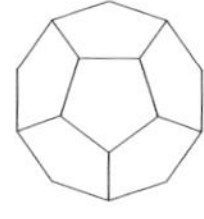

5. **Dodecahedron:** the most complex of the shapes, the dodecahedron is associated with the brow Chakra and Ether throat Chakra. Its twelve faces – the female principle – represent the mother of life. (The same twelve-fold symmetrical pattern can be seen in the chlorophyll molecule in plants, by which sunlight is transmuted into life-giving food.) The dodecahedron is made up of pentagons, which symbolize the creative flowering of life – that perfection is possible in the human form when we realize who we are as spiritual beings.

- (**mcs**) {a–b} for the one(s) needed.
  a. Look at the Platonic solid while it is spinning in front of your eyes. (**mcs**) if the spin needs to be (clockwise • counter-clockwise).
  b. The Platonic solid is placed in front of a specific area of the body. (**mcs**) (front • back) and for which area (pelvis / solar plexus / heart / throat / brow). (**mcs**) if the spin needs to be (clockwise • counter-clockwise).

22. SPINNING

Spinning strengthens the balance mechanism of the inner ear. It also affects the Reptilian Brain by releasing ingrained fight-flight responses so the higher thinking brain – the Prefrontal Cortex – is activated. You may experience some dizziness when you first practice this exercise, so it is best to start with only one or two spins and gradually increase the circling until you can do twenty-one spins, free of all dizziness.
See Further Reading: Christopher Kilham, The Five Tibetans

How To:

- Stand up straight with your arms outstretched at shoulder height; you can also do it with your left arm down. Both palms are open: left faces downward, right hand to the right. 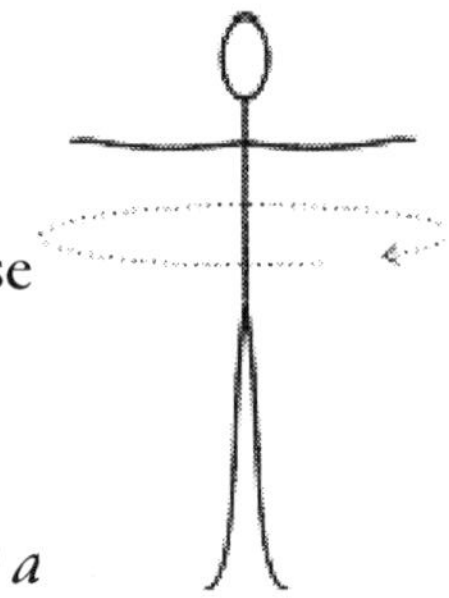
- Holding this arm position, spin a full circle in a clockwise direction (as though turning your head to the right).
- Repeat the spin 1–21 times without a pause. *In the beginning it is advisable to start with one or two spins only a some people feel unexpectedly dizzy and nauseous even after one spin. You can always add a spin each day until you are up to the full twenty-one.* 
- **It is important that when you finish spinning you stand with your feet apart, knees bent, your hands on your knees and your head down to re-establish your balance.** Take a full deep breath, inhaling through your nose. Exhale through your mouth with your lips pursed in an O. Repeat two full breaths before slowly standing up. **If in doubt about your balance, have a friend be present when you try the spinning so they can support you if you become dizzy.**
- Most people do the spinning clockwise. If doing it counterclockwise, observe carefully how you feel.

23. CHAKRA MOVEMENTS WITH THE SILK SCARVES

Silk Scarves for the Chakras: see ResonanceRepatterning.net/estore/

1. **Earth base of the spine Chakra movements**
   These movements help us to be grounded and centered. In societies close to the earth, walking bare-foot keeps people connected to the forces of the earth that constantly revitalize us. Wearing shoes, driving in cars, living in houses above the earth, disconnects us from the earth's forces and its grounding effect.

How To:
Do {a–c} in sequence.

a. (**mcs**) Client needs to wear the red Silk Scarf while doing the Earth movement? Needs to wear the red CYW Glasses?

b. (**mcs**) for the kind of Earth Chakra music needed.
Suggestions for Earth Chakra music: Drums of Passion; American Indian; African music; lullabies

c. (**mcs**) {1–4} for the Earth Chakra movement needed.
If possible, do the Earth movements with bare feet on the earth.

   1. Grounding movements: move your knees, bend close to the earth, feel your feet connected to the earth as you move. Earth movements are repetitive and rhythmic.

   2. Movements in slow motion.

   3. Earth Chakra Triad movements: move your neck, colon area and knees.

   4. Yoga movements, for those who know yoga.
   (**mcs**) for which inversion posture is needed. The (back roll • shoulder stand • plow • lying face down over a large ball, allowing your head to hang down to the floor).
   Reverse postures stimulate circulation of blood and energy to the head – reversing the polarity of feet on the ground. You can also lie on your back with your feet and legs in the air, or rest your feet on your bed or have your thighs at right angles to the floor with your lower legs resting on an armchair or bed.

2. **Water pelvis Chakra movements**
These movements are about fluidity; flowing round obstacles; tuning in to the power of water, or to its calmness and serenity.

How To:
Do {a–c} in sequence.

a. (**mcs**) Client needs to wear the orange Silk Scarf while doing the Water movement? Needs to wear the orange CYW Glasses?

b. (**mcs**) for the kind of Water Chakra music needed. *Suggestions for Water Chakra music: Ray Lynch: Deep Breakfast; Gypsy Kings; Debussy; Hawaiian hula; Belly dancing music; Latin music*

c. (**mcs**) {1–3} for the Water movement needed.
   1. (Whole body Katsugen • Hand Katsugen around the pelvic area).
   2. Dance with a wave-like motion, spiraling, circling.
   3. Water Chakra Triad movements: move your neck, chest, pelvis, and feet; or do the **Polarity Pyramid** – feet wide apart, knees bent, hands above knees with arms **straight**; rock from side to side to stretch and release tension in the pelvis and shoulders. This position is helpful for women who have menstrual pain.

3. **Fire solar plexus Chakra movements**
Fire movements are about action, energy, power, assertiveness, as well as being about fun and humor.

How To:
Do {a–c} in sequence.

a. (**mcs**) Client needs to wear the yellow Silk Scarf while doing the above Fire movements? Needs to wear the yellow CYW Glasses?

b. (**mcs**) for the Fire Chakra music needed. *Suggestions for Fire Chakra music: Drums of Passion; swing music; cha-cha; strong Beethoven; powerful tango music; or fun Charleston 1920s music*

c. (**mcs**) {1–7} for the Fire movement needed.
   1. Vigorous movements to revitalize and activate energy – vigorously moving the hands, arms, neck, spine, hips and feet to powerful music.

2. Dance with fiery activity (swing music is excellent for this kind of movement).

3. Fire Chakra Triad movements: move your head, belly area and thighs.

4. Hand Katsugen around your belly and solar plexus area.

5. Bouncing on a rebounder (or do the Chi Kung Bounce if no rebounder is available).

6. Yoga movements or postures for those who know yoga. (**mcs**) for which inversion postures are needed: The (shoulder stand • plow • face down on a large ball, relaxing your head toward the floor), all of which stimulate circulation of blood and energy to the positive fiery pole of the head.

7. Eye movements for the positive pole of the Fire Chakra Triad.

4. **Air heart Chakra movements**
Air movements are light and high; they are upward-moving and heart-opening.

How To:
Do {a–c} in sequence.

a. (**mcs**) Client needs to wear the green Silk Scarf while doing the Air Chakra movement? Needs to wear the green CYW Glasses?

b. (**mcs**) for the kind of Air Chakra music needed. *Suggestions for Air Chakra music: The Lion King: 'Circle of Life'; waltz music; Viennese waltz music; romantic music*

c. (**mcs**) {1–7} for the Air movement needed.
   1. Dance with shoulder and arm movements, open and up high in the air.

   2. Any movement that releases the shoulder blades and shoulder joints and rib cage. *See #10, #11, #17 of the Movement Options*

3. Air Chakra Triad movements: move your shoulders and stretch and circle your ankles.
4. Hand Katsugen in front of the heart area.
5. The Diaphragm Anxiety Release. *p.122*
6. Yawning and stretching.
7. The Polarity Pyramid Stretch:
    - Have your feet wide apart.
    - Bend your knees until your thighs are nearly parallel to the floor.
    - Place your hands above your knees with your fingers holding the **outside** of your thighs, your thumbs on the **inside** of your thighs. Now lean on your hands while **keeping your arms straight** and pushing your knees apart.
    - Keeping your arms straight gently tractions your spine. You can rock from side to side for a stretch and release as long as you keep your arms straight.
    - Now bring your right shoulder toward your left foot and then your left shoulder toward the right foot. Slowly and gently alternate this stretch, while keeping your arms straight.
    - Straighten your legs, hang over from the hips and shake out your jaw and shoulders. Gradually straighten up from the base of your spine.

5. **Ether throat Chakra movements**

Ether movements are subtle: slow, gentle, serene, balanced, with a feeling of connecting to spirit.

How To:

Do {a–c} in sequence.

a. (**mcs**) Client needs to wear the blue Silk Scarf while doing the Ether Chakra movement? Needs to wear the blue CYW Glasses?

b. (**mcs**) for the kind of Ether Chakra music needed. *Suggestions for Ether Chakra music: serene Bach: Swingle Singers sing Bach (Bach Hits Back); serene Mozart; serene religious music; Gloria, #13 by John Rutter; slow movements from Baroque music*

c. (**mcs**) {1–5} for the Ether movement needed.
   1. Any slow and serene movement. If doing the Ether movement with a partner make hand contact with both your palms touching; let the energy move you as you do Katsugen together with eyes closed, while playing Ether music.
   2. Dance with slow, undulating spinal movements.
   3. Hand Katsugen in front of the neck and throat area.
   4. Slowly move or circle all the joints of your body.
   5. Yoga movements or postures for those who know yoga. (**mcs**) for the balancing posture needed or stand still on one leg, then switch to the other leg.

24. LION POSE

- The Lion Pose of Hatha Yoga stretches the tongue and brings energy to the throat, mouth, face and eyes.
- It releases tension and frustration, and is helpful for discharging pent-up anger and emotional reactiveness in a healthy way so it doesn't become locked in your jaw, eyes and face.
- If you have a sore throat, try doing the Lion Pose about ten times.

How To:

- Take a deep breath.

- On exhaling through your mouth, stick your tongue out as far as possible to touch your chin! Simultaneously open your eyes wide and stretch your hands, fingers and arms in front of you, shaking with tension.
- At the furthest point of the tension and exhale, inhale through your nose, slowly and deeply relaxing your tongue, jaw, eyes, mouth, arms and hands back to normal.
- (**mcs**) Need to repeat the Lion Pose?

25. CHI KUNG ARM STRETCHES

- These three Chi Kung arm stretches activate energy flow in your arms and the whole of your body: wonderful to do outside in the sunlight and with bare feet.
- These stretches activate the flow of lymph in the upper body and are good to do on long airplane flights for support against jet lag.

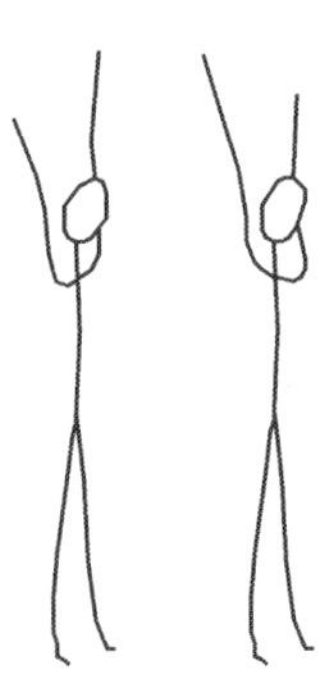

How To:

- **Arm Stretch #1**
  Standing, stretch your arms above your head. Alternately stretch the left and right arm and rib cage upwards.
- **Arm Stretch #2**
  Bring your arms up to shoulder height in front of you. As you inhale, **slowly** bend your elbows slightly, imagining energy coming in through your palms and flowing up your arms to your heart. As you exhale, **slowly** straighten your arms. While pressing your palms out, keep your fingers pointing up to the sky. Imagine energy flowing from your shoulder blades, down your arms and out through your palms, connecting your heart energy to the essence of all. Repeat a few times until you feel complete. Slowly lower your arms and take a pause to integrate what you have done.

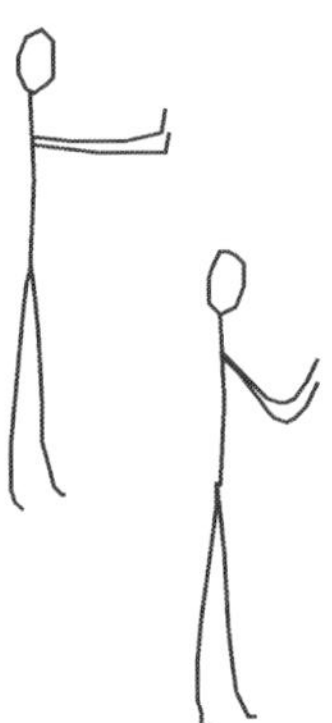

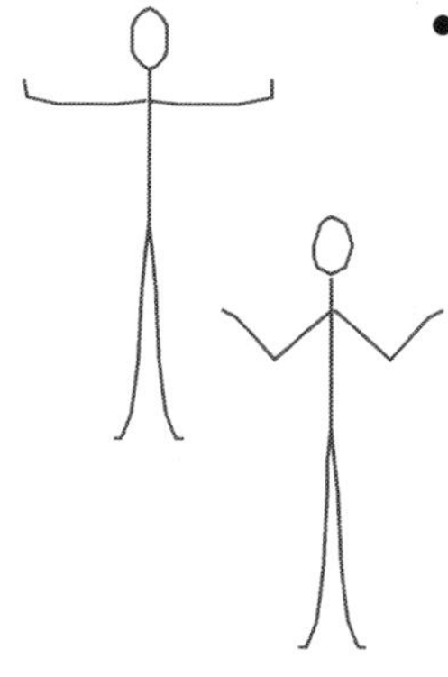

- **Arm Stretch #3**
  Bring your arms up to shoulder height on either side of you, palms facing the floor. As you inhale, **slowly** bend your elbows slightly and imagine energy coming in through your palms and flowing up your arms to your heart. As you exhale, straighten your arms, 'pressing' your palms out while keeping your fingers pointing up to the sky. Imagine energy flowing from your shoulder blades down your arms and out through your palms, connecting your heart energy to the essence of all. Repeat a few times until you feel complete. Lower your arms and take a pause to integrate what you have done.

26. FIVE ELEMENT MOVEMENTS WITH SOUNDS

- These movements with their corresponding Element sounds are part of a Chi Kung exercise for harmonizing the Five Elements of traditional Chinese Acupuncture.
- The five sounds, associated with the five Yin Meridians in certain Chi Kung schools, activate and balance the Yin Meridians of your heart, lungs, spleen, kidney and liver physically, emotionally and mentally.
- As each Yin Meridian is partnered with a Yang Meridian, all twelve Meridians, become harmonized through these powerful movements and sounds. *Be aware that there are many schools of acupuncture and Chi Kung, all of which may teach Chi movements if different ways. This is just one way.*

How To:
(**mcs**) I need to start by cleansing the bone marrow before doing any of the Five Element movements with sound?

Bone Marrow Cleanse

- With feet at hip-width apart, toes facing forward and knees slightly flexed, breathe in and raise your arms, palms up, on either side of your body; bring your hands over your head and direct your palms towards the top of your head. Hold this position and breathe deeply.

- Visualize white light from your palms pouring through your head and body.

- As you exhale, slowly bring your palms down in front of your body – a few inches away from your body and **facing the floor** – keep your palms and arms horizontal. Imagine white light cleansing every organ and cell right to your bone marrow as you bring your hands to hip level, and then visualize white light flowing down the bones of your pelvis, legs and feet.

Harmonizing Breath
After completing the Bone Marrow Cleanse (and after completing each Element sound and movement), do the Harmonizing Breath at least three times or, if more time, nine times:

- Inhale through your nose, keeping your tongue on the roof of your mouth.

- Exhale through your mouth, relaxing your tongue on the floor of your mouth.

Five Element Movements with Sound
(**mcs**) {a–e} for the Five Element movement and sound needed. *If you need the whole series, it may be done in the order given.* When complete with one movement and sound, do the three Harmonizing Breaths and then (**mcs**) for the next Five Element movement and sound you need.

a. **The Fire Element movement for the Heart Meridian (HAA)**
   As you tone the Haa sound, feel your physical heart vibrating and be aware that you are activating your heart's joy (the emotional level) and love and compassion (mental-spirit level).

   Repeat the Five Element movement and sound three times. The Heart movement is the only movement and sound that is repeated three times.

   - Toes face forward; knees are slightly flexed. Breathe in as you slowly raise your arms on either side of your body. Stretch your arms up over your head.

- With your fingers, gently grasp the Chi life energy, making a **soft** fist. Hold your breath while bending your knees and elbows, slowly coming into an imaginary sitting position (with your elbows bent and your gentle fists in front of your face).
- As you exhale with a long Haa sound, straighten your legs, with palms facing each other, open your hands and stretch your fingers apart and bring your hands above your head once more.

  As you exhale with the Haa sound, release anything in yourself that comes in the way of unconditional love and a vitally healthy heart.
- Repeat three times.
- Do three Harmonizing Breaths.

b. The Metal Element movement for the Lung Meridian (HEE)
As you tone the Hee sound, feel your physical lungs vibrating and be aware that you are activating your Lung Meridian's capacity to release grief (emotional level) and to let go of anything that disconnects you from the Divine. Feel your connection to the Divine within yourself and in others (mental-spirit level), which enables you to connect to your inner worth, to respect yourself and to value and respect others.

- Toes face forward; knees are slightly flexed. Inhale as you raise your arms in front of you to shoulder height with your palms facing the floor.
- Hold your breath and bring your wrists to your chest. Bend your fingers gently so your finger tips are facing your wrists.
- Exhale with a Hee sound, while moving your bent fingers out in front of you, still at shoulder height. When your arms are stretched in front of you and you have no breath left, suddenly open your fingers and stretch them strongly to release the energy to the partner Meridian of the Large Intestine, which allows us to let go of what we no longer need.

While making the Hee sound, be aware of releasing all toxins from your lungs and the partner Meridian to the Lung – the Large Intestine. Let go of anything that comes in the way of valuing yourself and feeling your connection to the Divine.

- Slowly lower your arms.
- Do three Harmonizing Breaths.

c. **The Earth Element movement for the Spleen Meridian (WHOO)**
As you tone the Whoo sound, feel your physical spleen area vibrating (under the lower left side of your rib cage), and be aware that you are balancing the emotion of sympathy or empathy (This is the emotional level of this sound. Many people are so sympathetic that in nurturing others they may feel victimized or used. Others may lack sympathy and not be available to help others in genuine need.)

As you tone Whoo, feel connected to the ideal mother archetype of service, devotion and nurturance (mental-spirit level). Feel that you are abundantly taken care of in this body by mother earth; feel contented with what you have, even while striving for more. Let go of all that comes in the way of helping and supporting yourself and others with kindness and generosity.

- Toes face forward; knees are slightly flexed. Place your palms, face up, on either side of your belly button, palms curved rather than straight.
- As you inhale bring your right hand above your head with the palm facing up to the sky and place your left hand, palm down to the earth, next to your spleen (the left side of your ribs). **Stay facing forward.**
- As you exhale, turn your upper body to the left.
- Hold this twist to the left as you breathe in, feeling your spleen area expanding with energy under your left rib cage as you breathe in.

- As you exhale with the WHOO sound, slowly face forward once more while bringing your palms back to their original position – curved palms facing up on either side of your belly button.
- Do three Harmonizing Breaths.

d. The Wood Element movement for the Liver Meridian (SSS)
As you make the SSS sound, feel your physical liver vibrate under your right rib cage; be aware that you are releasing old resentments and anger (emotional level) and opening yourself to a new vision and a new beginning (mental-spirit level).

- Toes face forward; knees are slightly flexed. Make strong, assertive fists on either side of your belly button with your hands-fists facing up.
- Inhale while bringing your fists up the midline of your body and above your head. Make a complete circle with your hands and arms and then place your elbows under the middle of your ribs (on a Liver Meridian acupuncture point called Gate of Hope). *If you bend forward slightly it is easier to place your elbows under the center of your left and right rib cage.*
- Once your elbows are under your ribs, exhale with a Sss sound. Keep your eyes wide open, look at the floor *avoid looking at a person* and breathe out past and present frustrations and anger through your eyes.
- Stand up. Do three Harmonizing Breaths.

e. The Water Element movement for the Kidney Meridian (SHEH)
As you make the Sheh sound, feel your kidneys vibrate on either side of your spine under the 12th floating rib, a little above your waist. Be aware that you are releasing fears (emotional level) and reconnecting to your essence – the source of your power, drive, courage and vital force (mental-spirit level).

- Toes face forward; knees are slightly flexed. Slightly bend forward and make fists with your palms, pressing them into your belly on either side of your belly button.
- Inhale and feel the kidney area in your back expanding against the pressure of your fists on your belly.
- Exhale with a long Sheh sound, releasing all toxins from the kidneys and anything that comes in the way of your being empowered and courageous.
- Stand up. Do three Harmonizing Breaths.

27. DANCING THE FIVE ELEMENTS

- The five Elements of Chinese Acupuncture are associated with particular qualities (or frequencies). Each Element correlates with a particular color, sound, emotion, smell, season, climate and certain mental qualities, to name just a few of the Element associations. Knowing the Five Element associations allows us to understand what energy frequencies are imbalanced and points us in the direction of establishing order and balance in the body-mind once more.
- Movements are also associated with the five Elements and can be used for calming an over-active Element or tonifying a depleted Element. In this way you can once more access its beneficial qualities within yourself.

How To:

- (**mcs**) for the Element movement needed. Use music appropriate for that Element, and then allow yourself to dance freely to the music, matching the characteristic qualities of the Element and owning that positive quality within yourself. Enjoy letting your body go with the music!
- You can wear the color scarf that corresponds to the Element, or wear the CYW Glasses with the color of the Element in one or both eyes.

Wood	**Color:** green **Quality:** assertive, strong, confident, outward-moving **Music:** Examples – cha cha cha; strong Beethoven
Fire	**Color**: red **Quality:** light and joyful, connecting with love and compassion to all **Music:** Examples – Dance Crazy; the Beatles, *Abbey Road* #3; joyful Mozart
Earth	**Color:** yellow **Quality:** rhythmic and repetitive, nurturing, gentle **Music:** Examples – drumming; Native American; lullabies
Metal	**Color:** white **Quality:** slow, balanced, connecting to your spiritual essence and the Divine in all **Music:** Examples – Bach, *Air on a G String* by the Swingle Singers; John Rutter, *Gloria* #13: 'The Lord Bless You and Keep You'; any spiritual calm music
Water	**Color:** blue **Quality:** powerful, energized, flowing **Music:** Examples – Ray Lynch, *Deep Breakfast*; Latin music.

E.
BREATH OPTIONS

Breath has been used for millennia to create a high degree of energy. Breath calms the mind and emotions and clears our energy channels. It has a long history of use for curing disease and helping us maintain our physical health by energizing our body and mind. Correct breathing, used in running marathons, has been shown to prevent athletic injuries.

Breath and past pain

I remember once doing a Resonance Repatterning session on a student involving his breathing. Through the muscle checking technique, we discovered an unconscious pattern associated with an early experience at the age of five that involved his mother and an accident. The young man initially had no memory of an accident at age five, until he suddenly remembered standing in front of the garage door waving goodbye to his mother who was in the car in front of him.

By mistake his mother, instead of putting the car in reverse, put her foot on the accelerator. The car moved forward and the child was locked between the car and the garage. His leg was broken. He shared that what was most painful for him was that his mother couldn't visit him in the hospital. Because she was an illegal immigrant, they couldn't risk her being sent back to Mexico. So the child, who only wanted his mother, felt abandoned, terrified and alone.

Ever since this accident, the young man realized he had constantly held his breath as though in a state of shock, and he still resonated with being alone, afraid and abandoned. The Energizing Option he needed was one of the Breath Options, after which his resonance with the past painful patterns shifted and he no longer resonated with the small child's perception of terror and pain.

THE FOUR OVALS FOR EACH OPTION

1. **Muscle check self (mcs) or use your felt sense for the Energizing Option you need**

2. **Read the introduction to the Energizing Option**
   Demo the 'How To' if doing with someone else, or use the video download if needed

3. **Do the Energizing Option**
   - Observe that you are doing it correctly
   - Breathe
   - (**mcs**) / **felt sense:** This is complete?
   - (**mcs**) / **felt sense:** Another Option is needed?

4. **After completing the Option**
   - Take a pause to integrate the positive change
   - Recheck your **felt sense:**
     a. Do you feel more relaxed?
     b. Are you breathing more easily?
     c. Do you notice any other positive change?
   - *RR Practitioners recheck *[cr] statements*

If we don't breathe, we don't live. How many of us are breathing? How many of us are fully living?

- The first and last breath marks the beginning and ending of life because breathing carries oxygen to every cell – the only cells that can live without oxygen are cancer cells.
- Perhaps more important, oxygen is the carrier for the **Prana** or **Chi life energy**. When we are filled with Chi energy, we feel on top of the world; when our Chi is depleted, we feel physically, emotionally and/or mentally flat or depressed.
- **The oxygen/carbon dioxide ratio**, controlled by the inhale and exhale, is essential for every life activity in the body. Carbon dioxide regulates the activity of the nervous system and controls the flow of blood to the brain (a low level of CO_2 in the blood reduces blood flow to the brain). CO_2 is needed for numerous highly significant biochemical processes, one of which is to break the chemical bond so the hemoglobin in our red blood cells releases its oxygen to all our trillions of cells. Without this process, there would be no oxygen at the cellular level and the cells would not be able to produce energy.
- Breath has been shown to **synchronize brainwaves** and to balance the left and right brain hemispheres.
- Breathing **activates endorphins**, which boost our immune system and bring a sense of joy.
- Breathing **moves lymph**. Our lymph system filters wastes and toxins; it returns blood proteins that seep into the fluid around the cells back to the bloodstream; and it returns fluids from around our trillions of cells back to the bloodstream. In cases of shock where the lymph system stops functioning, it can lead to death. *See #18 Lymphatic Purifying Breath*
- Certain breathing methods have been known to clear the arteries of 30–40% of their **plaque build-up** within three months of twice-daily practice. *See #2, Left Nostril Breath*

- With every exhale, we **release carbonic acid** and other gases. If carbonic acid builds up in our cells they become acidic, which leads to disease. The pH of the intracellular space can only vary between 7.34 and 7.40 or the cell dies. Relaxed exhaling helps maintain the appropriate acid/alkaline balance.

- Breathing **calms the mind and emotions.** Emotional responses are immediately mirrored in our breathing: when afraid, we often hold our breath or we breathe out and are unable to take a deep breath in (the collapsed breath); when we are upset, anxious or angry, we go into shallow fast breathing. Most of us have lost the natural gentle relaxed breathing of a healthy and contented baby.

- As we breathe slowly and rhythmically, we **reconnect to our feelings** and body sensations; we feel calm in the face of stress and emotional upset and we begin to experience more peace of mind.

We can use any one of the following twenty-seven breathing patterns when faced with a problem, a disharmonious situation, an exam, a presentation, a public performance, a sickness or pain. Some people believe that breath can help us cure any disease. The following breaths are an important Energizing Option to help us spiral up to our optimal frequency range. If we integrate some of these Breathing Options into our daily life, especially when we become aware that our breath is off track, we may experience for ourselves how they create a stable and calm state of mind and revitalize our body for more health.

1. SLOW GENTLE BREATHING

This slow, gentle, relaxed breathing is the basic breath that recharges and relaxes our body, emotions and mind. This is a good breath to do:

- when you want to re-energize and relax
- when you want to be centered within yourself before moving out into the world and handling your life
- when you are in a tense situation with highly-charged feelings and you need to stay calm
- when you need to balance your polarities: your masculine/feminine, outward/inward, Yang/Yin. We re-energize ourselves on the inhale (masculine, expansive, Yang) and we relax deeply on the exhale (feminine, letting go, Yin).

When you move back into sync with your optimal frequency range, you may observe that you suddenly take a deep breath, followed by a sigh and the Slow Gentle Breathing. The deep breath and sigh is a sign that you are releasing tension and stress and coming back into rhythm with yourself once more.

How To:

- Breathe slowly and gently in through your nose and out through your mouth. (You can also inhale and exhale through your nose. Try both ways and notice the benefits of each.) The inhale is energizing; the exhale is relaxing, a letting go. In – energize; out – relax.
- As you inhale, let your ribs and belly expand, all the way to the top of your chest. As you exhale, relax your ribs and gently pull your belly inward and upward. Feel your core muscles drawing your belly in.
- Do this gentle breathing until it flows easily and naturally and you feel calm, relaxed and re-energized.

2. LEFT NOSTRIL BREATH – *anulom-viloma*

- This breath, done three to ten minutes daily, cleanses the 70,000 energy channels or *nadis,* and is said to make the body healthy, lustrous and strong.
- Anulom Viloma helps clear negative thinking and has a calming effect on the mind.
- This breath has a beneficial effect in almost all disease conditions. After doing it ten minutes a day, two times daily for four months it is said to clear 30–40% of build-up in the arteries.

How To:

- Put the edge of your right index finger across your forehead just above your eyebrows.
- Close your right nostril with your right thumb and inhale slowly and completely through your left nostril.
- Close your left nostril with your middle finger and exhale completely through your right nostril.
- Continue inhaling **only** through your left nostril and exhaling **only** through your right nostril.
- Whenever your arm feels tired, relax it down. After a short rest, continue with the breath.

3. BREATH FOR MENTAL TENSION – *bhramari*

- When you feel agitated and stressed out, this Breath for Mental Tension steadies and calms your mind.
- It is said to be good for high blood pressure.
- The humming sound that goes with this breath increases ventilation of the sinuses.

How To:

- Place the pads of both your index fingers on your forehead and lightly place your middle fingers on your closed eyelids, resting your other fingers on your cheeks. With the pads of your thumbs on the flap of your ears, gently close your ears.
- Take a breath and exhale with your mouth closed, making a humming sound like a bee – pulling the core muscles of your belly inward and upward.
- When complete, inhale and hold your breath for five seconds, and then exhale and relax deeply with your eyes closed.

4. CALMING BREATH

- This breath is called the king of all breaths because it balances the two hemispheres of the brain, synchronizing alpha brainwaves (calming and healing) in both hemispheres.
- The Calming Breath sends the Chi life energy through the left and right nostrils. In this way it alternately stimulates the masculine, Yang, active, logical, outward-moving qualities of the right nostril/left brain and the feminine, Yin, relaxed, creative, inward-moving qualities of the left nostril/right brain.
- In India thousands of yoga students do this breath for ten minutes twice daily with exciting results in terms of improved health and well-being.
- This is a wonderful breath to do when you need to calm your mind and emotions and yet be quietly energized – before a test, giving a speech, or before meditation or prayer when you want your mind to be still and peaceful.

How To:

- Put the edge of your right index finger across your forehead, just above your eyebrows.

- Now close your right nostril with your right thumb and inhale through your left nostril. Hold your breath with both nostrils blocked, while relaxing deeply.
- Now open the right nostril and exhale through your right nostril. Hold your breath out with both nostrils blocked, while relaxing deeply.
- Keep your left nostril blocked and inhale through your right nostril. Then exhale and inhale through the left nostril.
- Continue exhaling and inhaling through the right nostril and then exhaling and inhaling through the left nostril. Block the nostrils at the top of the inhale and after the exhale for a few seconds.
- When you feel complete or you muscle check (**mcs**) that the breath is complete, relax your arm and breathe normally.

5. VITALITY BREATH

- The Vitality Breath is a powerful breath for activating the energy of the belly – known in China and India as the center of vitality for the whole body.
- Doing this breath is excellent when you feel tired, cold, you need to activate a sluggish digestion or when you need mental alertness.
- The Vitality Breath clears out clogged *nadis* – the 70,000 energy channels.
- This breath keeps the diaphragm mobile and supple, which helps to release anxieties and fears (and may stop hiccups).
- The Vitality Breath is said to have a cleansing effect on the blood.
- Many people do the Vitality Breath daily, twenty to fifty times or more. Start slowly and observe how you feel before working up to fifty or more of this powerful breath.

How To:

- Vigorously exhale through the nose while simultaneously and vigorously contracting the abdominal muscles in toward your spine.
- After exhaling, relax your belly, which allows the inhale breath to be automatically drawn in as the belly swells out.
- (**mcs**) for how many Vitality Breaths are needed. Often 5–20 are enough in the beginning. *When doing this breath as a Positive Action, you can work up to 40 Vitality Breaths for the first week and add 10 per week until you can do 100. Best to start slowly and listen to your body and how you respond to doing this breath before doing more.*
- When complete, relax and breathe regularly and rhythmically for at least five minutes.

6. OXYGEN BREATH

- All our trillions of cells can only produce energy and warmth through oxygen.
- If we don't have much energy, it could be that our cells aren't getting their supply of oxygen.
- If you can't think clearly, this too could be a lack of oxygen to your brain. (The brain needs more oxygen to function than any other organ in the body – even more than your heart.)
- If your vision is fuzzy, this may be a lack of oxygen to your eyes. (The eyes are second only to the brain in the amount of oxygen needed for their proper functioning.)
- One of the basics for thriving and being youthful into old age is oxygen: breathing and movement get oxygen and Chi to every part of the body. And of course attitude and what we eat are also foundational for good health at any age.

How To:
Inhale fully through your nose; relax and hold to the count of 10–15 seconds, then exhale slowly through your nose. Relax and breathe normally. Repeat until you feel complete.

7. CONTROL PAUSE BREATH FOR STABILIZING CO_2

- What many of us do not realize is that carbon dioxide (CO_2) is just as essential for life as oxygen. CO_2 is needed for numerous highly significant biochemical processes. For instance, CO_2 breaks the chemical bond that causes hemoglobin (which is carried in the red blood cells in our blood) to release oxygen to all our trillions of cells.
- CO_2 regulates the flow of blood to the brain. If there are low levels of CO_2 in the blood, this reduces blood flow to the brain. Our system is extremely sensitive to CO_2 levels in the air and in the body.
- The Control Pause Breath is used in Russian hospitals for curing people of asthma and emphysema.

See Further Reading: Teresa Hale, Breathing Free

How To:
- Sit comfortably.
- Breathe gently through your nose using shallow solar plexus breathing – observe your solar plexus swelling slightly as you inhale and relaxing in as you exhale.
- Now breathe in, relax and breathe out. Block your nostrils with two fingers and hold the breath out for whatever time is totally comfortable for you (2 seconds to 50 or 60 seconds). This is called the Control Pause.
- When you inhale again, it must be natural and easy. If you gasp for breath on the inhale, it means you held your breath out too long. Doing this breath is not a competition: simply hold the breath out for a few

seconds in the beginning. If you do this breath daily you will work up to an effortless 60-second pause while holding out the exhaled breath.

- After the Control Pause, return to the relaxed shallow breathing for 2–5 minutes.

8. THROAT BREATHING

- This breath brings the Prana or Chi life energy to your throat, neck, thyroid and parathyroid glands.
- This breath may help you when your throat is sore or your voice feels tense.
- For singers and teachers, or those who use their voice a lot, this breath should help you maintain a strong resonant voice.

How To:

- Straighten and elongate your neck, bringing it back in line with your spine. Gently bring your chin in.
- When you inhale and exhale though your nose, hear a slight hissing sound in the back of your throat, like the sound of waves on the shore. Your throat is slightly contracted as the breath passes through it.

9. CONTROL PAUSE WITH CREATING A SPACE

- Oxford physicist David Bohm says the energy contained in one cubic centimeter of space is more than the energy of all the matter in our known universe! In other words, 'empty' space contains enormous energy!
- While doing the Control Pause with Creating a Space, use this 'space' to change your attitude towards something that is difficult for you: picture a challenging situation in a positive light; visualize completing a project with ease and pleasure; if you sing, write, paint, dance, ski, run, play golf or tennis etc., see yourself doing your art or hobby perfectly and with joy.

How To:

- After doing a little relaxed shallow breathing, do the Control Pause Breath (see #7), holding the breath out.
- In the space when you are holding your breath out, visualize your situation in a positive light; or see yourself going into coherent action toward achieving your intention.
- After the Control Pause, spend 2–5 minutes doing slow, shallow breathing: a small in-breath and a relaxed out-breath.

10. CONTROL PAUSE WITH THYMUS TAP

- Our thymus gland, which is located under the sternum a few inches below where the clavicle bones meet, is associated with our immune system.
- Western medicine, in the not-so-distant past, was convinced that this gland shrivels in adults, proving that adults don't need it. (Some doctors still believe this.) However, when medical researchers did autopsies on healthy soldiers who had died at war, they found the thymus gland had not diminished in size at all. The thymus gland gets smaller when we are chronically sick or severely stressed, which of course diminishes the healthy functioning of our immune system.
- According to the research of Dr. John Diamond, the Thymus Tap stimulates the thymus (associated with the heart and the immune system) and energizes the twelve Meridian energy channels.
- If we want vital health, it is essential to keep our thymus gland and immune system in good shape. The Thymus Tap may help. (In addition, it may be wise to take kelp powder, a potent sea vegetable that helps eliminate radiation and strengthens the immune system.)

How To:

- After breathing in and out a few times, do the Control Pause *see #7*.

- While holding your breath out and closing your nostrils with the thumb and index finger of one hand, with your other hand do a slow Thymus Tap: tapping 1-2-3 in a waltz-heartbeat rhythm over your sternum about an inch or two below where your clavicle bones meet at the base of your throat.

11. CLEANSING BREATH

- This breath is great for clearing away negative thoughts and feelings and releasing tension, nervousness and anxiety.

How To:

- As you inhale, imagine energy flowing from the soles of your feet up your legs and body, up your arms and shoulders, sweeping all constrictions before it.

- Now exhale strongly through your mouth, squeezing your belly in vigorously, and release all your tensions, negative thoughts and feelings.

- Relax, sitting tall and straight. Notice how you feel. If you want, you can repeat the Cleansing Breath 2–3 times or as needed.

12. PELVIC ENERGIZER BREATH

- This breath brings blood circulation and energy to the organs of your pelvis – important for the womb and ovaries in women, and the prostate in men.

- It is also good for keeping the muscles associated with the bladder well-toned so we avoid problems with incontinence.

- This breath may be helpful for prolapses. Organs tend to prolapse due to the downward-pull of gravity. Keeping our core muscles strong holds our organs in their correct location.

How To:

- Breathe in through your nose and hold your breath.
- Still holding your breath, gently push the air into your lower abdomen so your belly swells out slightly.
- Still holding your breath, squeeze and release the anal sphincter seven times. Feel as though you are pulling these core muscles upwards towards your belly button.
- Relax and exhale through your nose. Repeat a few times, as needed.

13. STEAM ENGINE BREATH

- The Steam Engine Breath is similar to the vigorous Vitality Breath. This breath strongly stimulates the left and right side of your brain.
- This breath is excellent for strengthening your lungs and a weak digestive system.
- It is excellent to do when your energy feels low.

How To:

- Place the edge of your index finger on your forehead above your eyebrows. You will alternately block your left nostril with your middle finger and your right nostril with your thumb.
- Exhale and inhale vigorously through your left nostril by squeezing in your stomach strongly. Focus on the exhale; the inhale happens by itself.
- Now block the left nostril and exhale and inhale vigorously through the right nostril.
- Start the exhaling and inhaling through each nostril, gradually speeding up so you sound like a steam engine leaving a railway station. After reaching your quickest speed, begin to slow the breath down, like a steam engine coming into a railway station. Gradually bring the breath to a stop.

14. DOLPHIN BREATH

- This is a lovely breath that energizes your head, spine, back, shoulders and arms.
- The Dolphin Breath is both calming and energizing for your nervous system, which makes it an excellent breath to do when you feel anxious or stressed out.

How To:

- Place your tongue on the roof of your mouth and imagine you are inhaling energy, like a white light, from the crown of your head all the way down your spine.
- When you exhale, visualize a rainbow of colors like a fountain, spraying up your back, over your shoulders and down your arms. Repeat a few times.

15. CELLULAR BREATH

- The Cellular Breath is energizing and relaxing for your whole body.
- White light is a high frequency that contains the full spectrum of colors and is traditionally associated with healing.
- This is a wonderful breath to do when you are in a stressful environment, when people are talking negatively about others or the world, or when you are feeling negative about yourself.

How To:

- As you inhale through your nose, feel as though you are drawing in energy and white light through the entire surface of your body: the soles of your feet, your legs, back, arms, face, chest. Feel all your trillions of cells receiving this white light energy.
- When you exhale through your nose, radiate energy and white light from the entire surface of your body, feeling yourself surrounded by white light.

- Inhale and receive energy/light; exhale and radiate energy/light. When complete, relax and breathe naturally, noticing how you feel.

16. RAINBOW BREATH

Each color has its own unique frequency:

- **Red** is associated with the base of the spine and with grounding, stamina and the will to live.
- **Orange** is associated with the pelvis and with confidence and creativity. It is said to release muscle tension and strengthen bones.
- **Yellow** is associated with the digestive area and with intelligence, focus, power, vitality and optimism.
- **Green** is associated with the chest area and with cleansing, healing, regeneration of muscles and tissues; it is said to destroy harmful bacteria.
- **Blue** is associated with the throat and neck and with peace and calmness; it is soothing, cooling (good for irritations and itching).
- **Indigo** is associated with the brow and with inspiration and clear perception. It has been found to have a contracting effect (it has been used to shrink tumors, to stop bleeding and convulsions).
- **Violet** is associated with the crown and with inner stillness. It is said to strengthen our immune system.
- **White** is associated with purification and bringing balance.
- **Pink** is associated with love and peace. Along with turquoise, it is also known as the anti-wrinkle color.

How To:

- Decide or (**mcs**) which color frequency you need and where you need it: a particular organ; an area in pain; an area of your body; surrounding your body?

- As you inhale through your nose, take in the color your need; as you exhale, send the color to where you need it.

17. SACRAL BREATHING

- Our spine sits on the inverted triangle of bone called the sacrum. It is important that our sacrum stays aligned and the base horizontal (rather than tipping to left or right or rotating), or the alignment of our spine will be thrown off and back problems result.
- Our sacrum is meant to be stable, and yet it is also meant to move with each breath: expanding and relaxing.
- The energy of frustration and unresolved upsets easily stagnate at the negative poles of our body – in this case our sacrum and pelvis. It is good to use the Sacral Breath to relax tension and tightness in the sacrum and pelvis and to get the Chi life energy moving through this negative pole.

How To:

- Inhale, feeling your belly, pelvis and sacrum expand.
- As you breathe out, squeeze your belly in and feel your pelvis and sacrum relax. Repeat a few times or until you feel complete.

18. LYMPHATIC PURIFYING BREATH

- Most of us aren't aware of our lymphatic system, and yet without it we can't survive.
- Our lymph system removes dead cells and other toxic wastes from around our cells and sends them to the large intestines for elimination and to the liver – our body's primary detoxification plant.
- One of the many functions of our lymph system is to remove stuck blood proteins from around our trillions of cells and return them to our

bloodstream. As oxygen and nutrients seep out of the capillaries into the fluid surrounding the cells, blood proteins also seep out of the capillaries. Our lymph system returns these blood proteins to the bloodstream. If our lymph system is not functioning fully (often caused by a lack of exercise and a junk food diet), blood proteins collect around the cells, disturbing the positive/negative charge that allows cells to absorb nutrients and eliminate wastes. Excessive blood proteins around our cells can even be a major cause of death – as in cases of shock when the lymph system stops functioning. (In an emergency and any time you go through shock, remember to breathe deeply; then do the Lymphatic Purifying Breath.)

◎ It is amazing that we have twice as much lymph fluid bathing every cell and organ as we do blood. And yet the lymph system, on which our life depends, has no heart to pump its fluids around the body. So how does our lymph circulate? Through movement or exercise. Rebounding is one of the best ways to get the lymph moving (and you will observe how babies and children are constantly bouncing, moving up and down; and mothers holding their babies bounce them up and down – stimulating their lymph flow).

◎ Another major way to keep the lymph moving is through breathing deeply. Our lungs act as a suction pump, creating a vacuum that helps draw the lymph up the major thoracic lymph duct so it can be returned to the bloodstream (the veins) under the neck. And of course the third way to move lymph is with massage (good to give a self-massage towards the heart every day, especially before surgery).

How To:

- Inhale through your nose into your belly, letting it swell out. Hold your breath.

- Still holding the breath, expand your chest, which pulls the air from your lower lungs to your upper lungs. Then gently push the air to your lower lungs, letting your belly swell out. Repeat this up and down movement of your chest and belly three times, ending with the up movement of the expanded chest.

- Exhale with a sh–sh–sh–sh– sound, squeezing your belly in with each sh.
- Repeat a few times before relaxing and breathing slowly and deeply. Notice how you feel. Breathe deeply as much as possible during the day. (Different breaths have different effects: breathing deeply encourages lymph flow, whereas the shallow breathing associated with the Control Pause breaths is important to balancing the oxygen-carbon dioxide ratios in cases of emphysema and asthma.)

19. TAN T'IEN BREATH

- In China the Tan T'ien, just below the belly button, is known as the center of vital energy for the whole body.
- If our Tan T'ien is strong, we will have good digestion and lots of energy. It is said that total health depends on two things: a good digestion and good circulation.

How To:

- Suck air in quickly through your mouth into your upper chest and hold your breath.
- While holding your breath, push the abdominal muscles out seven times.
- Now exhale through your mouth in seven short bursts by squeezing in your abdominal muscles (like the Vitality and Stream Engine Breaths).

20. ORBITAL BREATH

- This Chi Kung breath revitalizes our central core. The two channels in Chinese Acupuncture that are associated with our core are known as the Governor Vessel, which flows up the spine, and the Conception Vessel, which flows up the front center of our body. These two vessels are reservoirs of energy that support the twelve Meridians, which in turn determine our physical health, emotional balance and mental well-being.

- The Governor Vessel (GV) is Yang or masculine, associated with action, focus, expansion and being out in the world. The Conception Vessel (CV) is Yin or feminine, and is associated with stillness, inward focus and deep relaxation. This breath helps to maintain balance in our Yang and Yin energies.

How To:

- Inhale, imagining energy flowing up your spine from your coccyx at the base of your spine, up your back, neck, over your head to the point just above your lip (the last point on the GV channel).
- As you exhale, imagine energy flowing down the front center of your body to the perineum and around to the base of your spine once more.
- Slightly arch your spine on the inhale and relax your spine on the exhale.
- Repeat a few times or for a few minutes, as needed.

21. CIRCULATION BREATH

- The Circulation Breath helps to get energy moving throughout your body.
- Energy moves blood and lymph, making energy circulation the foundation for our health.

How To: *for arms and chest*

- Inhale and imagine energy flowing from your left hand, up your left arm to your left shoulder, heart and the left side of your chest. As you exhale, imagine energy flowing across the right side of your chest and right shoulder, down your right arm to your right hand and fingers. Repeat the arm circulation a few times.

How To: *for legs and pelvis*

- Inhale and imagine energy flowing from your left foot up your left leg to your left hip and pelvis area. Now exhale and imagine energy flowing across to the right side of your pelvis and right hip, down your right leg to your right foot. Repeat a few times.

How To: *for the spine*

- Like the Orbital Breath *#20*, inhale energy imagining it flowing up your spine, over your head to the point above your lip and exhale down the front of your body to your pelvis and perineum.

22. MASCULINE ENERGY BREATH

- Both the Masculine and the Feminine Energy Breaths generate energy and move the Chi life energy down through your legs.
- The Masculine Energy Breath is great for releasing stagnation in your pelvis and legs, especially if you have weak legs, varicose veins or edema.
- It is an excellent breath to do if you are an athlete and want to maintain the vitality, strength and endurance of your leg muscles and tendons.

How To:

- Inhale sharply through your **nose,** expanding your upper chest, and hold your breath.
- Still holding, push the air into your lower lungs, expanding your belly.
- Exhale explosively through your mouth as though whistling: squeeze your belly in vigorously while imagining your energy shooting down through your legs to your feet. You can also open your fingers wide at the top of your thighs, palms facing each other, as you do the vigorous exhale.
- Take a pause before repeating or returning to your natural breathing once more.

23. FEMININE ENERGY BREATH

- The indicators for this breath are the same as for the Masculine Energy Breath.

How To:

- With the Feminine Energy Breath, suck air in sharply through your **mouth**, expanding your upper chest
- While holding your breath, push the air into your lower lungs by expanding your belly.
- Exhale explosively through your mouth as though whistling: squeeze your belly in vigorously, while imagining your energy shooting down through your legs to your feet. You can also open your fingers wide at the top of your thighs, palms facing each other, as you do the vigorous exhale.
- Take a pause before repeating or returning to your natural breathing.

24. CONTINUOUS BREATH

- The Continuous Breath recharges and relaxes your body, emotions and mind.

How To:

- Inhale fully, expanding your belly and ribs – front and back, left and right sides to the top of your lungs under your collar bone – until you can't breathe in any more air.
- Without a pause, slowly exhale, relaxing your ribs – front and back, left and right sides – and draw your belly inwards by using your core muscles. At the furthest point of the exhale, breathe more air out through your mouth, and again without a pause inhale once more.

25. FOCUSING BREATH

- This breath is associated with the Native American tradition. It is a good breath to do when you need to resonate with focused, clear, sharp thinking.

How To:

- Inhale into your lower abdomen while you focus in front of you. Hold your breath and soften your eyes.
- Still holding your breath, close your eyes, lift up your head and then rotate your head so you are facing to the right
- Now swivel your head to the left. At this point, still with eyes closed, explosively exhale your breath in a short burst through your mouth, open your eyes wide and focus strongly to the left, visualizing what it is you need to focus on doing, being or achieving.
- Face front again, relax and breathe normally.

26. BREATHING PATTERNS FOR THE CHAKRAS

- The seven major Chakras are concentrated reservoirs of energy that are closely associated with our nerve ganglia and glandular system.
- These energy centers control our physical functioning (elimination, procreation, digestion, circulation-respiration and speech); our emotional states (fear, cravings, anger, possessiveness and grief); and our mental well-being (contentment, moderation, tolerance and forgiveness, detachment with unconditional love, selfless service and harmony).
- In case it may prove helpful, I have categorized the breaths according to the qualities of the Chakras we may want to activate through breathing.

How To:
(**mcs**) {1–5} for which Chakra is needed and for the Breathing Pattern needed.

1. **Earth Chakra for grounding, stamina, the will to live, elimination and contentment.**
   (**mcs**) {1–2}.
   1. Cellular Breath #15
   2. Left Nostril Breath / Anulom Viloma # 2

2. **Water Chakra for being in the flow, living with creativity and moderation, and for releasing cravings.**
   (**mcs**) {1–5}.
   1. Calming Breath # 4
   2. Pelvic Energizing Breath #12
   3. Sacral Breathing #17
   4. Masculine Energy Breath #22
   5. Feminine Energy Breath #23

3. **Fire Chakra to support digestion, accessing your power, self-confidence, optimism, humor, tolerance and forgiveness.**
   (**mcs**) {1–4}.
   1. Vitality Breath # 5
   2. Steam Engine Breath #13
   3. Tan T'ien Breath #19
   4. Focusing Breath #25

4. **Air Chakra for your heart, circulation and lungs and to encourage communication of ideas and connecting to warm, affectionate feelings.**
   (**mcs**) {1–6}.
   1 Oxygen Breath # 6
   2 Control Pause Breath for stabilizing CO_2 # 7
   3. Control Pause with Thymus Tap #10
   4. Rainbow Breath #16
   5. Lymphatic Purifying Breath #18
   6. Circulation Breath #21

5. **Ether Chakra for new beginnings, feeling inwardly connected and experiencing life's beauty, harmony and wonder.**
   (**mcs**) {1–7}.
   1. Breath for Mental Tension # 3
   2. Calming Breath # 4
   3. Control Pause Breath for stabilizing CO_2 # 7
   4. Throat Breathing # 8
   5. Dolphin Breath #14
   6. Rainbow Breath #16
   7. Orbital Breath #20

27. FIVE ELEMENT BREATH

- The Five Elements of Chinese Acupuncture are a map of energy frequencies. As you learn the qualities associated with each Element, we begin to see clearly when our frequencies are out of sync and need support in order to maintain our physical health, emotional balance and a positive mental attitude.

- The Five Element sounds have a general strengthening effect on our Elements.

How To:

- **Fire Element** As you exhale, make a HAAA sound, which is associated with your Heart Meridian. As you tone, smile and feel unconditional love and compassion for yourself and others. Repeat and and rejuvenate your heart.

- **Earth Element** As you exhale, make a WHOO sound, which is associated with the Spleen Meridian. As you tone, be aware of grounding to the earth and feeling your center of calm from where you move into the world with abundance and generosity to those in need.

- **Metal Element** As you exhale, make a HEE sound, which is associated with the Lung Meridian. As you tone, feel inspired and connected to the Divine within yourself; feel your strength to stand for your spiritual values and to speak your truth with love and gentleness.
- **Water Element** As you exhale, make a SHEH sound, which is associated with the Kidney Meridian. Feel your immense power and energy; imagine using your energy to live your priorities with passion and positivity.
- **Wood Element** As you exhale, make the sound of SSS, which is associated with the Liver Meridian. As you make this sound, feel self-confident; that you can move into new beginnings; that you can assertively go into action for what you want, having a plan and achieving your goals.

F.
ENERGY CONTACT OPTIONS

These Options consist of energy contacts on or over the physical body using sound, light, north pole magnets, touch or essential oils. Energy Contacts balance the brain hemispheres and cranial rhythms, tranquilize fight-flight stress responses and tonify or calm Meridian flows and Chakra energy centers. Polarity, Jin Shin Jyutsu and Acupuncture energy contacts – among other Contact Options – have been used for over two thousand years and are renowned for the benefits they bring.

Energy contacts and phobias

A session that illustrates the power of these Energy Contact Options was shared by a practitioner. A client phoned her to say she had to go on a two-hundred mile journey and she had a phobia of cars (she would faint, become dizzy and get nauseous); she also had agoraphobia (great difficulty leaving the house).

The practitioner was busy but agreed to see the lady during her lunch break. As she didn't have time to identify the unconscious patterns associated with her client's phobias, she decided to go directly to the Energizing Options and she muscle checked to do #16, the Mu Acupuncture points from the Mu Point Repatterning, which is frequently used for phobias. The practitioner placed the ColorYourWorld Torch with various colors on her client's Mu Acupuncture points (the Mu points needed and the color for each Mu point having been identified by the muscle checking technique).

When the lady returned from her trip, she phoned to say that she had driven the two hundred miles with no fainting, dizziness or nausea. After her arrival she would normally have been housebound, but she had no trouble either leaving or returning to the house. She was so thrilled that she now wanted to work on her phobia of flying!

THE FOUR OVALS FOR EACH OPTION

1. **Muscle check self (mcs) or use your felt sense for the Energizing Option you need**

2. **Read the introduction to the Energizing Option**
   Demo the 'How To' if doing with someone else, or use the video download if needed

3. **Do the Energizing Option**
   - Observe that you are doing it correctly
   - Breathe
   - **(mcs) / felt sense:** This is complete?
   - **(mcs) / felt sense:** Another Option is needed?

4. **After completing the Option**
   - Take a pause to integrate the positive change
   - Recheck your **felt sense:**
     a. Do you feel more relaxed?
     b. Are you breathing more easily?
     c. Do you notice any other positive change?
   - *RR Practitioners recheck *[cr] statements*

We are energy beings. Our frequencies are vibrating at speeds beyond anything we can imagine.

Energy is characterized by its light and sound, which carry information to every cell of our body.

If our light is non-coherent, distorted information is transmitted at warp speed to our cells. Distorted information manifests as illness, pain, a lack of energy, upset emotional states or negative mental attitudes and thoughts.

If our light is coherent, life-giving information is transmitted at warp speed to our cells. This manifests as physical health, plenty of energy for everything we need to accomplish, positive feelings and an optimistic state of mind.

Most of the Energy Contact Options are drawn from or influenced by Chinese Acupuncture and the Chakra energy system of Ayurvedic medicine and Dr. Stone's Polarity Therapy. Their aim is to support coherent light and sound frequencies and the vitality of our body, emotions and mind for positive relationships and an energized healthy life.

1. BRAIN-ACTIVATING POINTS

- This contact is excellent when you need to think clearly and quickly or when your thinking is confused.
- Brain-Activating Points activates both the vital energy of the Kidney Meridian and the Fire Center of the belly. In Chinese Acupuncture the Kidney Meridian is associated with our reserves of energy and it fortifies our brain. In Polarity Therapy, which is based on the Ayurvedic knowledge of India, the belly has a direct relationship with the head, our level of vitality and the clarity of our thinking.

How To:

- Place the thumb and middle finger of one hand just under your collar bone about one-and-a-half inches on either side of your sternum – the central breastbone – on the two Kidney #27 Acupuncture points. These Kidney 27 points are called Store House (a store of energy, clear thinking, power and courage).
- Bring the fingers and thumb of your other hand together and place them over your belly button. It is sometimes more calming to place your palm over your belly button. Using your fingertips seems to have a more activating effect.
- You can also (**mcs**) for which hand needs to be above and which hand over the belly button.

2. THYMUS TAP

- The thymus gland is closely associated with the heart and the immune system. Tapping over the thymus is thought to stimulate the immune system and also centers you in your heart – bringing your awareness back to unconditional love.

How To:

- Tap on your sternum, about two inches down from the central hollow where your left and right collar bones connect.
- You can use any rhythm for the Thymus Tap, although the 1-2-3 waltz beat is similar to the heartbeat and is an energizing rhythm to use.

3. TONGUE ON THE ROOF OF YOUR MOUTH

- Placing your tongue on the roof of your mouth helps to synchronize the brainwaves of the left and right cerebral hemispheres and has a calming effect on the mind (probably why some systems of meditation recommend placing the tongue on the roof of the mouth).

- It is excellent to put your tongue on the roof of your mouth while doing most of the Spiral Up Energizing Options. Another opportunity for doing this Spiral Up Energizing Option is when listening to people.

How To:

- Place the top of your tongue on the roof of your mouth, just behind your upper front teeth, or further back on the hard palate, wherever it feels comfortable. Hold this tongue position, relax and breathe gently.

4. MEMORY/LISTENING EAR MASSAGE

- The ears are associated with our capacity to hear, and also with physical balance and memory.
- The ears are a reflex to the whole body. Massaging the ears, circling the ears and pressing into the ear Acupuncture points – several hundred of which are located on or in the ears – will energize and relax the whole body-emotions-mind frequency system and may have a beneficial effect on your hearing, memory and balance.
- Working on the ears has also been known to help with back pain.

How To:

- Place your thumb behind your ears and gently place your index fingers on the inside of each ear. *Avoid putting your fingers into the ear canal.* Press into the ear Acupuncture points and circle the ears slowly and gently.
- Gently stretch the flaps of the ears and pull the edges of your ears, massaging any sensitive points you find.
- You can work the top of your ears by putting your fingers behind your ears and your thumbs in front and repeating the stretching and pressing into the ear acupuncture points.

- You can cup your hands over your ears and circle the ears slowly and gently. This is relaxing and calming (especially when someone else does it on you).

5. ZIP-UPS

- The Zip-Ups strengthen and energize your core energy along the line known in Chinese Acupuncture as the Conception Vessel – a reservoir of Yin energy that supplies energy to the six Yin Meridians of the Spleen, Lung, Kidney, Liver, Heart and the Heart Protector function.
- Doing the Zip-Ups has an overall strengthening and energizing effect.
- If you do the Zip-Ups when you hear or see de-energizing images, sounds, words or actions, your frequencies will stay in sync with your optimal frequency range, which will help you stay energized, centered and calm.
- Doing Zip-Ups in stressful situations helps you maintain your center of balance.
- Doing subtle and gentle Zip-Ups for another person – as in a natural slow upward-moving gesture of your hand while talking – has a strengthening and calming effect on both you and on the other person. This is particularly useful when handling an upset child, in an emergency situation or, if possible, even when threatened by an attacker.

How To:

- Holding your upward-facing palm – right or left – about one inch in front of your pelvis, move it **slowly** up the center of your body from your pelvis to your chin, just below the mouth.
- Avoid moving your hand **down** your midline or down someone else's midline. Only upward moving.
- You can do a more subtle Zip-Ups in front of your heart, moving your hand just a few inches **up** the midline.

6. PULLING YOUR FINGERS

- Each finger and toe is associated with one of the five major energy reservoirs of the body, known in India as the Chakras.
- The five energy reservoirs are located in the center of the body: at the base of the spine, the pelvis, the solar plexus, the heart, and the throat. Each one is closely associated with the nerve plexuses and glands of the body. These reservoirs of energy control all aspects of our physical health, how we feel and how we think.
- Each finger and toe is associated with one of the five major energy reservoirs. By working into our fingers – pressing, holding, massaging and pulling – we activate the energy associated with its respective Chakra.
- Wherever we are, we can work on our fingers as a way to change our resonance with a problem, to stay centered and energized in a difficult situation or simply to keep our Chakras balanced and revitalized.

Dr. Randolph Stone, who developed Polarity Therapy, used to say that spending ten minutes a day working on your fingers, toes and feet was the best health insurance in the world. He would remind his students that wherever there is pain, the energy that corresponds to that Chakra is blocked, either physically, mentally or emotionally. When the lines of force are activated and balanced through polarity contacts, pain often disappears and there is a sense of well-being and heightened energy.

- A lady in her 80s was in bed, unable to move because of back pain. A Resonance Repatterning practitioner suggested that she work into her fingers while she was lying in bed. She did so and was surprised at how quickly she was able to start walking again.

- Teenagers and college students love this Spiral Up Energizing Option when they are feeling frustrated, nervous, lacking in self-confidence or while taking an exam. You have probably observed that many children naturally do quite a few of these Spiral Up Energizing Options, instinctively feeling drawn to do them, like shaking out their wrists when stressed or pulling their fingers when they need energy.

How To:

- (**mcs**) I need to work on my thumb (throat center) • index finger (heart center) • middle finger (solar plexus center) • ring finger (pelvic center) • little finger (base of spine center)?
- Press with the tip or side of your index finger and thumb into each finger and toe: side to side and front and back, especially working into pain spots and each joint, where energy is blocked.
- Finally hold each finger firmly at the base joint and pull; repeat the finger pulling from the middle joint and finally from the top joint.

7. HARMONIZING CONTACT

- This contact uses the power of the belly button – the center of vital energy for the body, where the fetus is connected to life through the umbilical cord – combined with an equally powerful Acupuncture point on the Triple Heater Meridian.
- One of the functions of the Triple Heater Meridian is to balance our temperature and bring harmony to all functions of the body-mind system.
- The contact point for the Triple Heater Meridian is a spirit level point known as 'Heavenly Window'. This point brings a sense of light and harmony when you are experiencing darkness, disharmony or a lack of love.

How To:

- (**mcs**) for which hand to use over the belly button. Bring all your fingers and thumb together and place them on or over the belly button.
- Place your middle or index finger in the hollow behind the right mastoid bone (behind the ear) and under the base of the skull, in the V where the mastoid and skull meet. Hold until you feel that it is complete.
- Switch hands and contact the left Triple Heater point in the hollow behind the mastoid bone of the left ear and under the skull, while the fingers of your other hand make a contact over the belly button.

8. YIN BALANCING POINTS

- ◎ This contact uses Acupuncture points on the Conception Vessel (CV). The Conception Vessel is known in Chinese Acupuncture as one of the eight 'Extraordinary Vessels'. It is a reservoir of Yin feminine energy that supports the six Yin Meridians of the Heart, Lung, Spleen, Kidney, Liver and Heart Protector.
- ◎ The quality of Yin energy supports you in being grounded and calm, and gives you the capacity to flow with the circumstances of your life, to accept, free of resistance, what you cannot change.

How To:

- Place the middle finger of your right hand on the lower Conception Vessel point – point 6, called Sea of Chi, located on the midline of the body a little more than an inch below the belly button.
- Place the index finger of your left hand on the upper Conception Vessel point – point 24, called Receiving Fluid, located in the indentation of the chin below the lips. This point is a powerful spirit-level point that helps you reconnect to a higher source of sustenance when you are in great need of inner support and strength.

- Close your eyes and relax deeply as you hold these two points. Or, while holding these two points, you can do Katsugen, allowing your body to move in any way it needs in order to balance your energy.

9. YANG BALANCING POINTS

- This contact uses two Acupuncture points on the Governor Vessel (GV), which is known in Chinese Acupuncture as one of the eight 'Extraordinary Vessels'.
- The Governor Vessel is a reservoir of Yang masculine energy that supports the six Yang Meridians of the Small Intestine, Stomach, Large Intestine, Bladder, Gall Bladder and Triple Heater.
- Yang energy is outward-moving, supporting you in being strong, confident, powerful and actively engaged in handling the world 'out there'.

How To:

- Place the middle finger of the right hand on the lower Governor Vessel point – point 1, called Long Strength, located at the base of your spine under the coccyx.
- Place the index finger of your left hand on the upper Governor Vessel point – point 28, called Mouth Crossing, located on the gum between the two upper front teeth. You can place your finger just above your upper lip, rather than directly on your gum.
- Close your eyes and relax deeply as you hold the two points; feel strong and confident; feel that you are empowered to successfully move into the world to achieve your goals and do right action.
- You can also do Katsugen as you hold the two points, allowing your body to move in any way it needs in order to balance your energy.

10. JIN SHIN JYUTSU® – The 26 Safety Energy Locks

- Jin Shin Jyutsu® Physio-Philosophy is an ancient Japanese art of harmonizing life energy in the body.
- The art was revived in the early 1900s by Master Jiro Murai, who devoted his life to the research and development of Jin Shin Jyutsu.
- His student Mary Burmeister brought the art from Japan to America in the 1950s.
- **Using Jin Shin Jyutsu** Our bodies have energy pathways that feed life to every cell. When one or more of the paths become blocked, the resulting stagnation of energy can disrupt localized areas in the body and eventually disharmonize the complete path or paths of the energy flow.
- Jin Shin Jyutsu uses twenty-six bilateral (right side and left side) 'safety energy locks' along these energy pathways. Holding these energy locks with a contact, in specific combinations and in a specific order, brings balance to mind and body.
- Practicing Jin Shin involves knowledge of the six depths, the pulses, the exact combinations of points for each 'Flow' and the order for doing the 'flows'. Attending Jin Shin Jyutsu seminars is necessary for this level of expertise.
- *The following notes were originally collated by Chloe Wordsworth from Mary Burmeister's seminar and are printed with permission of the Scottsdale Jin Shin Jyutsu School and edited by the school.*
- In Resonance Repatterning we use one or two of the 26 safety energy locks with a finger contact as a means for changing our resonance. We also use light/color, essential oils and tuning forks on the points and may even use toning while holding a point.

How To: *as used in Resonance Repatterning*

- (**mcs**) for which safety energy lock(s) is needed. If more than two are needed, (**mcs**) for how they need to be combined or for the order.
- (**mcs**) CYW Glasses are needed? (**mcs**) for details on which color for which eye.
- (**mcs**) {1–3} for the kind of contact needed on the safety energy lock(s). *Jin Shin points are different from Acupuncture points; Jin Shin 'locks' consist of an area of energy, as against an Acupuncture point that is an exact point.*

  1. A finger contact while (toning a note • doing Harmonic Overtones?) (**mcs**) for which finger. (**mcs**) for the details.
  2. A (tuning fork • ColorYourWorld Torch) is needed on the safety energy lock(s)? (**mcs**) for details.
  3. An Essential Oil is needed on the safety energy lock(s)? (**mcs**) for details on which Essential Oil.
     pp.237–241 Client places the Essential Oil on the point.

JIN SHIN JYUTSU® – THE 26 SAFETY ENERGY LOCKS

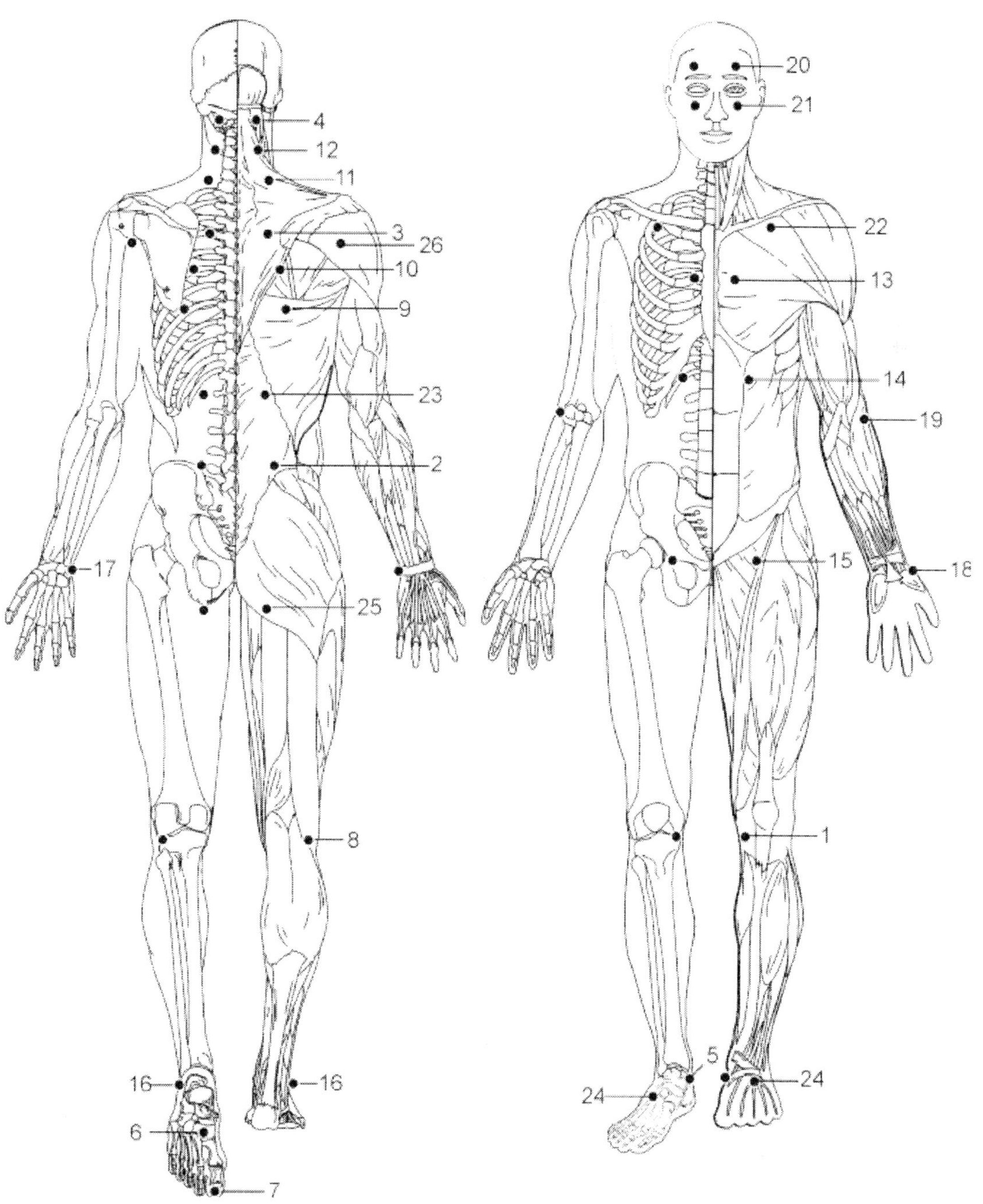

#1: The prime mover • Connects extreme height with extreme depth

Location

- Inside area of the knee.

Physical effects

- The first point is the masculine principle where all flows start.
- By keeping #1 clear, all flows can be kept clear – hold every day.
- It helps you unload, to exhale down the front;
- For anything stuck above the waist on the front, #1 will help descending functions. For example, choking; breathing difficulties; chest discomfort; heart conditions; headaches; digestive disorders; gas.
- #1 has a relationship to the opposite #10. For heart and lungs you may want to release the #1 flow first.

Mental/emotional effects

- Clearing chaos.

Additional details

- Client holding the thumb energizes the #1.
- #1 and the thumb hold helps #16, which harmonizes attitudes and helps with headaches.

#2: Life force for all creatures • Wisdom

Location

- On the back along the crest of the hip.

Physical effects

- The second point is the Mother principal, the feminine: it is about receiving and inhaling.
- Holding #1 and #2 harmonizes the masculine and feminine energies.

- #2 is the 'osteopath' for body alignment.
- #2 helps the ascending function. Because it helps energy ascend up the back, it is good for back troubles.
- Harmonizes blood pressure.
- Recharges the energy battery. Energizes the back and clears the mind.
- Releases leg tension.
- Releases pelvic/pubic tension.
- #2 helps with respiration: when jogging, place the thumb on the ring finger nail (the finger associated with #2); this contact helps when you are out of breath and need to adjust to high altitudes (airplanes, hiking, etc.)

Additional details

- Client holding their ring finger energizes #2.

#3: Understanding • The door swings open to release and receive

Location

- The top of the scapula (shoulder blade) outside the inner corner of the scapula.

Physical effects

- For all respiratory functions: shortness of breath, fluid in the lungs, coughing.
- Helps all immune system functions.
- Releases shoulder tension.
- Fever and cold release.
- Allergies.
- Fatigue.

Mental/emotional effects

- Neutralizes negative attitudes.

#4: Intelligence • The window letting in air and light

Location

- Base of the skull on either side of the spine.

Physical effects

- Rules the motor system of the body.
- Helps sinuses.
- Helps leg tension/stress, head discomfort.
- Good for the eyes, throat, insomnia, heart palpitations and irregularities.
- Detoxifies and energizes the system.

Mental/emotional effects

- Heightens/uplifts consciousness; clears the mind; balances the will, modulates the ego.
- When horizons seem limited and doors closed through negative, self-destructive thoughts, this safety energy lock allows you to open again to receive the energy of life.

Additional details

- When #4s are closed there is death; it is critical to keep them energized by holding these points.
- To harmonize, hold #4 on one side and the opposite cheekbone.
- If the #4s are stuck, holding #18 first may help.
- When pregnant it is good to do the #4s every day.

#5: Regeneration • Putting aside the old and putting on the new

Location

- On the area by the inside ankle bone.

Physical effects

- Energizes the bladder and kidneys.
- Relieves chest and shoulder tension and back and hip stress.
- For sprains.
- It is a good point for reproductive vitality.
- For arthritis: put the right hand on #5 and left hand on #16 (both are held on the same foot).

Mental/emotional effects

- Overcoming fear by connecting to spirit.

Additional details

- The index finger can be held to energize #5.

#6: Balance • Discrimination

Location

- Middle of the arch of the foot.

Physical effects

- Governs the chest, shoulders, arms, hands and respiration.
- Helps dizziness.
- Helps the reproductive organs.
- Helps digestive discomfort, back and hip stress, head tension (particularly migraines).
- For ridges on the nails: hold the right little toe with your left hand and place your right hand on the right #6.

Mental/emotional effects

- Where the buried jewel of the mind can be accessed.
- Balances masculine and feminine.
- Promotes beauty and harmony.

#7: Victory • Perfect life power

Location

- The tip of the big toe slightly on the underside of the toe.

Physical effects

- Helps the center of the brain (pineal and pituitary area).
- Helps with temper tantrums.
- Head discomfort; digestive stress; hip and back stress.
- Helpful for seizures: with your right hand contact point #7 on right big toe and with the left hand contact point #7 on left big toe.

Mental/emotional effects

- Brings focus and clarity.
- Clears the head.

Additional details

- To harmonize the entire system, sit on the client's left side and hold both #7s with the left hand and place the right hand on the solar plexus.

#8: Rhythm, strength and deep relaxation

Location

- Top of the fibula on the outside of the lower leg, beneath the knee.

Physical effects

- All skin symptoms: itching, eczema and rashes.
- Burns.
- Deep tension in the body; relaxes and regenerates muscles.
- Stimulates lymph flow; clears the body of toxins.
- Regulates the body thermostat: right #8 warms and the left #8 cools. For hot flashes hold right hand on left #8.

- Balances hormones (e.g. excessive body hair).
- Menstrual cramps, menopause and reproductive problems; use after a hysterectomy.
- Adjusts metabolism and body chemistry.
- Alleviates gas.
- Hemorrhoids and rectal problems: for self-help: hold #8 and the swollen area.

Mental/emotional effects
- Brings a sense of splendor to the body.
- Symbol of infinity and vitality.

#9: End of a cycle, beginning of another • Every end is the seed of a fresh beginning

Location
- Bottom third of scapula (shoulder blade) between scapula and spine.

Physical effects
- Benefits the organs in the waist area (pancreas, adrenals, kidneys, liver, spleen, stomach and gall bladder).
- Helps in chest congestion, back and hip stress, leg and foot discomfort.
- Dissolves calcifications.
- High blood pressure (hold #9 and the same side of the coccyx).

Mental/emotional effects
- For new beginnings and letting go of the past, clearing the deck and starting a new cycle.
- Newborn babies: hold #9 and #26 and opposite #2 to ease entry into the world.
- Brings completion and closure to what you have accomplished.
- Brings power and authority.
- Helps create a humanitarian attitude.

Additional details

- If you cannot reach #9 on yourself, hold the high #19 instead (on the biceps area of the upper arm).

#10: Air • Outpouring of limitless life power

Location

- Middle third of the scapula (shoulder blade) between scapula and spine.

Physical effects

- #10 provides limitless energy for the body and all its functions.
- For speech problems or loss of speech function through strokes. For stuttering: hold left #10.
- Cerebral palsy, Down's Syndrome, Bell's Palsy, Parkinson's or autism.
- Improves vocal functions: may be helpful for polyps on vocal cords and for singing.
- For heart attack or heart problems hold #10 at the 5th thoracic vertebra and the left little finger.
- Harmonizes hips, knees, blood pressure and respiration.

Mental/emotional effects

- Helps mental and emotional stresses and strains.
- For feminine and masculine balance.
- #10 and #1 represent limitless life power.

Additional details

- If you cannot reach #10 on yourself, hold the high #19 instead (biceps area of the upper arm).
- #10 allows energy to ascend up the back.

#11: Justice • Unloading excess baggage • The hub

Location

On the ridge of the shoulder.

Physical effects

- Back problems: hold #11 and the index finger for 15 minutes.
- For back tension: hold #11 and #15. For reducing digestive discomfort: hold #11 and #25.
- Immune system: hold #11s and #3s together.
- #11 and #12 help prevent strokes.

Mental/emotional effects

- Releases 'garbage' on all levels.
- Releases the tendency to dwell on negativity.
- Brings the power of quick decisions.

Additional details

- Harmonizing the #11s helps the assimilation and elimination functions of the body.

#12: Not my will but Thy will • Submission of personal consciousness

Location

- Middle portion of the neck on either side of the spine.

Physical effects

- Helps relieve stress in the organs around the waistline such as liver, spleen, stomach, pancreas, gall bladder, kidneys, adrenals. For sinus problems: hold #21 on the side of the affected sinus and the opposite #12.
- Stroke: hold #12 and opposite #20, 21 and 22.

- For alcohol hangovers: place right hand on left shoulder (fingers pointing down), with the pad of the thumb on the left side of the neck.
- Neck tension.

Mental/emotional effects Helps relieve stress of daily life.

- Hold left #12 to clear destructive thoughts, right #12 for mental and emotional stress.

Additional details

- #12s bring a feeling of love and peace.

A quick way to open up #12 is to hold #16 and #12 together.

#13: Equilibrium • Love thine enemies

Location

- 3rd rib down from the clavicle.

- **Physical effects** Supportive for breast cancer. Maintain the energy flow of the #13s as a preventive measure against breast cancer.
- Strengthens immune system (helps thymus gland).
- Helps reproductive function.
- Chest congestion.
- Appetite imbalances/eating disorders.
- Neck and shoulder imbalances.
- For sore throat: hold #13 and the opposite #11.

Mental/emotional effects

- Youthfulness; helpful for avoiding wrinkles.
- Increases productivity.
- Change your image.

- Extreme emotional distress.
- Promotes enthusiasm and curiosity.

Additional details
- Hold middle finger to energize #13.

#14: Equilibrium • Sustenance

Location
- Base of ribs on front of body.

Physical effects
- Governs hips and thighs.
- Helps disperse fat around the middle (use #14s and the right ring finger).
- For sleep disorders including snoring, sleep apnea and nightmares.
- For epilepsy, unconsciousness, convulsions in children.
- For indigestion.
- Heart stress.
- Brain stress.
- Harmonizes eye conditions.

Mental/emotional effects
- Helps to adapt and adjust lack of balance in one's lifestyle.

Additional details
- Hold the ring finger to energize #14.
- Spirit into action.

#15: Joy and laughter • Wash our hearts with laughter

Location

- Groin: along the crease created where the thighs join the body.

Physical effects

- To release tension or pain in the groin and pubic bone.
- For pain in the hips, leg trouble, broken bones or sprained ankles.
- Hip, leg, knee and foot disharmony.
- Stimulates the immune system.
- Calms the nervous system and brings physical balance.
- For varicose veins and blood clots.
- Respiration, reproduction or elimination: use #15 and the opposite #11 and #2.
- Back problems: use #15 and either #10 or #11.
- Abdominal stress; bloating.
- Heart function.

Mental/emotional effects

- Eases mental stress and brings joy and laughter.

#16: The basis of all human activities

Location

- In the area round the outer (lateral) side of ankle bone.

Physical effects

- Tones muscles; skeletal balance.
- Head and back discomfort.
- Reproductive function.
- Clears migraines and frontal headaches.
- Assists in the healing of scar tissue.

- Chronic stiff neck: hold the neck and the same side #16.
- For paralysis, stroke and breast conditions: hold #16 with #17, #18 or #19.
- Voice and speech problems: hold #16 and # 9 or #19.
- For swollen eyelids: hold #16 on ankle bone on same side as the swollen eye.

Mental/emotional effects

- For those who are weepy and cry a lot.
- Helps in general relaxation.

Additional details

- Hold thumb for energizing #16.

#17: Transformation power • Creative imagination

Location

- Outer (lateral) side of wrist, at the base of little finger.

Physical effects

- Helps the reproductive function, heart and spleen.
- For hearing.
- Harmonizes acid/alkaline balance.
- For nervous system.
- For ankle and back tension.
- Rest.

Mental/emotional effects

- Activates intuitive nature.
- Balances the system in cases of over-effort.
- Calms nervous system.

Additional details

- Holding this point acts as natural smelling salts.

#18: Body consciousness • Functions affecting human consciousness

Location

- On the wrist at the base of thumb.

Physical effects

- Sleep disorders, insomnia.
- For headaches/congestion located in the back of the head.
- Back stiffness; rib cage distortions.
- Hiccups.

Mental/emotional effects

- Clears the mind and the head.
- Helps attune to one's personal rhythm.

Additional details

- Hold little finger to harmonize #18s.

#19: Authority and leadership • Perfect balance

Location

- Bend of elbow. With the palm up, #19 is located at the elbow crease on the same side as the thumb.

Physical effects

- For overall well-being.
- Breathing: chest, lung and breath congestion.
- Heart issues and breast problems.
- Digestion.
- Bed wetting.
- For ringing in the ears.
- Painful feet: hold #19s.

Mental/emotional effects

- For a sense of liberation.
- For confidence.
- For emotional balance.

Additional details

- Balances weight distribution.
- Clears physical symptoms in the body.
- Use #19 as an alternative for #9 if you cannot reach #9 on yourself.

#20: Everlasting • Eternity

Location

- In the middle of the forehead, above the center of the eyes.

Physical effects

- Helps head, ears, eyes, equilibrium, heart function and chest function.
- Benefits the bladder.
- For high blood pressure.
- For frontal headaches: hold #20 and opposite #4.

Mental/emotional effects

- Harmonizes mental tension.
- Promotes common sense and logic.
- Assists in memory retention (beneficial in cases of senility).

#21: Profound security • Escape from mental bondage

Location

- On the cheek bones below the center of the eyes.

Physical effects

- Weight problems.
- For wrinkles: hold #21 and the opposite #23.

Mental/emotional effects

- When practicality is needed.
- Insecurity.
- Releases tension and worries; erases inertia.

Additional details

- Hold thumb to energize #21.

#22: Completion • Gathering and dispersal

Location

- Between the collar bone and first rib.

Physical effects

- Helps stabilize high blood pressure, prevent strokes and vascular stress.
- Thyroid and parathyroid function.
- Harmonizes mental, emotional, physical, and digestive stress.

Mental/emotional effects

- Helps develop reason.

Additional details

- Converging of all energy.
- Hold index finger to harmonize #22.

#23: Proper circulation • Controller of human destiny

Location

- Base of the rib cage at the back.

Physical effects

- For weight imbalance.
- Muscle function.
- For blood sugar metabolism: diabetes, hypoglycemia.
- For bloating and digestive troubles.
- Blood circulation, blood composition (cholesterol), blood chemistry.
- Adrenal function.
- Brain function.
- #23 and #3 together are important in regulating the immune system and balancing respiration.

Mental/emotional effects

- Harmonizes addictions and cravings.
- For fears.
- For tantrums and obstinacy.
- Helps turn hate to love.
- For selfishness.
- For those who are temperamental, negative, impatient, hyperactive.
- For shyness: use #23 and #21.

Additional details

- #23 can be used in many combinations.

#24: Understanding • Harmonizing chaos

Location

- Between the 4th and 5th metatarsal bones (4th toe and little toe) on the top of the foot.

Physical effects

- Harmonizes chaos in the physical body.
- Helps the skeletal system.

Mental/emotional effects

- Helps prevent jealousy and stubbornness.
- Brings understanding.

#25: Quietly regenerating

Location

- On the back of the thigh just below the sitting bones.
- To locate this safety energy lock: sit on your hands, palms up.

Physical effects

- Helps clear fatigue and recharge energy.
- Quietly regenerates the whole body-mind system and brings alertness.
- Tones the muscles ('the lazy person's jogging').

Mental/emotional effects

- Brings relaxation on all levels.

#26: Director • All-encompassing

- **Location** Outer edge of the scapula (shoulder blade) at the back of the armpit.

Physical effects
- Brings energy to the whole body-mind system.
- Use if you feel physically shaky.
- For tingling in the arm, wrist or elbow.
- Hold left #26 for tumors or cysts anywhere in the body.

Mental/emotional effects
- Brings a sense of peace, harmony and the splendor of limitless life.

Additional details
- #26 with opposite #24 brings quietness and relaxation.

SUMMARY OF JIN SHIN SAFETY ENERGY LOCKS THAT MAY BE HELPFUL TO KNOW

Experiment with these contacts and see if they help.

- Adrenals: 9
  Allergies: 3
  Arthritis: 1, 5+16

- Back troubles: 2, 6, 8, 10, 11, 13, 15, 16, 11+15, 10+15
  Bladder/kidneys: 5, 17, 20, 23
  Blood disorders: 8, 17
  Blood pressure, high: 2, 3, 9, 11, 12, 20, 21, 22
  Breasts: 9, 13, 16, 17, 19, 23, 26
  Breathing: 1, 2, 3, 7, 9, 10, 15, 19, 23

- Cancer fears: 9, 13, 23, 26
  Cerebral palsy: 10
  Convulsions: 14
  Coughs: 3
  Cysts: 23, 26

- Digestion: 14, 23
  Dizziness: 6

- Ears: 4, 17
  Eating disorders: 13
  Elimination: 1, 15
  Energy: 2; 10; 19
  Epilepsy: 7, 14
  Eyes: 8, 14, 16 *swollen eyelids*

- Fatigue: 4, 10
  Fevers: 3
  Foot pain: 19
  Fountain of youth: 13+21, 21+opposite 23

- Gas: 1, 8

- Joy: 15

- Hangover: 12
  Hair: 6
  Harmonizing masculine and feminine: 2, 10, 23
  Headaches: 1, 6, 16, 18, 20
  Hearing: 17
  Heart problems: 1, 10, 13, 14, 15, 17, 19, 20
  Hemorrhoids: 8
  Hormones: 8, 9, 10, 11, 23

- Immune system: 3, 8, 11+3, 13, 15, 17, 23
  Indigestion: 1, 14, 23
  Insomnia: 18 (see sleep)

- Joints: 5+16, 15, 26

- Labor pain: 8, 16
  Leg problems: 2, 4, 15, 9+4
  Liver: 9, 12
  Low energy: 2, 4, 10, 20, 22, 25 *hold for 15 minutes*, 26
  Lungs: 1, 2, 3, 7, 9, 10, 13, 15, 19, 23
  Lymph system: 17, 22

- Menstrual problems: 8, 13, 15, 17
  Mental & emotional tension: 2, 4, 6 *help with anger*; 5 *fears*; 7 *temper tantrums*; 7, 8 *deep tension*; 11, 12 *anger and frustration*; 13 *extreme emotional distress*; 13, 14 *brain stress*, 15, 17 *calms nervous system*; 16 *weeping, crying a lot*; 17 *feeling shaky*; 17, 18 *mental tension, sadness, depression, senility*; 19 *emotional balance*; 21, 23 *fear, tantrums, obstinacy*; 24 *chaotic thinking*; 25, 26 *brings calm*
  Migraine: 6, 7, 16, Muscle tension: 8, 9, 16,17, 23, 24 *achy all over*, 25

- Nails: 6
  Neck problems: 13, 15+16 *on same side*, 16
  Nervous system: 17, 20

- Paralysis: 16
  Postural problems: 6

  Reproductive organs: 6, 8, 13, 15, 17 Respiratory problems: 1, 2, 3, 7, 9, 10, 15, 19, 23

- Scar tissue: 8, 16
  Shoulders: 3, 5, 13
  Seizures: 7
  Sinuses: 4, 12 + opposite 21
  Skin: 5, 8, 13, 21, 23 Sleep: 14, 18 *insomnia*; 18 *sleep disorders, snoring, apnea*
  Snoring: 14
  Sore throat: 10, 13+opposite 11

  Speech problems: 10, 16 + 19, 16 + 9 Spleen: 9, 12, 17
  Sprained ankle: 5, 15
  Stomach: 12, 21
  Strokes: 10, 11, 12, 12 + 20, 12 + 21, 12 + 22, 16, 20, 22
  Stuttering: 10

- Thrombosis: 15
  Thymus: 13
  Temperature imbalances: 3, 8
  Tinnitus: 19
  Toxicity: 8
  Tumors: 23, 26

- Varicose veins: 15
  Voice problems: 10, 16 + 9, 16 + 19, 16 and hold all fingers

- Weight issues: 14, 21 + 23, 23
  Well-being: 25, 26

- Youthfulness: 13, 20, 23

11. CRANIAL CONTACTS

See spiralup127.com for video/audio downloads of the cranial contacts and all Energizing Options.

Cranial contacts (making contacts on the bones of the skull to activate the cranial rhythms) are powerful:

- **The cranial bones and rhythms.** The sutures of the cranial bones connect the five major cranial bones to form the skull.

- Previously, the cranial bones were thought to be unmoving in an adult (based on autopsies done on dead bodies!), but in fact on live bodies the sutures expand and relax, which allows for the subtle movement of the cranial bones. Each cranial bone expands and relaxes in its own unique way that cannot be seen with the naked eye.

- **The cerebro-spinal fluid.** Movement of the cranial bones is created by the movement of the cerebro-spinal fluid in the ventricles of the brain and spinal cord. Dr. Randolph Stone describes the cerebro-spinal fluid as the most highly vibrating energy in the human body.

- When there are accidents, shocks and emotional traumas, the movement of the cranial bones loses its correct and symmetrical rhythm, which directly affects the flow of the cerebro-spinal fluid throughout the body along with its energizing and healing power and the calming effect it has on the mind and nervous system.

- **The associated brain areas.** The cranial bones are associated with their corresponding brain areas: the **frontal** bones with clear thinking and focused attention; the **parietals** with knowing where we are in space (so we don't bump into a curb when driving, for example) and with helping us evaluate how something feels – pleasurable or threatening; the **occipitals** with vision; and the **temporals** with sound, speech, comprehension and memory. The **sphenoid** is a butterfly-shaped bone in the center of the brain on which the pituitary sits. It seems to have an association with feelings, and is 'contacted' via touch on the temples.

The cranial holds are light energetic contacts. Those who have studied cranial-sacral therapy, know that using cranial holds professionally is a lifetime practice. But even holding the cranials lightly can have a beneficial and deeply calming effect both on yourself and the person you are working with.

How To:

- (**mcs**) Practitioner needs to do the cranial contact on the client? *Go to {1} below.* (**mcs**) Client needs to do a self-cranial contact? *Go to {2}.*
- (**mcs**) for the cranial contact(s) needed {a–e} either with #1 or #2 above.
- (**mcs**) The cranial hold needs a contact with (the fingers • the ColorYourWorld Torch • a tuning fork)? (**mcs**) for details on color / tuning fork needed. The stem of the tuning fork is placed on the cranial bone, or the two tines can be moved over the cranial bone. (**mcs**) for details.
- If a contact is needed and you have studied Dr. Upledger's Cranial-Sacral work, you can follow the cranial rhythm as you maintain the cranial contact. If not, simply make a light contact, as in Polarity Therapy.

1. **The practitioner doing the cranial contact(s) on the client**
   If a contact is needed, the client lies down on his/her back and the practitioner sits north of the client's head.
   a. **Frontal bones**
      Place the tips of your index, middle and ring fingers on the forehead halfway between the eyebrows and the hairline. The contact is very light, as though you are lifting the forehead toward the ceiling.

   b. **Sphenoid**
      Place your thumbs very gently on the client's temples, outside the orbital ridge of the eyes (at the side of each eye). The rest of your fingers rest comfortably under the back of the client's neck.

c. **Temporals**

Place the pads of your thumbs on the inside of your client's ears and your fingers behind the ears where the ears meet the skull. Do not block the ear canal. Slightly stretch the ears downwards and outwards and then relax. While still holding the contact, you may be able to follow the 'unwinding' or Katsugen movement-release that sometimes occurs. The client may find their head gently moving; explain that this is the natural 'unwinding' of tension as the cranial rhythm is re-established.

Another beautiful balancing is to place the length of your thumb over the mandibular joint on the cheek outside the ears, and place all your fingers behind the ears. Gently and slowly circle forward in a clockwise direction. This circling of the ears has a deeply relaxing effect.

d. **Parietals**

Follow a line from the top of the client's ears to the top of the head, and then place your index, middle and fourth fingers at this point on either side of the dome of the client's head. Make a light contact, feeling as though magnets on your fingertips are drawing the client's head toward you (if the client is lying down and you are sitting above his/her head). Allow for any Katsugen unwinding to occur.

e. **Occipital stretch**

This Polarity contact is different from the cranial hold taught in the Cranial Sacral seminar, but is also very effective.

Bring the fingers of both hands under the ridge of your client's skull on either side of the spine; with their head resting on your palms, give a gentle, stretching pull with your fingers under their occipital ridge.

DIAGRAM OF THE CRANIAL BONES

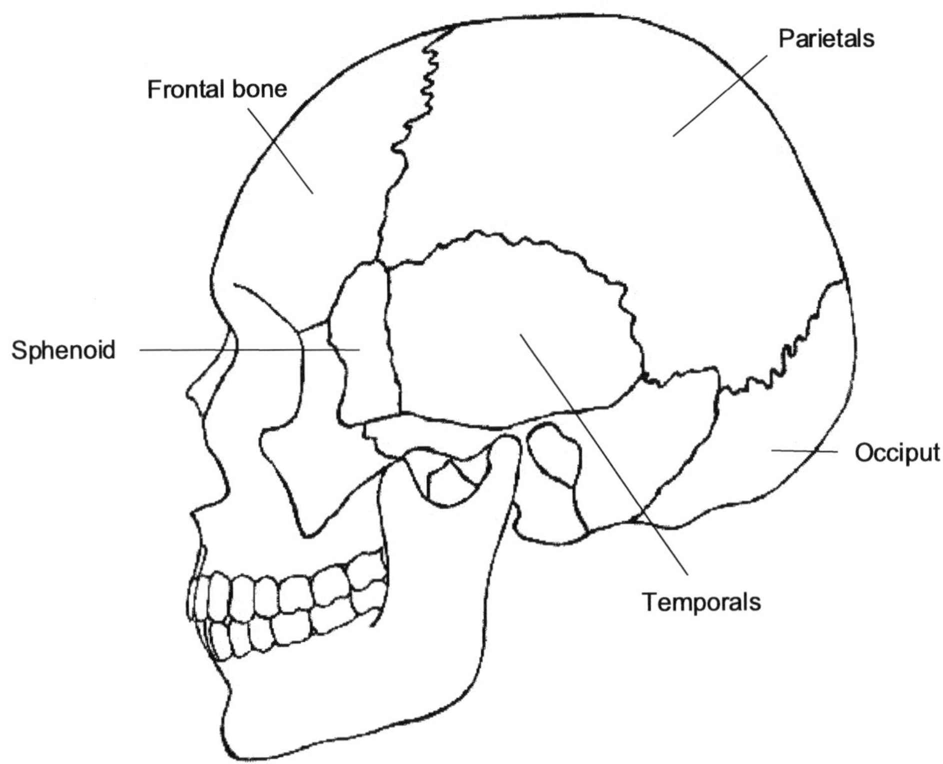

2. **The client doing the cranial contacts on themselves**
   a. **Frontal bones**
   If a finger contact is needed, place your ring fingers, middle fingers and index fingers on your own forehead halfway between your eyebrows and your hair line. Imagine magnets on the tips of your fingers gently pulling your forehead forwards (if you are sitting up). If using a tuning fork / CYW Torch, (**mcs**) where to place ie move it on your forehead.

   b. **Sphenoid**
   Place the tuning fork / CYW Torch or your (index • middle) finger(s) on your temples *outside the orbital ridge of each eye.*

c. **Temporals**
Place the pad of your index fingers inside your ears and your thumb behind the flap where you ears meet your skull. Stretch your ears gently downward and outward. Now allow the inner directed movement of Katsugen to determine how you gently pull, circle or vibrate your ears – with the intention of activating and balancing the cranial rhythm of your temporals.

d. **Parietals**
Place the tips of your ring, middle and index fingers very lightly on either side of the dome of your head, with your ring fingers in line with the tip of your ears. Feel as though magnets are gently lifting your skull upwards (if you are sitting). If a Tuning Fork / CYW Torch is needed, (**mcs**) where on either side of the dome of the head to place or move it.

e. **Occiput**
Place the fingertips of both hands on either side of the midline of the back of your head. It is best doing this contact lying down so you can relax the back of your head into your fingertips. If a Tuning Fork / CYW Torch is needed, (**mcs**) where on the back of the head to place or move it.

12. SNS BALANCING

- This Polarity contact helps to balance the sympathetic nervous system (SNS) and has a calming effect on the whole system.
- It is highly recommended to use this contact after any shock, accident, stress or trauma.

How To:

- Place the tip of your right middle finger under your coccyx and place the tip of your left index finger at the top of your spine in the hollow under the occipital ridge of your skull.

13. PNS BALANCING

- This Polarity self-help contact is important to do after any shock, accident or stress that has upset you, or if you need to calm your mind, especially for those with insomnia.
- It supports the balancing of the parasympathetic nervous system (PNS), which allows for bonding, safety, calmness and relaxation.

How To:

- Lie on your left side with your upper right knee bent and your lower left leg straight.
- Bend your left arm and place your left hand on the right side of your neck.
- Place your right hand over your right hip. Your fingers curl gently round your right sitz bone.
- Relax and breathe deeply.

14. POLARITY CONTACTS

TRANSFORMING CHAKRA PATTERNS *seminar.*
For the video downloads of the Polarity Contacts see spiralup127.com

15. MERIDIAN MASSAGE

- There are twelve Meridians in traditional Chinese Acupuncture which govern our physical, emotional and mental functions.
- Three Yin Meridians flow down the inside of your arm from your chest to your fingertips. Three Yang Meridians flow from your fingertips up the back of your arm, over the shoulder to the side of your face.
- Three Yang Meridians flow down the body to the feet and three Yin Meridians flow up the body from the inside of the feet to your chest, where the cycle begins once more.

How To:

- (**mcs**) where you need to begin: with #1, 2, 3, 4. Wherever you begin, continue in the sequence given. For example, if you start with #3, then go to #4, then #1 and #2.
- (**mcs**) if you need to touch the skin lightly or if you need to be above the skin without actual contact.
- (**mcs**) for the number of repetitions needed. *Usually one or two.*
- If working with a client, he/she will do the Meridian Massage on him/herself as you demonstrate and do the Meridian Massage along with your client.

1. **Three Yin Meridians: the Heart, Lung, Heart Protector**
   Lightly stroke down the **inside** of your arm, from your armpit to your palm and fingertips. Repeat on the other arm.

2. **Three Yang Meridians: Small Intestine, Large Intestine, Triple Heater**
   Lightly stroke up the **outside** or top of the arm, from the fingers, back of your hand, over the back of your shoulders, up your neck to the side of your face. Repeat on your other arm.

3. **Three Yang Meridians: Bladder, Gall Bladder, Stomach**
   Place your index fingers at the inside corners of your eyes above your tear ducts (Bladder Meridian); brush your hands over your head, down the back of your neck, down your back and buttocks and the back of your legs. Let your thumbs stroke down the side of your ribs and the outside of your legs so you include the Gall Bladder and Stomach Meridians in this downward-moving energy massage. Finish by stroking down the outside of your feet to your toes.

4. **Three Yin Meridians: Kidney, Liver, Spleen**
   Start at your big toes and stroke up the **inside** of your arch, over your ankles, up the inside of your legs, the front of your body on either side of the midline to your chest and armpits.

16. MU ACUPUNCTURE POINTS

The Mu Acupuncture Points are special points that powerfully activate coherent energy of each Meridian with all its characteristic positive qualities. Dr. John Diamond's research demonstrated that using consonant sounds along with its associated Mu point strengthens that Meridian.

How To:

a. (**mcs**) A (midline • bilateral) Mu point is needed? (**mcs**) for the specific point. *More than one Mu point may be needed*

b. (**mcs**) {1–4} for the type of contact needed.

1. **A Finger Contact**
   (**mcs**) for which finger and whether (*Client* • practitioner) needs to make the contact. (**mcs**) for the level of touch (gentle • stimulating). *If working with a client it is better for the client to do the contact on their own Mu point.*

2. **The ColorYourWorld Torch**
   (**mcs**) for the (color • gemstone • geometric pattern • Sanskrit chakra pattern) needed.

3. **A Tuning Fork**
   (**mcs**) for details of which tuning fork. Usually the stem of the tuning fork needs to be held on the Mu point 1–3 times.

4. An Essential Oil
   (**mcs**) for details. (**mcs**) The Essential Oil needs to be inhaled through the (left • right) nostril? (**mcs**) The Essential Oil needs to be placed on the Mu point? *Let client do this on themselves.*

c. (**mcs**) (*Client*) needs to wear the CYW Glasses? (**mcs**) for details.

d. Have the client do the consonant sound with the Mu point contact.

MIDLINE MU POINTS

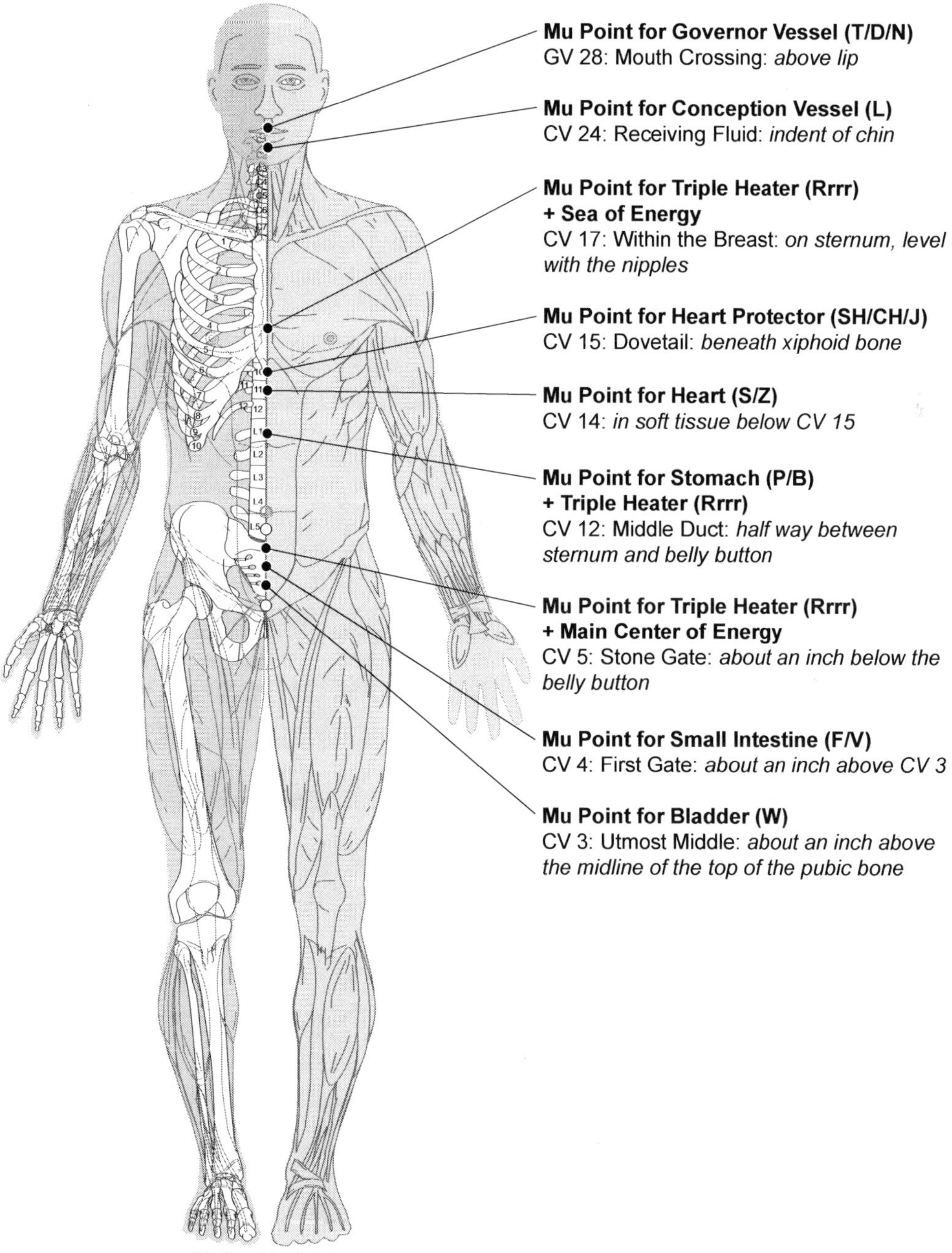

Mu Point for Governor Vessel (T/D/N)
GV 28: Mouth Crossing: *above lip*

Mu Point for Conception Vessel (L)
CV 24: Receiving Fluid: *indent of chin*

Mu Point for Triple Heater (Rrrr)
+ Sea of Energy
CV 17: Within the Breast: *on sternum, level with the nipples*

Mu Point for Heart Protector (SH/CH/J)
CV 15: Dovetail: *beneath xiphoid bone*

Mu Point for Heart (S/Z)
CV 14: *in soft tissue below CV 15*

Mu Point for Stomach (P/B)
+ Triple Heater (Rrrr)
CV 12: Middle Duct: *half way between sternum and belly button*

Mu Point for Triple Heater (Rrrr)
+ Main Center of Energy
CV 5: Stone Gate: *about an inch below the belly button*

Mu Point for Small Intestine (F/V)
CV 4: First Gate: *about an inch above CV 3*

Mu Point for Bladder (W)
CV 3: Utmost Middle: *about an inch above the midline of the top of the pubic bone*

Midline Mu Points

BILATERAL MU POINTS

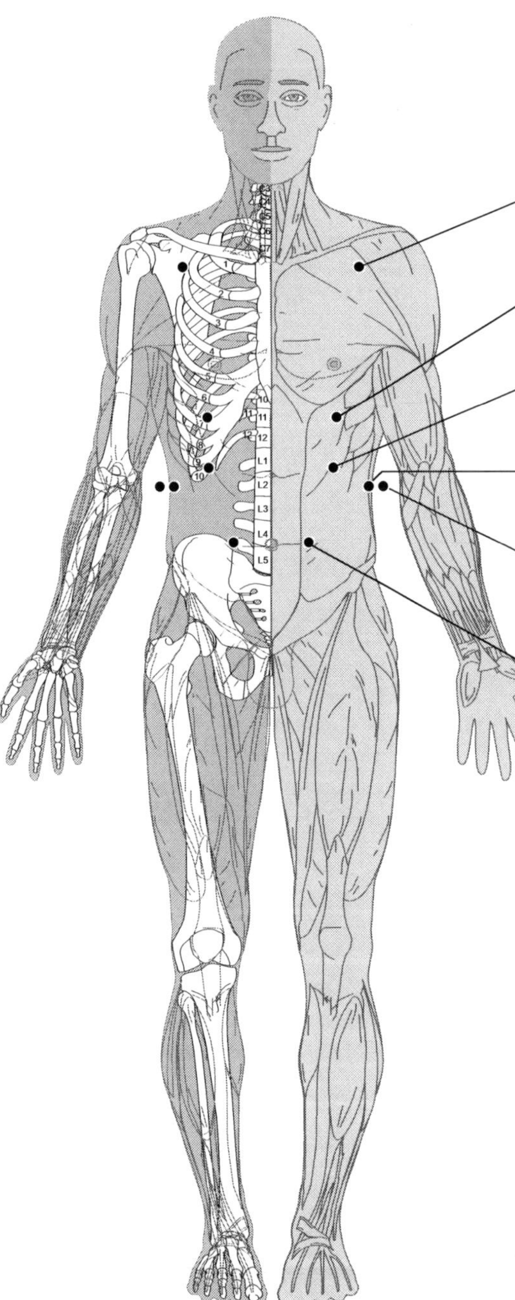

Mu Point for Lung (Q)
Lung 1: Middle Palace: *about an inch below the clavicle where it connects to the shoulder joint*

Mu Point for Gall Bladder (Y)
Gall Bladder 24: Sun and Moon: *in line with the nipple under the chest*

Mu Point for Liver (TH)
Liver 14: Gate of Hope: *in line with the nipple under the rib cage*

Mu Point for Spleen (H)
Liver 13: Chapter Gate: *at 11th floating rib at the side of the waist*

Mu Point for Kidney (K/G)
Gall Bladder 25: Capital Gate: *at 12th floating rib at the back of the waist*

Mu Point for Large Intestine (M)
Stomach 25: Heavenly Pivot: a*bout two inches on either side of the belly button.*

Bilateral Mu Points

G.
ESSENTIAL OIL OPTIONS

Essential Oils have been used since ancient times in Egypt, Greece, India and China. Essential Oils are renowned for balancing mental and emotional states and re-harmonizing the physical body. Modern research is now proving their effectiveness for regaining and maintaining our health and for preventive 'medicine'.

Essential Oils and bacteria

There is a powerful example from a medical doctor, Dr. Valnet, MD, proving the effectiveness of essential oils. He used vaporized Lemon essence (from a diffuser) to kill meningococcus bacteria in 15 minutes; diphtheria bacilli in 20 minutes; typhoid bacilli in 1 hour; staphylococcus aureus in 2 hours; pneumococcus bacteria in 3 hours.

Lemon is also good for throat infections and is used for cleansing the skin and reducing wrinkles; it is an excellent substitute for commercial deodorants; and because it is known to be mentally uplifting, it is often used for any kind of mental upset.

And lemon is just one of hundreds of essential oils!

THE FOUR OVALS FOR EACH OPTION

1. **Muscle check self (mcs) or use your felt sense for the Energizing Option you need**

2. **Read the introduction to the Energizing Option**
   Demo the 'How To' if doing with someone else, or use the video download if needed

3. **Do the Energizing Option**
   - Observe that you are doing it correctly
   - Breathe
   - **(mcs) / felt sense:** This is complete?
   - **(mcs) / felt sense:** Another Option is needed?

4. **After completing the Option**
   - Take a pause to integrate the positive change
   - Recheck your **felt sense:**
     a. Do you feel more relaxed?
     b. Are you breathing more easily?
     c. Do you notice any other positive change?
   - *RR Practitioners recheck *[cr] statements*

The ancient use of Essential Oils

- Using Essential Oils is one of the most ancient of the healing arts. Essential Oils were used in ancient Egypt, India and Rome in baths, inhaled, ingested and placed on the body. *Only certain Oils can be taken internally (swallowed) and usually in a highly diluted form.*

- The average Essential Oil may contain 80–200 **natural** chemical constituents (not synthetic), each of which contributes to the overall benefit of the Oil to the body, emotions and mind.

- There is research documenting that most viruses, fungi and bacteria cannot live in the presence of certain Essential Oils like cinnamon, oregano and thyme.

- Research has also shown that cancer patients respond positively to the daily use of frankincense.

- It is well documented that therapeutic lavender oil heals burns. As most lavender is a hybrid, or is mixed with cheaper lavendin that actually makes the burn worse, caution about using only the highest quality oils is needed.

- Because the fragrances of the oils goes directly to the limbic brain, oils have a unique effect on the emotions, bringing a sense of calm, uplift and joy.

- Because of their effectiveness in relation to emotional states, Essential Oils are often used in the following Resonance Repatterning processes: Fusion, Diffusion, the Energy Constriction Release, as well as the Suppressed Emotion-Image Repatterning taught in the ENERGETICS OF RELATIONSHIP seminar for cases of shock or trauma.

- As an Energizing Option, Essential Oils can be be used along with any other Spiral Up Energizing Option in this book, if you (**mcs**) or feel that this would be helpful.

How To:

- From the following list of 18 Introductory Essential Oils, or from the charts, or from a list of any Oils that you have available to you, (**mcs**) for which Essential Oil needed, or choose an oil based on your knowledge and training.

- (**mcs**) The Essential Oil needs to be inhaled through the nose?

- (**mcs**) The Essential Oil needs to be placed on (the feet • the hands • an area of the face • the ears • the neck • the throat • a vertebra of the spine • pulse points of the wrists • a cranial bone or on the scalp • around the orbital bone surrounding the eyes (NOT IN THE EYES) • a Chakra area • an Acupuncture point • a Jin Shin Jyutsu safety energy lock)? (**mcs**) for details.

- Place a drop of the Essential Oil on the palm of your hand, generally with a few drops of a vegetable carrier oil (jojoba oil, olive oil, apricot oil or almond oil). If the skin is not sensitive or reactive to the Essential Oils, you can place the oil undiluted on an area – otherwise it needs to be mixed with a vegetable carrier oil before placing on the skin.

- Client applies the Essential Oil to the area where it is needed, unless he/she gives permission to the practitioner to apply the Oil and the practitioner is a certified massage therapist.

18 INTRODUCTORY ESSENTIAL OILS

The following information represents the traditional uses of 18 Essential Oils the author generally carries with her and uses most frequently. Each person collects their own favorites. You will soon discover the ones you want to have available at all times. Three of these oils (#1, 6, 15) are special YoungLiving combinations.

Disclaimer:
Essential Oils have been used for thousands of years. I list, for information only, what many people, including researchers, have experienced as a result of using Essential Oils. Use your own discretion before using any oil.

1. **THIEVES** immune system support; kills mold and fungus

2. **LAVENDER** burns; sunburn; cuts; wounds; stretch marks; bruises; calms the mind (used since ancient times for insomnia); throat infections; laryngitis; palpitations; high blood pressure

3. **CLOVE** has been used for skin cancer; infected wounds; toothache; pain

4. **HELYCHRYSUM** stops bleeding; reduces pain from cuts; regenerates nerves; hemostat (balances the blood / thins blood)

5. **LEMON** Dr. Valnet, MD, used vaporized Lemon essence to kill meningococcus bacteria in 15 minutes; typhoid bacilli in 1 hour, staphylococcus aureus in 2 hours, pneumococcus bacteria in 3 hours, diphtheria bacilli in 20 minutes. Good for throat infections and it is used for cleansing the skin and reducing wrinkles, Lemon is an excellent substitute for commercial deodorants. It has been used for mental upset and is mentally uplifting

6. **VALOR** bruising and structural alignment; a wonderful fragrance for using instead of a deodorant

7. **PEPPERMINT** irregular menses; hot flashes; shock; headaches; digestion; pain reduction; mental alertness and focus

8. **SAGE** in ancient Rome it was written, "Why be sick when you have sage growing in your garden;" adrenals; nerves; sage tea is used as part of a cancer protocol *See Rudolph Breuss, The Breuss Cancer Cure*

9. **GRAPEFRUIT** for the skin; cleanses blood; supports the liver; helps eliminate toxins; has been used as an anti-depressant for drug withdrawal; fatigue (Palmarosa is used for nervous exhaustion); supports the lymphatic system; has been used as a tea for weight loss

10. **EUCALYPTUS** bronchial troubles; lungs; antibiotic effect; hyperactivity

11. **CORIANDER** research at Cairo University has shown that Coriander lowers glucose and insulin levels and supports pancreatic function

12. **SACRED FRANKINCENSE** (Boswellia carterii) good for everything; depression; research has shown that it is anti-tumoral and repairs damaged DNA

13. **OREGANO** anti-bacterial, anti-viral, anti-microbial; general tonic

14. **THYME** asthma; anti-bacterial, anti-fungal, anti-microbial, anti-viral; insomnia; amazing properties that support longevity

15. **PURIFICATION** antiseptic; bug bites; stings; scorpion stings

16. **CINNAMON** used for diarrhea; for warts; alzheimer's

17. **GALBANUM** wrinkles; scar tissue; wounds; anti-spasmodic; pain relief

18. **OTHER** (Sandalwood, Myrrh, Melaleuca, Bergamot, and options from the charts on the following pages)

SOME USES OF ESSENTIAL OILS

SKIN	SKIN (cont.)	SKIN (cont)	JOINTS / MUSCLES	HORMONAL
• Cajeput *skin spots, oily skin* • Cardamom *acne, psoriasis* • Cedarwood • Chamomile, German *degeneration of skin, abscesses, burns, cuts,acne, eczema, infected nails* • Chamomile, Roman *wrinkles, cysts, regeneration of cells* • Clary Sage *dry skin* • Clove *skin cancer, infected wounds* • Coriander • Cypress *scar tissue* • Dill *Roman gladiators rubbed their skin in this* • Elemi *wounds, reduce scarring, wrinkles, rejuvenates skin* • Galbanum *wrinkles, scar tissue, wounds*	• Geranium • Grapefruit *dissolves fat* • Helychrysum • Idaho Tansy *tones entire system* • Jasmine *dry, oily, irritated* • Lavender *prevents build-up of skin oil that bacteria feed on, cuts, wounds, tissue regeneration, burns, sunburns, stretch marks, bruises* • Lemon *cleanser, reduces wrinkles* • Lemongrass *tissue regeneration* • Mandarin *for all types of skin problems* • Mountain Savory *burns, cuts* • Myrrh *chapped, cracked, wrinkles* • Myrtle *tonic for skin*	• Neroli *wrinkles, thread veins, helps to shed old skin* • Orange *wrinkles, tissue repair* • Palmarosa *stimulate new skin growth, regulate oil production, moisturizes* • Patchouli *wrinkles, itching, bites* • Pine *skin parasites* • Rose *wrinkles, skin disease* • Rosewood *eczema, dry skin* • Sage *"sacred herb"* • Sandalwood *skin revitalization, dry-dehydrated skin* * Valor: bruising • Vetiver *oily, aging, irritated skin* • White Lotus *liver spots* • Yarrow *heals wounds* • Ylang Ylang	• Basil *for tired overworked muscles* • German Chamomile *inflamed joints* • Birch *arthritis, tendonitis* • Elemi *sore muscles* • Roman Chamomile *tension & restless legs* • Cajeput *stiff joints* • Galbanum *anti-spasmodic, pain relief* • Ginger *arthritis, rheumatism* • Juniper Berry *sore muscles* • Lemongrass *regenerates ligaments & connective tissue* • Marjoram *soothes muscles* • Nutmeg *muscles, joints, muscle pains* • Orange *sore muscles* • Pine *stressed muscles & joints*	• Clary Sage *pms, menstrual cramps, pre-menopause, dementia* • Coriander *menstrual pain* • Cypress *menstrual pain* • Fennel *stimulates estrogen production & balances menstrual cycle* • Grapefruit *pre-menstrual tension* • Peppermint *hot flashes, irregular menses* • Pine *hormone-like* • Sage *balance of estrogen, progesterone & testosterone* • Spearmint *stimulates menses* • Spruce *hormone-like, cortisone-like* • Blue Tansy *hormone-like* • White Lotus *promotes menstruation* • Yarrow *balances hormones* • Ylang Ylang *impotence*

TOXINS ELIMINATION	WARTS	ANTIBIOTIC EFFECT	DIABETES	EYES
• Grapefruit • Cedarwood • Juniper Berries • Fennel	• Cinnamon *(very strong – dilute)* • Lemon • Melaleuca alternifolia	• Eucalyptus • Bergamot • Juniper • Lavender • Tea Tree	• Coriander *research at Cairo University: lowers glucose & insulin levels & supports pancreatic function* • Dill • Pine	• Clary Sage • Lemongrass • Frankincense • Sandalwood & Juniper (astigmatism & poor sight) • Lavender, Frankincense & lemongrass (cataracts) (if skin-sensitive, dilute in carrier oil and rub round ocular bones of eyes and on cheeks)

SOME USES OF ESSENTIAL OILS

IMMUNE STIMULANT	ANTI-BACTERIAL / ANTI-FUNGAL / ANTI-INFECTIOUS / -INFLAMMATORY / -VIRAL	NERVES	MENTAL / DEPRESSION	LUNGS / THROAT SUPPORT
• Black Cumin • Frankincense *(treats everything)* • Lemon *(Dr. Valnet, MD, "vaporized essence can kill meningococcus bacteria in 15 minutes, typhoid bacilli in 1 hour, staphylococcus aureus in 2 hours, pneumococcus bacteria in 3 hours, diphtheria bacilli in 20 minutes & inactivate tuberculosis bacteria")* • Lemongrass *(lymph flow)* • Mountain Savory *(general tonic & stimulant)* • Nutmeg • Oregano *(general tonic)* • Geranium *(Lymphatic massage)* • Juniper *(Lymphatic massage)* • Rosemary *(lymphatic massage)*	• Bergamot • Cinnamon Bark • Clove • Eucalyptus globulus *staph, strep, pneumonia* • Laurus nobilis • Lemon • Lemongrass *anti-fungal* • Marjoram • Melaleuca • Mountain Savory • Neroli • Oregano • Peppermint • Pine • Ravensara • Rosemary • Rosewood *candida* • Thyme	• Eucalyptus *(hyperactivity)* • Blue Tansy *(calming)* • Chamomile *(calming)* • Geranium *(neuralgia)* • Helichrysum *(regeneration)* • Lavender *(calming)* • Lemon *(well-being)* • Melissa • Peppermint *(shock, regeneration)* • Rose *(balance, harmony)* • Rosemary *(endocrine balancing)* • Sage *adrenals & nerves* • Thyme *tonic* • Valerian *(tranquilizing)*	• Basil • Clary Sage • Frankincense • Geranium • Grapefruit • Juniper Berry • Lavender • Lemongrass • Melissa • Neroli • Peppermint • Pine *(use in bath for mental/ emotional fatigue)* • Rosewoood • Sandalwood • Thyme • Vetiver *(post-partum depression)* • Ylang Ylang	• Bergamot *(sore throat)* • Eucalyptus • Fir • Frankincense • Galbanum • Ginger • Lavender *(throat infections, laryngitis)* • Lemon *(throat infection* • Melaleuca alternifolia *(sore throat, bronchitis, tonsillitis)* • Melissa • Myrtle • Oregano *(viral, bacterial, respiratory)* • Pine • Rosemary *(asthma)* • Thyme *(asthma)*

INSOMNIA	HEMORRHOIDS	FATIGUE	HEMORRHAGE	THYROID
• Bergamot *(calming)* • Clary Sage • Cypress *(dissolves fat)* • Lavender • Neroli • Ravensara *("the herb that heals")* • Thyme	• Clary Sage • Cypress • Melaleuca quinquenervia • Myrtle • Orange *blood in feces* • Peppermint *dissolves fat* • Yarrow	• Grapefruit • Melissa • Nutmeg • Palmarosa *(nervous exhaustion)* • Black Pepper *(stamina & energy)* • Spruce *(general tonic)*	• Cistus • Geranium *hemostatic, stops bleeding* • Lemon *(stops bleeding – dilute)* • Orange • Rose *nose bleeds, stops bleeding*	• Clove • Myrtle *(balances hyper-thyroidism, normalizes hormonal imbalance of thyroid)* • Spruce *(hyper-thyroidism)*

DYSENTERY	BONES
• Elemi *amoebic dysentery*	• Valor

SOME USES OF ESSENTIAL OILS

PARASITES	CALMING / STRESS	HEART SUPPORT	HAIR	TEETH
• Bergamot *intestinal parasites*	• Bergamot *(anxiety)*	• Cardamom	• Cedarwood	• Cajeput *(toothaches)*
• Chamomile, Roman	• Cedarwood	• Helichrysum	• Laurus nobilis *(hair loss after an infection)*	• German Chamomile *(teething pains)*
• Citronella *(intestinal parasites)*	• Chamomile	• Lemongrass *(dilates blood vessels & strengthens vascular walls)*	• Lavender *(dandruff)*	• Roman Chamomile *(toothaches)*
• Clove *(intestinal parasites)*	• Coriander	• Marjoram *(regulates blood pressure)*	• Rosemary	• Clove *(dental infection, heals mouth sores, abscesses / dilute 1–2 drops in water & gargle / apply heat & rub on gums)*
• Fennel *(expels worms)*	• Grapefruit	• Melissa *(palpitations, nervous tension)*	• Sage *(hair loss, dandruff)*	• Geranium *(gingivitis)*
• Hyssop	• Lavender	• Neroli *(arrhythmia, insomnia, nervous tension, palpitations)*	• Yarrow *(promotes hair growth)*	• Melaleuca alternifolia *(gum disease)*
• Lemon	• Lemongrass	• Orange (palpitations)	• Ylang Ylang *(thick, shiny, lustrous, controls split ends & hair loss)*	• Myrrh *(gum infections, mouth ulcers)*
• Melaleuca quinquenervia *(amoebas & parasites in blood)*	• Melissa *(anxiety, calming, uplifting, brings out gentle qualities)*	• Pine *(high blood pressure)*	• Rosemary, Lavender & Thyme *(stimulate hair growth / use in base of almond, coconut or olive oil – massage scalp & leave on for 2 hours or overnight)*	• Sage *(gingivitis)*
• Mountain Savory	• Myrtle *(calming for anger)*	• Thyme *(cardio-tonic)*		
• Neroli	• Neroli	• Ylang Ylang *(tachycardia, arrhythmia)*		
• Peppermint *expels worms*	• Tangerine *(sense of happiness*			
• Rosewood	• Ylang Ylang *(anxiety)*			
• Tarragon	• Rose			

CIRCULATION	HEADACHES	HERPES	ANTI-CANCER	DIGESTION
• Cyprus *(strengthens capillary walls)*	• Eucalyptus	• Bergamot *(herpes simplex, cold sores)*	• Frankincense	• Fennel
• Laurus nobilis *(palpitations, angina, anti-coagulant)*	• Coriander	• Eucalyptus radiata	• Geranium	• Ginger
• Lavender *(palpitations, high blood pressure)*	• Clary Sage	• Bergamot *(herpes simplex)*	• Lavender	• Grapefruit
• Lemon *(varicose veins)*	• Citronella	• Geranium	• Lemongrass	• Juniper Berry
• Melaleuca alternifolia *(reduces phlebitis)*	• Cajeput	• Lavender	• Melaleuca alternifolia *(protects against radiation)*	• Laurus nobilis
• Mountain Savory *(general tonic for circulation)*	• Basil *use for migraines*	• Melissa *(one-time application of true Melissa oil led to remission of herpes simplex)*	• Mountain Savory *(possibly anti-HIV activity)*	• Lemongrass
• Neroli	• Grapefruit *(palpitations)*	• Ravensara	• Peppermint *anti-cancerous, anti-tumural growth)*	• Peppermint
• Peppermint *(varicose veins)*	• Laurus nobilis *(migraine)*	• Rose	• White Lotus *(anti-cancerous)*	• Sage
• Sandalwood	• Lemongrass	• Tea Tree		• Spearmint
	• Peppermint			• Tarragon
	• Thyme			• White Lotus
	• Valerian *(migraines)*			• Yarrow

GUARANTEED QUALITY OF ESSENTIAL OILS

Essential Oils need to be produced from organically grown plants, which are picked at the right time of day, pressed with the correct pressure for each type of oil and at the optimal heat for that Oil. In addition, each batch of oils needs to be laboratory tested.

At the time of printing, only one European company laboratory tests its oils. In the USA, Young Living Oils tests every batch of oils three and sometimes four times. Young Living Essential Oils are from organically grown plants; they are weeded by hand; cut at the appropriate time; the pressure and heat used are optimal for each plant, and all chemical solvents are avoided in the extraction process.

Gary Young has dedicated his life to historical, botanical and medical research on the therapeutic effectiveness of Essential Oils.

If you have questions or want to purchase Young Living Essential Oils or become a distributor, you are welcome to contact any Young Living distributor, or Shady Sirotkin: oilsofthegods@igc.org will answer your questions.

For those who want to buy organically grown oils more economically, but with no guarantee of laboratory testing:
labofflowers.com
materiaaromatica.com
naturesgift.com

POSITIVE ACTIONS

THREE WAYS TO USE POSITIVE ACTIONS

1. In a Resonance Repatterning session, we may do a **Specific Positive Action** for a few days to anchor our new resonance with the positive beliefs, feelings and needs that emerged in the session.

2. Also in a Resonance Repatterning session, we may do a **Strategic Positive Action** to directly support resonating with achieving the particular goal or intentions of the session.

3. **Separate from doing or receiving a Resonance Repatterning session**, we may want to **scan the list of 26 Positive Actions** when we want or need to make a life-style change, improve our health or change a difficult relationship.

Scanning the Positive Action list for a healthy and a vital life may stimulate ideas that lead to a new unthought-of direction in your life.

- **Positive Actions we resonate with reinforce neural connections in the brain, heart and body for new positive behaviors and habits.** As we repeat positive actions, no matter how small the action, neural connections and pathways become hard-wired so we spontaneously start doing those things that are most energizing for us.

- **When we go into unhesitating action free of self-doubt, it sends a message to our emotional Limbic brain and the Pre-Frontal Cortex of our higher thinking brain, that all things are possible.** If we avoid action, are filled with self-doubt or think that our intentions and goals are impossible, then our

Limbic and Pre-Frontal Cortex make it difficult, exhausting or impossible for us to go into action to achieve what is most important to us!

- **Positive Actions keep us wired for wellness: everything in the universe conspires to keep us healthy and uplifted, on condition that we go into coherent action aligned with our intentions.**

INDEX OF POSITIVE ACTIONS

Scan the list below to see which Positive Action you feel you need for revitalizing your body and mind or (**mcs**) {1–26} to discover the Positive Action that most supports your Resonance Repatterning session or the lifestyle change you want to make. Then turn to the numbered item on the pages that follow. *Some of the Positive Actions can be found on pp.9–12 / blue pages*

1. Spiritual Well-Being 247
2. Light, Color and the Eyes 247
3. Sound 249
4. Water 250
5. Breath 250
6. Warmth 250
7. Relaxation and Joy (humor) 251
8. Movement 251
9. Creative Self-Expression and Play 252
10. Human Connection 253
11. Gratitude and Appreciation 253
12. Communication 254
13. Body Work / Touch 254
14. Chakra Positive Actions 255
15. Connection with Nature and Animals 255
16. Flower Power 255
17. Food 256
18. Naturopathic Self-Help 257
19. Cleansing Baths to Detoxify 259
20. Energy Balancing 259
21. Toxicity Awareness and/or Avoidance when possible 260
22. Dental Awareness 261
23. Technology Self-Help 262
24. Therapeutic / Practitioner Support 262
25. Written Support 263
26. Reading 263

POSITIVE ACTIONS

Information on these suggestions will be posted on Chloe's Blog at spiralup127.com or you can request information on the suggestion you are interested in. Some of the Positive Action suggestions are taught in Resonance Repatterning seminars.

1. SPIRITUAL WELL-BEING

(**mcs**) {1–14}

1. (Attend • Sit quietly in a) (church / temple / mosque / other).
2. (Be with people with spiritual values • Be in the company of a spiritual teacher.
3. Chant / Sing spiritual songs.
4. Meditate.
5. Pray.
6. Read (spiritual literature • mystic poetry • *The Inner Way* by Anthea Guinness).
7. Silence in nature.
8. (Spiritual environment • Go to a place that is a spiritual environment for you).
9. Spiritual music or talks.
10. Spiritual practice.
11. Spiritual retreat.
12. Spiritual symbols or mandalas.
13. (Yoga • Chi Kung • Tai Chi) (daily • weekly • seminar) for harmonizing your energies, re-centering yourself and creating physical-emotional-mental balance.
14. Other.

2. LIGHT, COLOR AND THE EYES

(**mcs**) {1–28}

1. Sunlight:

   (**mcs**) {1–3}

   1. Be out in the sun for 10–20 minutes of daily sunbathing.
   2. Be in full spectrum light (not direct sunlight).
   3. Use full spectrum light bulbs.

2. Blinking.
3. Breathing light and energy into your eyes.
4. Circling your eyes.
5. 'Cross-eye' movements with focus on your thumb moving towards your nose.
6. Juggling.
7. Eye baths with (pure water • Eye Bright).
8. Glasses: (pinhole • full-spectrum) glasses • ColorYourWorld Glasses.
9. (Warm • Cold) eye wash with pure water.
10. 'Looking' at the sun with eyes closed.
11. Near-far movements.
12. Negative north pole magnets on/around the eyes.
13. Palming.
14. Patch over the dominant eye and flashing different colors to stimulate the weaker eye.
15. Peripheral vision movements.
16. Swinging.
17. Tibetan eye chart.
18. Visual field with eyes closed and allowing sunlight in through closed lids.
19. Other: eye movements from A NEW VISION by Chloe Faith Wordsworth
20. Avoid fluorescent lighting.
21. Blinking in sunlight.
22. Color breathing.
23. Color for clothing.
24. (ColorYourWorld Torch on pineal gland – forehead • violet light back and forth on the forehead above the eye brows).
25. Color focusing on a (Chakra • Meridian point • specific area of body).
26. Color: (looking at it • visualizing it).
27. (Gazing at candles • Star gazing • Moon gazing).
28. Other.

3. SOUND

(**mcs**) {1–20}

1. Affirmation or intention (say it aloud).
2. Ayurvedic sounds for the Chakras. *See* SPIRAL UP! *table of contents*
3. Chakra affirmations. *See* CHAKRA *book*
4. (Harmonic Overtones • Intervals) – (listening to • doing) them.
5. Humming.
6. Laughing.
7. Listening to music (classical • slow movements from Baroque music – Bach, Vivaldi, etc. • high frequency non-digital tapes • high frequency filtered classical music).
8. Listening to (bird song • sound of dolphins • sound of wolves • other animals/on CDs • slowed-down angelic choir of crickets. *See ResonanceRepatterning.net/estore*
9. Listening to the sound of (rain • the ocean • water • the wind • other sounds of nature) (with • without) music superimposed.
10. Meridian Consonant sounds.
11. Meridian quality affirmations. *See* MERIDIAN *book*
12. Poetry: reading aloud (with exaggerated tonal quality and elongating words for creative freedom of expression).
13. Prayer: hearing or saying.
14. Reading aloud (wisdom books • poetry • funny books • classics • other). Excellent to do for 30 minutes each day.
15. Repeating certain words aloud (love • trust • faith • courage • thank you • other).
16. Singing.
17. Talking to a friend.
18. Toning (alone • with others).
19. Using Tuning Forks on a particular area.
20. Other.

4. WATER

(**mcs**) {1–7}

1. Filtered water.
2. Shower filter.
3. Spring water.
4. Structured water: read *Dancing with Water – A Guide to Naturally Treating, Structuring, Enhancing and Revitalizing Your Water* by M.J. Pangman and Melanie Evans; browse ***cnswater.com*** for information on the Clayton Nolte water structuring device.
5. Sun-color filtered water.
6. Water of life: read *van der Kroon, The Golden Fountain: The Complete Guide to Urine Therapy*
7. Other

5. BREATH

(**mcs**) {1–3}

1. Breathing pattern. *See Energizing Options pp.163–185*
2. Jin Shin Jyutsu breathing points (#1, 2, 3, 4, 7, 11, 15, 23).
3. Other.

6. WARMTH

(**mcs**) {1–9}

1. Acupuncture balancing.
2. Cayenne pepper.
3. Exercise.
4. Garlic and ginger root.
5. Infra-red sauna.
6. Sunlight.
7. Vitality Breath.
8. Silk or wool wrapped around the waist in winter.
9. Other.

7. RELAXATION AND JOY (HUMOR)

(**mcs**) {1–19}

1. Calming Cross-Overs when emotionally exhausted.
2. Get-away to the sea, a lake, the mountains.
3. Hot Springs.
4. Humor: Find three things to laugh about each day • Watch humorous movies • Videos for (laughter • specific Chakra or Meridian balancing).
5. (Meditation • Retreat).
6. Naps.
7. Nature: (walking • relaxing) in a restful or scenic area.
8. Plants: (looking at • smelling • growing • listening to them).
9. (Reading for relaxation • Reading humorous books).
10. Self-massage: (sesame • olive oil • Neem oil • Other).
11. Skin brushing (with natural bristle brush).
12. (Slant board • Hanging upside down).
13. Smiling.
14. Sleep: (**mcs**) How many hours? How many hours before midnight. If you have insomnia, some people receive relief using the NIR (Near Infra Red red light in the nose for 10–20 minutes daily).
15. Thai Massage / other types of body work.
16. Time-out.
17. Vacation.
18. Zip-ups.
19. Other.

8. MOVEMENT

(**mcs**) {1–19}

1. Aerobics.
2. Aikido or other martial arts.
3. Bicycling.
4. Brain Gyms.
5. Chi Kung.
6. Dancing (Belly, Ballroom, Swing, Salsa, Swing, Latin, Country Western, free dancing, Contra dancing, other).

7. Egoscue.
8. Feldenkrais Awareness Through Movement / Bones for Life.
9. Five Tibetans.
10. Gyrotonics.
11. Katsugen.
12. Rebounding , running on rebounder, running barefoot on grass *See Positive Action #26 Reading (#10) for books on running; optimal diet and running.*
13. Six Fundamental Movements. *See Energizing Options p.131*
14. Somatic Movements. *See Energizing Options p.138*
15. Swimming.
16. Tai Chi.
17. Yoga.
18. (Walking • Ruthy Alon's Walk for Life).
19. Other.

9. CREATIVE SELF-EXPRESSION AND PLAY

(**mcs**) {1–22}

1. Acting (theater arts • improvisation).
2. Biking.
3. Camping.
4. Coloring (mandalas • geometric shapes).
5. Concerts.
6. Dancing.
7. Day dreaming.
8. Drawing.
9. Drumming.
10. Hiking.
11. Juggling.
12. Jumping.
13. Mirror work (for accepting your body • for accepting your face • for looking into your eyes).
14. Painting.
15. Playing a musical instrument.

16. Sculpting.
17. (Singing • Karaoke).
18. Skipping.
19. (Swimming • Surfing).
20. Theater.
21. Writing: (poetry • a book • a script • journaling • letter to self or someone else • using left and right hand to access different voices • other).
22. Other.

10. HUMAN CONNECTION

(**mcs**) {1–7} with:

1. An intimate.
2. Family member.
3. Prenatal self-healing with mother / father.
4. Social bonding, relaxing with others / having fun with others.
5. Colleague.
6. Friend.
7. Other:

   (**mcs**) {1–6} for what needed:

   1. Awareness of the heart connection / Heart Entrainment. *p.22*
   2. Appreciation.
   3. Forgiveness: "I let go of the pain associated with (*name person*) for (*name what was done*) and I open my heart to love."
   4. Radiating heart's love to (a person you love • a person you have trouble with).
   5. Holding time with (child, partner, other).
   6. Other.

11. GRATITUDE AND APPRECIATION

(**mcs**) {1–10}

1. Name what you are grateful for.
2. Appreciation of (self • other).

3. (Bonding • Hugs • Holding time) with your (child • partner • sibling • parent).
4. Celebrate what you appreciate about your life.
5. Chakra Positive Actions. *See* CHAKRA book
6. Changing your negative (language • thoughts).
7. Communicate your appreciation to (someone).
8. Seeing the new possibility in a situation.
9. Write out the positive qualities and strengths of both your parents. If possible, share with your parent(s) the qualities you admire and appreciate.
10. Other.

12. COMMUNICATION

(**mcs**) {1–9}

1. Communicate verbally with a specific person.
2. Communicate non-verbally by (touch • hugs • holding).
3. Communicate with (*name person you have trouble communicating with*) about the issue. Listen and give feedback on what you hear. Hear (__'s) point of view calmly and lovingly.
4. Forgiveness communication: asking for forgiveness / saying sorry.
5. Listen and reflect on the (words • feelings • meaning) you are hearing.
6. Write (apology • thanks • appreciation • other).
7. Write out the strengths of both your parents/someone who is a challenge for you and communicate this with the person.
8. Write appreciations (of self • other) and share with the person.
9. Other.

13. BODY WORK / TOUCH

(**mcs**) {1–14}

1. Alexander.
2. Chiropractic (Straight • 1st and 2nd cervical adjustment • Toffness • Network • B-E-S-T • other).
3. Ear coning.

4. Feldenkrais bodywork.
5. Foot reflexology.
6. Lymphatic massage.
7. Massage / Thai body work.
8. Ortho-bionomy.
9. Rolfing / Rosen Method (for suppressed emotions held in muscles).
10. Self-massage (using oils • with skin brushing).
11. Specific practitioner of body work.
12. Polarity Therapy.
13. Jin Shin.
14. Other.

14. CHAKRA POSITIVE ACTIONS

See spiralup127.com for videos on the Polarity Contacts for each Chakra and the TRANSFORMING CHAKRA PATTERNS *book.*

15. CONNECTION WITH NATURE AND ANIMALS

(**mcs**) {1–4}

1. Be with specific animal (domesticated animal • dolphin • whale • zoo animal • other).
2. Listen to animal recordings (wolf sounds • dolphins • bird songs • the cricket song. *See Resonance eStore*
3. Be out in nature.
4. Other.

16. FLOWER POWER

(**mcs**) {1–6}

1. Essential Oils.
2. Flower essences.
3. Go for walks and smell flowers; look at flowers.
4. Grow flowers and plants.
5. Look at flower pictures. *See ResonanceRepatterning.net/estore/*
6. Other.

17. FOOD

a. Foods to avoid

(**mcs**) {1–4}

1. Avoid (caffeine • black tea • sugar • alcohol • coffee • carbonated drinks • meat • chicken • fish • dairy • hydrogenated fats • margarine • bread, pasta and wheat products • gluten • all oils (especially if you have cancer or heart trouble, but eat flax and other seeds, avocado, unsalted raw nuts) • non-organically grown fruits and vegetables: avoid insecticides, nitrates, nitrites, genetically modified).
2. Avoid specific ('bad' carbohydrates – pasta, white bread, donuts, cakes, pastries, sugar, candies).
3. Avoid excess protein.
4. Other.

b. Foods that may be needed

(**mcs**) {1–21}

1. A detoxifying and rebuilding diet including (organic juices • wheat grass juice • sea vegetables (dulse, kelp, nori) • orange Essential Oil • raw foods • colon cleanse • liver cleanse • kidney cleanse).
2. Candida diet • re-establishing positive gut flora for autism, dyslexia, ADD, ADHD, depression, schizophrenia. *Read: Gut and Psychology Syndrome by Dr. Natasha Campbell-McBride, MD*
3. Combining of foods; (no protein with processed carbs, etc).
4. Diabetes diet: plant-based diet, mostly uncooked. *Gabriel Cousins, Tucson AZ*
5. Juices (fresh organic fruit • fresh organic vegetables).
6. High Lignan flaxseed / flaxseed oil, if freshly pressed.
7. Fruit (acid • sweet).
8. (Garlic • Dr. Schulze Super Plus: phone 1-800-herbdoc).
9. Grains (rice • millet • quinoa • buckwheat • Pinole: organic corn (non-GMO) • kamut • barley • spelt • rye • amaranth – mixed with other grains when cooking).
10. Diet and heart program from the book, *Caldwell Esselstyn, MD*
11. Diet and heart program from the book, *Dr. Dean Ornish, MD, Program for Reversing Heart Disease*

12. Noni. *See realnoni.com*
13. Purifying diet of fruit and green juices.
14. Raw foods.
15. Seeds: (sesame • sunflower • pumpkin • flaxseed • chia • Brazil Nuts – high in selenium) – soak or grind and add to grains or make into a fruit smoothie.
16. Seaweed: (dulse • kelp • nori • kombu • arame • hijiki) soak, add a little freshly made flaxseed oil and organic apple cider vinegar. *See Maine Sea Vegetables for seaweeds that are organically grown and toxicity-free*
17. Sulfur and silicon foods. *See David Wolfe Eating for Beauty.*
18. Vegetables: specific ones needed, including mushrooms.
19. Vegetarian diet.
20. Organic apple cider vinegar: teaspoon with pinch of cayenne and ½ teaspoon of honey in a glass of water first thing in the morning.
21. Other.

18. NATUROPATHIC SELF-HELP

(**mcs**) {1–37}

1. Acidophilus.
2. Ag-Cidal (Colloidal silver: used intravenously for Lyme disease. *See Hippocrates Institute 561-471-8876*)
3. Aloe Vera (organic whole leaf).
4. B Vitamins.
5. Castor oil (compresses • massage) on (troubled areas, the breasts, sore bones, congested large intestine, over kidneys for kidney stones).
6. Cayenne (a pinch with lemon, honey).
7. Cell Salts.
8. Life Tonic: liquid herbal immune builder: 1-972-416-0228
9. (Chlorella • Blue-green algae • Synergy • Hawaiian spirulina).
10. Chlorophyll.
11. Cinnamon (also excellent for diarrhea).
12. Compresses (garlic • ginger • castor oil • honey • cold water).
13. Essiac herbal detoxifier.
14. Earthing (sheet • computer mat).

15. Herbs/herbal tinctures (Sunrider • Nature's Sunshine • Ayurvedic • Dr. Schulze: 1–800–herbdoc; Dr. Robert Morse).
16. Heat: (Infra-red Sauna • Sauna • Steam room; heat lamp on belly).
17. Homeopathic remedies.
18. Lemon and honey water.
19. (Manchurian mushroom tea • RM-10 (used successfully for cancer: gardenoflifeusa.com.
20. (MSM • Sulphurzyme: Young Living Essential Oils).
21. Neti – yogic practice for cleansing the nose and sinuses and stimulating the brain: use celtic sea salt and water in Neti pot, or Colloidal Silver dissolved in water: 1-888-328-8840).
22. Nutribiotic, a grapefruit extract anti-parasitic, a water purifier.
23. Optimal time for eating (breakfast • lunch • evening meal).
24. Organic vegetables, fruits and juices (not pasteurized juices).
25. (Oxygen • Hydrogen peroxide).
26. Ozone: research shows it is excellent for joint problems, back pain, bladder problems, diabetes, scleroderma, MRSA etc. Longevity Resources in Canada: 877-543-3398 for machine).
27. Papaya enzymes, especially for digestive help.
28. Primal Defense for getting good organisms back in the gut: gardenoflifeusa.com.
29. Anti-oxidants (Pycnogenol • Resveratrol from red grapes • Negative north pole magnets • NingXia Red: Young Living.
30. Silver (colloidal • intravenous – for such problems as Lyme Disease; check Hippocrates Institute in Florida).
31. Sleep.
32. Swedish Bitters for digestion.
33. Turmeric and honey (used for infections, inflammation, cancer).
34. True Rife machine.
34. Ume plum paste (½ teaspoon in warm water for acidity and digestive troubles, alkaline balancing).
35. Water (in or under water • baths).
36. Water of life *(Resources: Coen van der Kroon, The Golden Fountain, The Complete Guide to Urine Therapy).*
37. Other.

19. CLEANSING BATHS TO DETOXIFY

(**mcs**) {1–5}

1. Essential Oil bath.
2. Apple cider vinegar bath. Read *Apple Cider Vinegar Nature's Health Elixir* by Alicia Smith
3. Epsom salts bath (for back pain, tight muscles and detoxification).
4. Sodium bicarbonate (soak for 1½ hours for detoxification) • Bentonite bath.
5. Other.

20. ENERGY BALANCING

(**mcs**) {1–20}

1. Acupuncture (Meridian • scalp • ears).
2. Aromatherapy.
3. Biofeedback.
4. Breema.
5. Chakra Spiral Up Energizing Options and Positive Actions. *See* CHAKRA *book*
6. Cranial Sacral therapy.
7. Essential Oils.
8. Feldenkrais bodywork.
9. Flower essences.
10. (Geometric patterns • Five Platonic solids).
11. Homeopathy.
12. Jin Shin Jyutsu.
13. Magnet therapy.
14. Meridian Massage.
15. Polarity Therapy or self-Polarity. *See spiralup127.com for video downloads*
16. Reiki.
17. Shiatsu.
18. Trager.
19. Watsu.
20. Other.

21. TOXICITY AWARENESS AND/OR AVOIDANCE WHEN POSSIBLE

(**mcs**) {1–26}; (**mcs**) {1–5} for Cleansing Baths #19 if appropriate.

1. Air pollution.
2. Asbestos.
3. (Building materials • Household laundry products).
4. Carbon-monoxide.
5. Chlorine – and fluoride – from (showers • baths • swimming pools • drinking water).
6. Cigarette smoke.
7. Direction of bed for sleeping (earth's magnetic lines) and avoid sleeping with a cordless phone or digital clock by the bed.
8. Drugs.
9. Electro-magnetic pollution; smart meters *See KlinghardtAcademy.com for information of the effect of smart meters on autism, cancer, MS, Parkinson's etc., and having your electric company replace the smart meter with the old type of meter. See TakeBackYourPower.net for documentary on smart meters.*
10. Environmental pollution.
11. Feng Shui mis-alignment/clutter.
12. Geopathic stress.
13. (Hair spray • Hair dye • Home cleaning supplies • cosmetics).
14. (High-voltage lines • Household electrical pollution • Work pollution – computers • televisions • machines • hair dryer • cell phone towers near your residence).
15. Insecticide spray (in air • on food) • Genetically engineered foods *95% of corn in USA is GMO.*
16. Ley lines
17. Location of place where living or sleeping.
18. Makeup
19. Metal: mercury, arsenic, fluoride, lead, other.
20. Parasites.
21. (Radiation • X-rays).
22. Situation feels toxic to you (your resonance needs to shift).

23. Smart meters: *Digital Meters are being substituted by electrical companies for the old-fashioned manual reading meters. This allows electrical companies to read electricity usage in detail from a distance. The new Digital Meters put out a huge electro-magnetic field that has been found to negatively impact many people's health, including those with heart pacers. Phone your electrical company; speak to the supervisor and request that your Digital meter be changed back to the old manual meter. They immediately respond and change your meter back to manual, if you insist, particularly when they installed it without your permission and when many are questioning its negative health effects. See also #9*).
24. Water pollution (from tap water • well water)
25. (Toothpaste • Shampoos) with sodium lauryl sulfate and fluoride, etc.
26. Other.

22. DENTAL AWARENESS

(**mcs**) {1–13}

1. Atomodine rubbed on gums or ulcers: Edgar Cayce.
2. Electric toothbrush (sonic).
3. Essential Oils: diluted (cinnamon bark • clove • birch • myrrh • tea tree • thyme • Thieves) diluted and rubbed into gums or as mouthwash *YoungLiving.com* and 1-800-herbdoc for Dr. Schultz herbal mouth wash. Young Living Denterone toothpaste and mouth wash have reportedly stopped gum infections, bleeding and caries development in teeth.
4. Avoid fluoride. *See Fluoride the Aging Factor by Dr. John Ylamouylannis*
5. Ipsab rubbed on gums: Edgar Cayce
6. Mercury amalgam fillings removed by wholistic dentist
7. Read *Cure Tooth Decay* by Ramiel Nagel: a revolutionary insight into why our teeth decay and what we can do to stop it.
8. Roll air-ball around your mouth (fill mouth with air and push out the cheeks as you move the air around your mouth)
9. Root canals: if you have root canals you need to take extra care of your health (with organic green juices, healthy organic food, meticulous dental care, flossing, Hydrofloss, Essential Oils) or have them removed. *See Root Canal Cover-Up by George E. Meinig*

10. Slide tongue in circles around your upper and lower teeth: this creates saliva, which helps eliminate bacteria.
11. Hydrofloss water pick with (a teaspoon of colloidal silver, or a little Hydrogen peroxide or 10 drops GSE *grapefruit seed extract* or **very** diluted thyme Essential Oil to clean gums and prevent gum disease.
12. Check for impacted wisdom teeth.
13. Hydrogen peroxide.
14. Other.

23. TECHNOLOGY SELF-HELP

(**mcs**) {1–12}

1. Beamer Pad.
2. (Biofeedback • Neurofeedback).
3. Coherence system for electro-magnetic pollution.
4. (Earthing sheet while sleeping • Earthing pad while sitting at computer. Read *Earthing* by Clinton Ober, Stephen T. Sinatra, MD, and Martin Zucker).
5. Getting something fixed (car • bicycle • machine).
6. Heat lamp – Infrared heat lamp or infrared sauna.
7. Magnets – only North Pole magnets.
8. Heavy metal detox.
9. Ozone Therapy – Robert J. Rowan, MD, 800.791.3445
10. Pulsors.
11. (Scalar Technology • True Rife machine).
12. Other.

24. THERAPEUTIC / PRACTITIONER SUPPORT

(**mcs**) {1–4}

1. (Acupuncture • Herbal acupuncture)
2. Birth trauma release work (Dr. Emerson; Dr. Ray Castellino; other).
3. Chiropractic.
4. Couples therapy.
5. Cranial sacral.

6. Energetic work (Polarity • Shiatsu • Jin Shin Jyutsu • Feldenkrais • Donna Eden Energy Medicine • other).
7. Family Systems work.
8. Hakomi.
9. Nutritionist.
10. Oriental massage; Thai massage.
11. Osteopathic.
12. Psychotherapy / Gestalt / other.
13. Resonance Repatterning (in-person • long-distance proxy session • telephone session • with a specific Resonance Repatterning
14. Support group. Other.

25. WRITTEN SUPPORT

(**mcs**) {1–3}

1. Need a copy of something from your Resonance Repatterning session.
2. Need to (write to someone • receive written communication).
3. Other.

26. READING

(**mcs**) {1–16}

1. Colloidal silver for (viral • bacterial • fungal) problems
2. *Depression-Free Naturally* by Joan Mathews Larson
3. *Earthing*: 'The most important health discovery ever?' Clinton Ober, Stephen T. Sinatra, MD, Martin Zucker
4. *Energy Medicine* by Donna Eden; *Energy Medicine The Scientific Basis* by James Oschman
5. Health books: (herbs • psychology • vegetarianism: *The China Study* by T. Colin Campbell; *Healthy at 100* by John Robbins • *Heart Health: Reverse Heart Disease* by Dean Ornish; *Prevent and Reverse Heart Disease* by Caldwell B. Esselstyn, MD • *My Beef with Meat – The Healthiest Argument for Eating a Plant-Strong Diet* by Rip Esselstyn • *Healing the Gerson Way: Defeating Cancer and other Chronic Diseases* by Charlotte Gerson; *Conscious Eating* by Gabriel Cousens, MD; Re-establishing

healthy Gut Flora for autism, dyslexia, ADD, ADHD, depression, schizophrenia: *Gut and Psychology Syndrome* by Dr. Natasha Campbell-McBride , MD); *Eating for Beauty* by David Wolfe.

6. (Cleansing • Fasting).
7. Colon cleansing, liver cleanse, kidney cleanse and overall health-rejuvenating support (Richard Schulze: 1-800-herbdoc).
8. Juicing (Norman Walker).
9. Parasite detoxification.
10. Running: *Born to Run* by Christopher McDougall; *The Perfect Mile* by Neal Bascomb; *Barefoot Running Step by Step* by Ken Bob Saxton; *Eat and Run* by Scott Jurek; *Thrive* by Brendan Brazier.
11. Self-help (articles • book).
12. Spiritual literature.
13. Wisdom literature.
14. Water: *Dancing with Water: The New Science of Water* by M.J. Pangman, Melanie Evans. *The Water Prescription for Health, Vitality and Rejuvenation* by Christopher Vasey, ND.
15. Poetry.
16. Other.

A SCIENTIST SPEAKS

THE SCIENCE OF SPIRALS: A THIRTY-YEAR ADVENTURE BY JAMES L. OSCHMAN, PHD

It is easy to write a contribution for a book about my favorite subject. I have learned a great deal about the profound significance of spirals, and can remember vividly the enlightening steps along the remarkable and exciting journey. During the thirty or so years of this adventure there were long periods when nothing happened. But I waited patiently, knowing that something would show up somewhere that would take me to the next level of understanding. My notes, lecture materials and this brief account document the voyage.

SPIRAL UP! has taken me further along this fascinating path of discovery. I find it very exciting that Chloe's work shows us how to experience for ourselves the wonders of the spiral. The somewhat detailed description and the references that follow are for those who wish to dig more deeply into the science of the spiral.

For me, it all began in a Rolfing® class in Boulder, Colorado in the early 1980s. I had become fascinated with Dr. Ida P. Rolf's ideas about human structure. She had made the remarkable discovery that human structure has significant "plasticity." Specifically, the cumulative physical distortions and compensations in the musculoskeletal system arising from injury or emotional trauma could be "unwound" or re-balanced by stretching key parts of the connective tissue.

In other words, anatomical imbalances from any cause are not permanent. The Rolfer learns to see these imbalances and correct them. This was fascinating to me because conventional medicine had no such concept of the ability of the human structure to be changed, except by surgery.

For example, one Rolfer "fixed" a fallen arch with his bare hands in about five minutes by lengthening key components of the fascia in the foot and leg. An orthopedic surgeon watched the procedure and said that he could do the same thing surgically for about $3,000. It occurred to me that this might be an old price, given the spiraling costs of medical care. I looked on the web and found a description of the process of correcting "flat feet": "Before the operation, I was told I needed six procedures: posterior tibial tendon repair, F.D.L. tendon transfer, calcaneal osteotomy, lateral column lengthening, iliac aspiration and gastric release. Though I have insurance, my out-of-pocket costs could be more than $4,000."[1] Recovery would take 14–16 weeks. He was given a 12-week prescription for oxycodone. At week 10 he would be able to start physical therapy.

One moral of this story is that it is good to know that there are hands-on methods that can produce the same outcome as surgery in only a few minutes, with no post-treatment recovery time, and no painkillers needed.

The plasticity of the human body Dr. Rolf had discovered arises from the remarkable properties of the connective tissue and fascia, the most extensive and interconnected system in the human body. Dr. Rolf became excited that an academic scientist had taken an interest in her work. Because of this, I was invited to be a "research auditor" in one of the 5-week classes in which Rolfers® obtain their basic training. I was not learning how to do the process, I was learning about the ideas behind it.

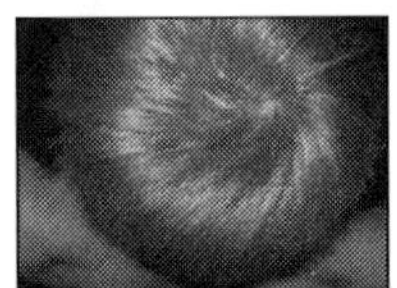

One day I was sitting next to one of the teachers, Jan Sultan, and he drew my attention to the top of the head of a student lying on a table while he was being given a practice session. Jan pointed to the spiral in the person's hair.

What he said next was absolutely astonishing to me: "Everyone has a spiral like that on the top of their head, and it continues all the way down through their body."

This was a completely new concept for me, and I was fascinated. What could this mean? This was the beginning of a life-long study that continues to this day, and that makes me want to digest and share Chloe's new book, SPIRAL UP!

When I got home to Woods Hole, Massachusetts, after the Boulder class, I started to investigate spirals. A key question that seemed relevant had emerged from my other life-long passion, the study of collagen, the structural protein found in connective tissues and fascia. The collagen molecule, the most abundant protein in the animal kingdom, is a triple helix. Why did Mother Nature, in her infinite wisdom and evolutionary experience down through the ages, select the spiral or helix for this basic building block of animal life?

To me, this was a deeply significant question that haunts me to this day. Perhaps it is a clue we can add to Dr. Rolf's insights about human structure and how the spiral at the top of the head extends through the body. Perhaps it is one of the great secrets of life that all serious biologists long to find!

I made a simple little drawing of the helix and spiral (A), and I now add a modern drawing of the collagen triple helix next to it (B). Notice that each of the helical collagen molecules has a layer of water wound around it. This is called the hydration shell. It is also helical, and it is very significant, as we shall soon see. (I view the helix as a special kind of spiral, and *vice versa*).

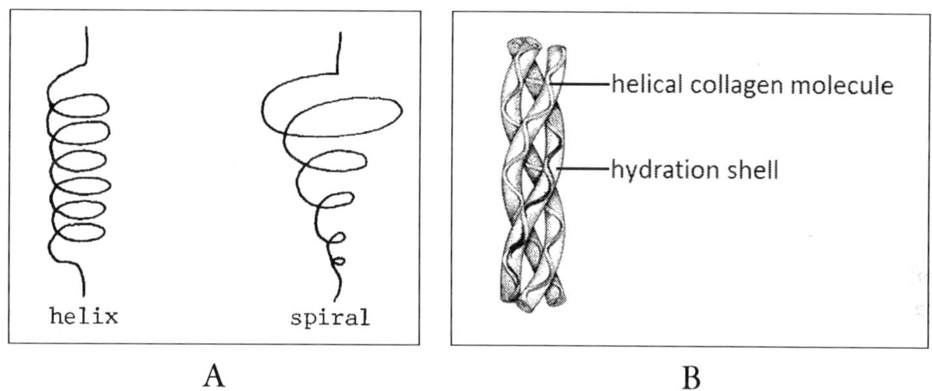

A B

I went to the exceptional library at the Marine Biological Laboratory and searched and searched, but could not find a good explanation of precisely what the fundamental property of spirals and helices might be. But Woods Hole is an amazing place, and answers to profound questions are sometimes found in unlikely ways. Lewis Thomas describes the magic of Woods Hole in his delightful essay, "Lives of a Cell: notes of a biology watcher" (1984). He describes fundamental equations drawn in the sand, casual discussions with Nobel Laureates in bathing suits, meetings of top scholars in a particular field at the local deli or coffee shop, and so on. These are the real stories of how science progresses in the special informal atmosphere of a small New England fishing village with two major international centers for marine and oceanographic research.

I posed my spiral question to a biochemist. He told me that proteins are helical because that is the way the amino acids that comprise them go to together. Specifically, it is an inherent property of the chemical bonds that bind the parts of proteins to each other. This was a very good explanation of **how** proteins become helical, but it still did not answer the question of **why** they are helical. Reader, be patient, because we will find the answer to that question a little later.

As often happens in Woods Hole, the next step in my inquiry took place at the beach. A chance conversation with one of the distinguished summer investigators at the lab, Dr. John Metuzals from the University of Ottawa, quickly led to a discussion of spirals and helices. John described how the nervous system has a fundamental spiral organization. He had discovered that the giant nerves of the squid, a favorite research animal at Woods Hole, are helical in their internal and external structure. Like me, he had obviously become fascinated with spirals.

Dr. Metuzals suggested that I look at the discussion of spirals in the classic, *On Growth and Form,* by Sir D'Arcy Wentworth Thompson. First written in 1917, the book was revised by Thompson in 1942. Following this thread, I found that Thompson had worked out the mathematics of the spiral and had made a few suggestions as to why certain animals had a spiral structure, but he did not give any unifying principles of the spiral form. And I was definitely looking for a unifying principle!

Thompson referred to a little book by Sir Theodore A. Cook entitled *The Curves of Life*. The book was first published in 1914, and was reprinted in 1979 by Dover Publications. The book contains 426 illustrations of spirals and helices found in nature, science and art. The spiral form is fundamental to the structure of shells, leaves, horns, the human body, drawings of Leonardo, the Leaning Tower of Pisa, staircases, galaxies, and many other structures found throughout nature and architecture.

I copied pictures of many different helical structures and thought about them in the hope of having an "ah-ha" moment.

I had pictures of microtubules in cells, actin and myosin molecules in muscles, the ventricles of the heart, the horns of sheep, sea shells, hurricanes, whirlpools, bones, single-celled organisms, propellers, screws, springs, ropes and cables, the cochlea of the inner ear, spiral galaxies, growing plants, spiral radio antennas, spiral staircases, traces of subatomic particles in cloud chambers, feathers, bird wings, fingerprints, umbilical cords, the ducts of sweat glands, fly egg cases, elephant tusks, ruminant intestines, myofibers in the walls of arterioles and capillaries, the Milky Way, sunflowers, and so on.

I studied every sentence in Cook's book, looking for clues. I finally found a vague statement that the spiral was the fundamental energy structure in the universe. Yes – but why? More details, please!

In support of his statement that the nervous system is organized helically, Dr. Metuzals referred me to a paper by A.A. Schaeffer from the University of Kansas, published in 1928, entitled "Spiral Movement in Man."[2] Shaeffer blindfolded people and told them to walk, run, swim, row, or drive their automobile in a straight line. He traced their movements on a large open field in the flat country of western Kansas and eastern Colorado. Other studies were done on the ice on the large Wachusett reservoir in Clinton, Massachusetts. Swimming, rowing and paddling studies were done at Cold Spring Harbor, Long Island, New York. The movements were recorded either by drawing them or by using a special camera.

When told to follow a straight path, blindfolded persons walk, run, swim, row and drive automobiles in "clock-spring" paths. They think they are moving in a straight line, but they are not! Some of these spiral patterns are shown below.

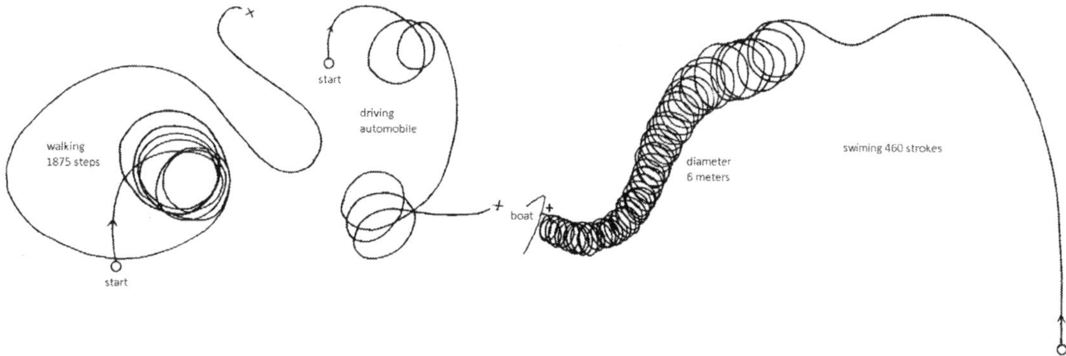

The studies were done in part to try to understand the well-known phenomenon of people who lose their way – in a forest, snowstorm or fog – by going round in circles. Schaeffer concluded that the mechanism causing the spirality of the path in humans and other animals must be located in the central nervous system. He did not explain this in any more detail.

Dr. Metuzals also told me that the spinal cord spirals where it goes through the neck into the brain. I have never been able to find a reference to this and never had a chance to ask him about it.

I gave some talks at Rolfing classes and at annual Rolfing conferences on the physics and quantum physics of connective tissue. In due course, I was invited to teach a class on biophysics for the Rolf Institute's pre-training or comprehensive studies that was designed to give Rolfing candidates the background they needed for their Rolfing classes.

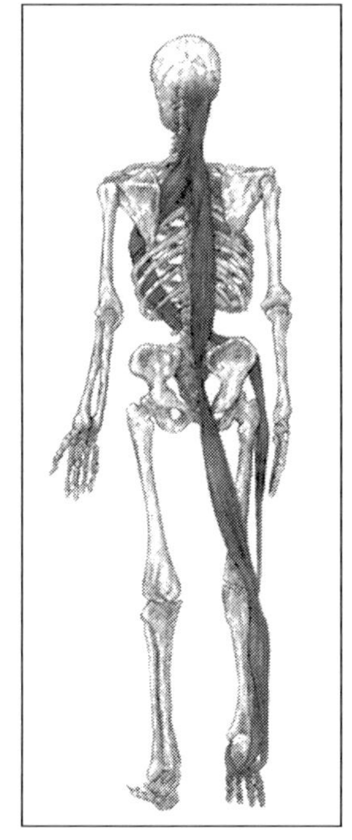

For a number of years, I taught this course with Tom Myers, who was also fascinated with spirals. We would both present our spiral ideas to the class. Eventually, Tom wrote his famous book, *The Anatomy Trains*[3] that is used as the text in anatomy classes for body-workers and movement therapists around the world. In the book, he describes the spiral line (shown to the right) that is at least a part of the head-to-foot system that started this inquiry. The detailed anatomy of the spiral line as described by Myers is shown in the box on the next page.

A detailed description of the spiral line taken from *The Anatomy Trains* is available on the internet.[4] In that excerpt, Tom acknowledges me for giving him a key article by a famous anthropologist, Raymond A. Dart, MD, of the University of the Witwatersrand in Johannesburg, where Dart was Dean of the Medical School. Tom said, "I thank Dart for the inspiration and Oschman for pointing his finger in the right direction, but the progressive development of the Anatomy Trains system

The spiral line loops around the body in a double helix, joining each side of the skull across the upper back to the opposite shoulder, and then around the ribs to cross in front at the level of the navel to the same hip. From the hip, the spiral line passes like a 'jump rope' along the anterolateral thigh and shin to the medial longitudinal arch, passing under the foot and running up the back and outside of the leg to the ischium and into the erector myofascial to end very close to where it started on the skull.

Myers 2009, p.131

involved a lot more perspiration, including the work of demonstrating the reality of the myofascial lines through dissection, the results of which appear in the photos accompanying this article and on our DVD, *Anatomy Trains Revealed*." I, in turn, must acknowledge Peter Levine as the person who originally gave that article to me.

Dart believed in the universality of spiral movement. He began his article, "Voluntary Musculature in the Human Body: The Double-Spiral Arrangement,"[5] with this statement:

> I recall an elderly otologist, named Miller, 30 years ago in New York City, demonstrating by means of examples ranging from the spiral nebulae to the human cochlea and from the propagation of sound into the propulsion of solid bodies, that all things move spirally and that all growth is helical.

Dart had severe scoliosis, and he had a child who had night terrors, and another who was spastic. Searching for help, he encountered a practitioner of the Alexander technique, who was able to resolve all of these health issues by bringing awareness to postural twisting and "relationing" of the parts of the body. Through careful observation and anatomical considerations, Dart developed his understanding of the "spiral mechanism of the body." He concluded his paper:

> In the members of my family and in myself, the "undoing" of previously unrecognized leftward twists, whether congenital or acquired, has been a major preoccupation of the past 7 years. That

> employment has led me to recognize and to correlate many facts about the body and its functioning, both as a whole and in parts, which had previously eluded my notice. Amongst those anatomical facts, the double-spiral arrangement of the voluntary musculature is basic. In ontogeny, as in phylogeny, man grows and moves spirally.

A part of this system was also described by Yoshio Manaka in his acupuncture text, *Chasing the Dragon's Tail.*[6] For Manaka, as well as for myself, there was profound energetic significance to this system because of its analogy to a coil and a core, otherwise known as a solenoid *(illustrated in the diagram on the right side).* Manaka viewed the place where the *obliquus internus* muscles attach to the anterior superior portions of the iliac spine *(arrow)* as the location of the important acupuncture point known as Gall Bladder 29. He states that the continuous muscular band or "coil" relates to the physico-electrical medium of the Yang Qiao Mia and probably the Yang Wei Mai as well. He is referring to the Extraordinary Vessel points, sometimes called master points or respectable points (descriptions dating to the Jin dynasty, 1115–1234 A.D.).[7]

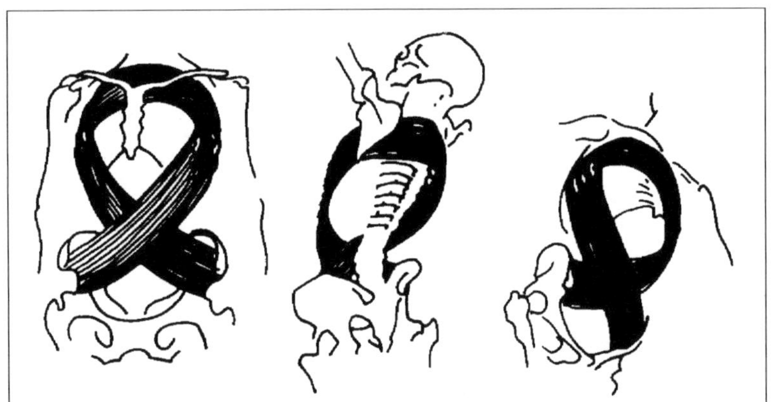

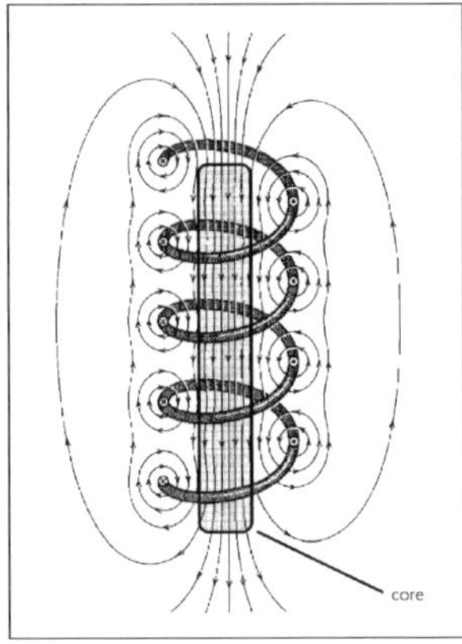

For me, the coil-core arrangement of the spiral myofascial line (coil) and the deep front line (core) probably serve a bioelectrical function comparable to the solenoid. Specifically, placing a conductive core inside the solenoid greatly increases the size of the field produced in the surrounding space.

In the human body, the main source of electrical energy that flows through the spiral musculature is the heart. This is the same electricity that gives rise to the electrocardiogram. The core musculature consists of the erector spinae and the psoas. And there is a large conductive core known as the descending aorta.

The resulting biomagnetic field is shown to the left below, in a diagram from Richard Gordon's book on Polarity Therapy.[8] A similar diagram, shown to the right, adorns the cover of the proceedings volume of a prestigious organization that sponsors conferences every other year on the topic of biomagnetism.

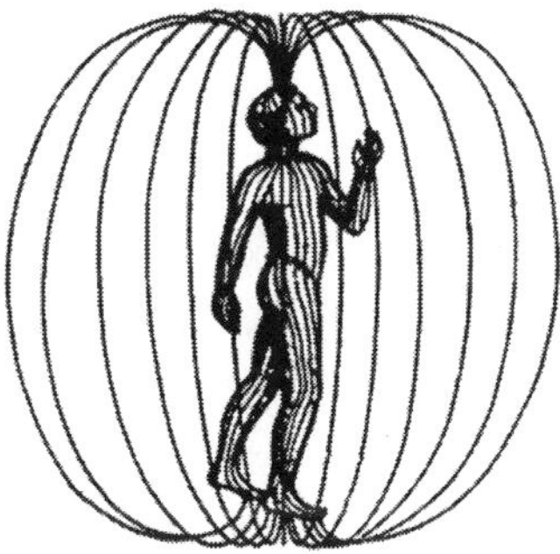

Notice that there is something resembling a vortex at the top of the head, where the lines of force of the biomagnetic field converge at the crown. Many iconic illustrations like this have existed since ancient times in the mystical/esoteric literature. Some of these are shown below.

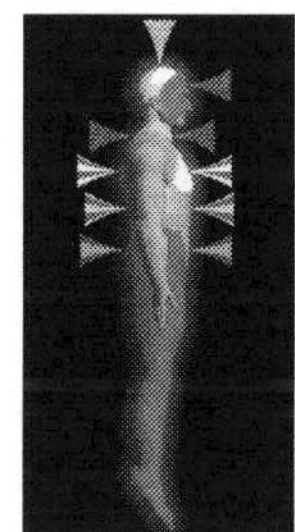
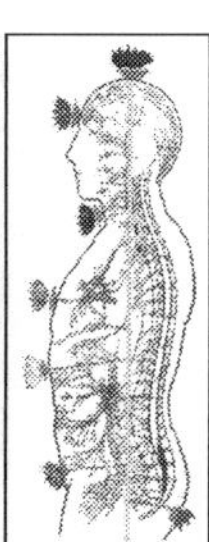
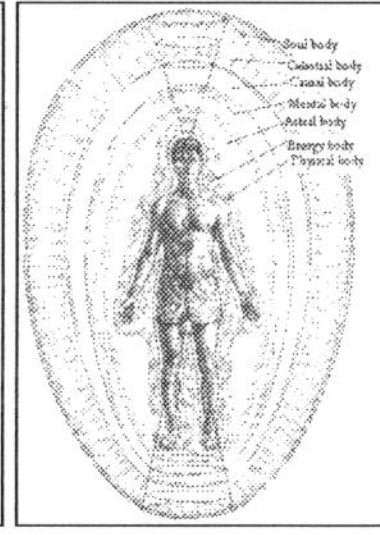
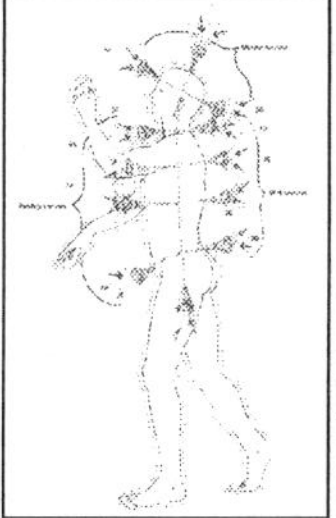
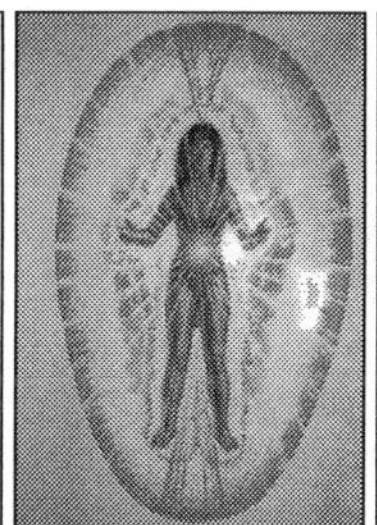
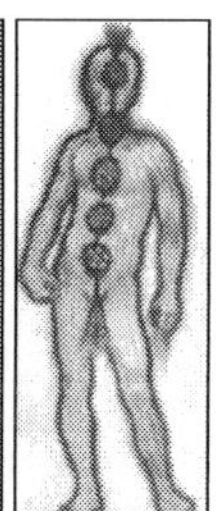
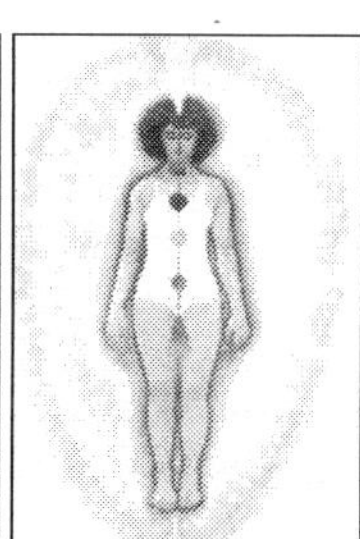

No respectable scientist, wanting to stay respectable, would even consider the idea that there is a vortex of energy entering the body through the top of the

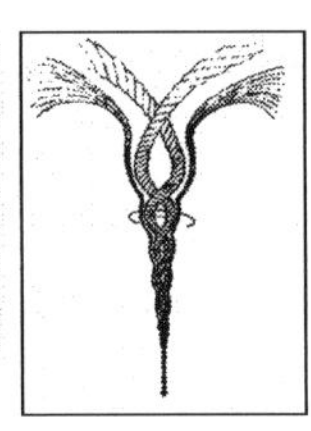

head. The a respectable scientist did just that. In this diagram, we see on the left one of the iconic images of an energy vortex at the top of the head, from Barbara Brennan's book, *Hands of Light*.[9] In the center is an image made by Charles G. Overby II from Princeton University, who meditated in a dark room with an ultraviolet camera with an image intensifier focused on the region above his head. An unmistakable vortex of some sort appears above his head.[10]

Here we are briefly departing from conventional science to consider the possibility that these images may be related to something that is real and significant. In a rare book by Peter V. Ind, *Cosmic Metabolism and Vortical Accretion,*[11] we find an endeavor to show that many material objects come into existence by being "spun out" of the ether or quantum vacuum in a tornado – or hurricane-like vortex, which Ind diagrams as shown on the right above.

From all of this came the idea that the vortex above the head draws in very high energy particles such as neutrinos that then pass through the body and deliver a tiny fraction of their enormous energy and information in a way that gives rise to and informs the material body. This is, of course, an outrageous speculation that would get nowhere in the halls of academia. However, there are places where we can find support for the idea.

On April 16, 2005, I presented a workshop entitled *The Intelligent Body* at the Sutherland Cranial College in London. I gave a presentation on Quantum Jazz, a term developed by Mae-Wan Ho to describe the remarkable aspects of biological coherence she had recorded with a special polarizing microscope she and her colleagues had invented. My presentation was followed by a talk by Stephen M. Levin, MD, developer of the biotensegrity concept. The following day Dr. Levin and I were invited to attend some workshops the organizers had quickly and cleverly organized to demonstrate the phenomena Stephen and I had discussed at the workshop.

One of the exercises involved placing one's hands next to but not touching the head of a person lying on a treatment table. Somehow I did not pay close enough attention to the instructions, so I really did not know what I was supposed to do. Knowing about the power of intention, I decided to test P.V. Ind's idea of vortical accretion by imagining a vortex of energy coming down through my head and out my hands and into the head of the person before me. So I closed my eyes and visualized this flow of energy for a few minutes. The results were astounding. The person who was on the table and the person sitting next to me (one of the school directors) both felt an incredible wave of energy during this process. The school director said she was almost blown off her seat!

While an experiment like this does not mean anything, I kept it in mind as a possible clue about the vortex or spiraling of energy.

A few years later, on March 30, 2008, I gave a presentation at the UK Reiki Federation Annual Festival at the University of Leicester. I described the possibility of the vortical flow of energy through and around the body, and the experience I had had three years earlier at the Sutherland Cranial College. One of the people attending the meeting was a small slender gentleman who spoke up about his experiences as an advanced martial arts master. He told us that he used the vortex image exactly as I had described it. He could, for example, have six strong men attack him, but they could not touch him.

I do not know what school of martial arts he belonged to, but it could have been Aikido, the art that practitioners use to defend themselves while also peacefully protecting their attackers from injury. One of the methods of Aikido is called "Tenkan." It is described as the force of the tornado or cyclone. The master is in the center of a vortex and the attackers are flung around the edges of this cyclonic force.

You can see a demonstration of this phenomenon in a rare film of the founder of Aikido, Morihei Ueshiba O-Sensei, published by Aikido Journal.[12] During the 6-second part of the film between 1:18 and 1:23, you will see the master attacked by seven strong men. They do not appear to be able to touch the master, and all of them quickly end up on the floor of the dojo.

The attack of 7 men *at 1:18*

The result *at 1:23*

Eventually I did sort out the significance of the spiral. Here is the answer to the big question, published here for the first time: **The spiral has profound energetic significance because of the way it deals with the intersection of forces.** Helical and spiral structures have the ability to allow energy fields to intersect with each other at an angle.

Consider, for example, bringing a piano up the stairs and into your home. Yes, you can employ a number of people to lift the piano straight up and then carry it up the stairs. This requires strong people and a lot of effort. But it is much easier to have a ramp – in physics it is called an inclined plane. Once the ramp is in place, one or two people can push the piano into the house with a modest effort.

In the first case, lifting the piano, force must be exerted perpendicular to the gravity field. In the second case, with the ramp, force is directed at an angle to the gravity field. While you have to push farther, you do not need nearly as much force to move the object.

Here is my little diagram of the inclined plane. You can guess its antiquity by the label, which was made with an ancient device known as a typewriter:

This idea of the intersection of forces made a lot of sense. I imagined wrapping an inclined plane around a cylinder and made this simple sketch:

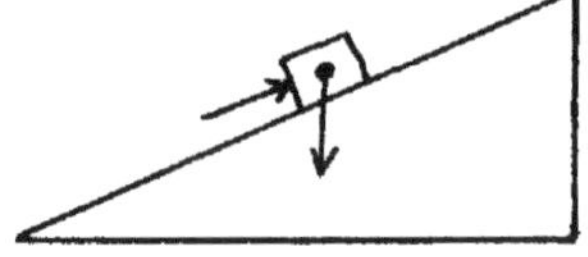

inclined plane

This resembles the threads of a bolt, the turns of a coil or the turns of a spring. If a cone is used instead of a cylinder, a spiral is produced. From this it can be seen how the screw, bolt and propeller can allow a rotational force to be applied at an angle to overcome a resisting force.

A relatively weak force can have a large effect. With a good screw jack, one person can lift a very heavy weight. With a good propeller, a modest wind can be used by a windmill to lift water from a deep well or to produce substantial electricity. A screw can penetrate straight through hard wood with a little rotational effort applied to a screwdriver.

I tried these ideas on the various spiral and helical drawings I had spread out on the table. It made sense that the various collagen-containing components of the musculoskeletal system – bones, tendons, ligaments, cartilage – had their strength and elasticity (resistance to deformation by outside forces) and resilience (ability to be deformed and then return to the original form) because of their spiral and helical designs. At the molecular level, the same sturdy design is present in actin, myosin, keratin and DNA.

These concepts explain the shapes of shells of organisms of all sizes. The spiral shape of the nautilus, for example, prevents predators from biting through its shell, because any compressive force is shunted off at an angle.

I reached the conclusion that there is no theoretical limit to the mechanical advantage (or emotional advantage) that can be obtained with the application of the spiral principals. Forces can intersect at any angle. If you are not getting the effects you are looking for, change the angle!

The final step in the unfoldment of the spiral story takes us to the quantum level and **the mechanism of the formative process**. This is a major unsolved problem in biology. The healing of an injury must reference the original blueprint of the organism – the plan that enables the body to grow into its adult form. This simple fact brings embryology, developmental biology, wound healing and cancer research together at the forefront of medical theory and practice.

The effectiveness of any science-based medical system is vitally dependent on detailed and accurate understandings of these phenomena. Rupert Sheldrake has developed a model known as **morphic resonance** or **the morphic field** to explain the origin of form in living things. This model and Dr. Sheldrake have been rather violently attacked by conventional academics. However, I find nothing inherently wrong with the model, find much support for it, and think it may well be the best explanation.

We are taught that DNA is the blueprint of the organism. It is not. Conventional science has fields such as embryology and developmental biology that describe the formation of organisms, but the basic mechanisms by which this occurs remain elusive. Hence we need to be creative to solve this fundamental problem, and should not reject any idea until we know more.

Rupert Sheldrake has proposed that memory and morphology depend on morphic resonance – a **resonance across time**. For details, see his books, including *The New Science of Life*. The basic ideas:

- Morphogenetic fields give rise to all forms.
- Matter assumes form when it resonates with a field.
- The fields involved are not classical electromagnetic fields.
- Morphogenetic fields are derived from a body's own past actions and from the structures and actions of ancestors.
- Fields act across space and time.

In presentations at three water conferences in 2013, in London, Germany and Bulgaria, I described the idea that the water layers that exist around all molecules in the body couple information to and from the morphic field.

For example, we can look at the collagen molecule mentioned before. I have drawn some of the water molecules adjacent to the collagen, representing them as spinning tops. This concept brings in the latest information on quantum coherent spinning of water molecules developed by Mae-Wan Ho in London[13] and Emilio del Giudice in Milano.[14] This is not the place for a detailed description, but those who wish to explore further can look at the references cited here.

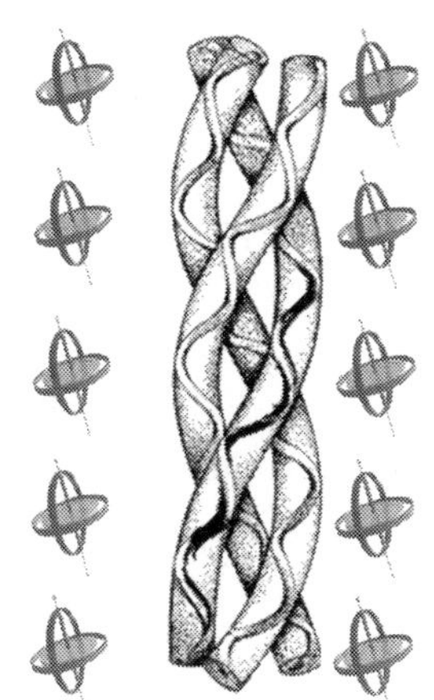

The morphic field is seen as a phenomenon taking place in the fabric of space. Five books by Vladimir B. Ginzberg show that what we used to refer to as "empty" space actually has a spiral grain.[15] This is an ideal medium for spiral spin waves, such as those produced by spinning water molecules, as shown above.

For those wishing to dig very deeply into the history of the spiral, Ginzberg has published a remarkably detailed history of the subject from ancient to modern times.[16] Every generation of scientists since Archimedes has had one visionary scientist who has recognized that the spiral is the true secret of matter and energy.

Of all of the topics I have studied, the spiral has to be the most fascinating, probably because it touches on all of the other subjects that have interested me. It is my wish that this personal story of discovery and the story of the science behind the spiral will be of value to those who explore the wonders of Chloe's SPIRAL UP! I also hope it convinces you that there is no limit to the power of the spiral to enhance your life, health and happiness.

James L. Oschman, PhD
Author of *Energy Medicine: The Scientific Basis*

ENDNOTES

1. http://www.nytimes.com/2010/05/04/health/04case.html?_r=0
2. *Journal of Morphology and Physiology* 45(1):293–398.
3. Myers T. *Anatomy Trains: Myofascial Meridians for Manual and Movement Therapists.* 2nd edition. Edinburgh: Churchill Livingstone, 2008.
4. http://oldsite.anatomytrains.com/uploads/rich_media/BodyReading_JF2012.pdf
5. Dart RA. 1950. "Voluntary Musculature in the Human Body: The Double-Spiral Arrangement." *The British Journal of Physical Medicine* 13(12):265–268.
6. Manaka Y. *Chasing the Dragon's Tail: The Theory and Practice of Acupuncture in the Work of Yoshio Manaka.* Paradigm Publishers, 1995.
7. Matsumoto K, Birch S. *Hara Diagnosis: Reflections on the Sea*. Paradigm Publications, 1988, page 363–364.
8. Gordon R. *Your Healing Hands: The Polarity Experience.* North Atlantic Books, 2004.
9. Brennan B. *Hands of Light: A Guide to Healing Through the Human Energy Field.* Bantam, 1988.
10. Overby CG III. "Subtle Energy Imaging with Active and Passive Electronic Devices" in *Proceedings: Bridging Worlds and Filling Gaps in the Science of Healing*, by Jonas WB, Schlitz M, Krucoff MW, and RA Chez (ed.). Conference held at Keauhou Beach Resort, Hawaii, November 29–December 3, 2001: 463–473.
11. Ind PV. *Cosmic Metabolism and Vortical Accretion.* Zeigenhaus Publications, 1964. *Ed.: Available on the internet.*
12. Highlights of a rare film presenting Morihei Ueshiba O-Sensei, the Founder of Aikido, published by Aikido Journal. http://www.youtube.com/watch?v=8V7NHLlmT3Y&list=PLECFD39131FC5C3D0&index=42
13. Ho M-W. The best resource for her work is *Science in Society,* published by The Institute of Science in Society, www.i-sis.org.uk
14. del Giudice E and Tedeschi A. "Water and the autocatalysis in living matter." *Electromagnetic Biology and Medicine* 28(1), 2009.
15. Ginzberg V. *Spiral Grain of the Universe.* Univ Editions 1996.
16. Ginzberg V. *Prime Elements of Ordinary Matter, Dark Matter and Dark Energy.* Helicola Press, 2006.

AFTERWORD
BY JAMES OSCHMAN, PHD

This book is an extraordinary gift that Chloe has given us. She has dedicated her life to exploring numerous methods available to find peace, happiness, comfort, longevity, joy, laughter, freedom from pain, mobility and success. She has traveled the world, worked with some of the most remarkable healers of our times, and studied the wisdom of ancient cultures, gathering a broad range of techniques. And she has put it all together for us in one significant resource: SPIRAL UP!

There are several aspects of this book that excite me very much:

- I appreciate Chloe's emphasis on the fact that you do not have to push hard to get great results for yourself. A simple and effective method applied once or a few times or for a short period of time can change your life quickly and permanently. The reason for this she mentions is that **living systems are non-linear**. In a linear system, the harder you push the bigger the change you get. In a non-linear system, even a tiny input of energy or information of the right kind can cause a huge shift towards resolving physical and emotional aches, pains or discomforts that keep you from being comfortable in the world and that block you from living the life you would like to live.

  To understand the basis for non-linear phenomena, you can look at the Award Ceremony Speech for the 1997 Nobel Prize in Chemistry, presented to Ilya Prigogine.[1] The complex field of thermodynamics has a concept of entropy, which describes a universe and a living system that is essentially disintegrating, falling apart over time. Prigogine replaced this rather depressing idea with a completely new and much more positive and optimistic vision of life. It is a vision in which chaos or disorder actually lays the foundation for a new and more ordered and coherent systems.

  Stated differently, all of the physical and emotional aches, pains or discomforts you can find within yourself represent opportunities for transformation into new levels of functioning – opportunities to *Spiral Up*. The key is the input of appropriate energy to the right place, whether it is sound, light, movement, breath, energy contacts, or essential oils.

Prigogine showed us how energizing changes are possible and sustainable. His work was distinguished by elegance and lucidity which earned him the epithet "the poet of thermodynamics." Chloe has transformed the great discoveries from science and therapeutics into a poetry of the human spirit!

- Chloe recognizes that you already know which of the multitude of approaches she has outlined will work best for you. **You know much more about yourself than you think you know**. At every step Chloe encourages you to look within for the answers: "You already 'know' what you need. Trust yourself."

  My advice: always listen to the whispers – the faint murmurings from your unconscious mind, a source of incredibly accurate wisdom. In our culture we are taught to ignore intuitive insights as worthless noise or nonsense, when in fact they provide extremely accurate information. For those who do not believe this because there is no scientific basis for it, I have written an article on the biophysics of the unconscious mind, in collaboration with a distinguished psychiatrist, the late Maurie D. Pressman MD.[2]

- I also appreciate Chloe's mention of the great value of doing processes and exercises outside in your **bare feet**. For the past ten or so years I have been working on a research project that explores the remarkable physiological and emotional benefits from going barefoot.[3]

  A couple of years ago I gave a two-day workshop at the Craniosacral Therapy Educational Trust in London. On the first day, I summarized our research on the benefits of going barefoot. At the beginning of the second day, one of the participants was bursting with excitement. He told the group that he had been doing his QiGong exercises, heel raises, for 20 minutes a day for 20 years. But he had forgotten that his teacher had told him to always do the exercises outside, on the grass or bare earth, without shoes. "This morning I went into the garden and did my exercises barefoot, and the difference was incredible!"

- I also value Chloe's focus on **coherence**. This is a topic I have been researching for a long time. Coherence has a particular meaning in biophysics. Here is the way the story unfolded for me.

In the late 1960s I was working in the Zoology Department at the University of Cambridge in England. One day a colleague told me about some research by Mark S. Bretscher at the Medical Research Council Laboratories in Cambridge. He had discovered that a protein in the red blood cell membrane extends across the cell surface. This may not seem like a big deal, but it was revolutionary at the time. Nobody had ever thought of proteins crossing cell membranes. Like all new discoveries, it was initially rejected by the scientific community. Bretscher wrote three scientific articles about it.[4] Soon it was discovered that some proteins go back and forth across the cell surface from 7 to as many as 14 times!

I made a little diagram to show what he had found. The protein could be at the surface of the membrane (A) or it could be partly in the membrane (B or C) or it might extend all the way across, from the inside of the cell to the outside (D). Using radioactive tracers, Bretscher was able to show that D was correct. The other diagram shows a protein that crosses the membrane 7 times.

The trans-membrane proteins Bretscher had discovered came to be known as integrins. They occur in all cells and are profoundly important in linking activities inside every cell with activities in the surrounding matrix. In a recent article, we have suggested that **the integrins are the places where essential oils and many other frequency therapies have their effects.**

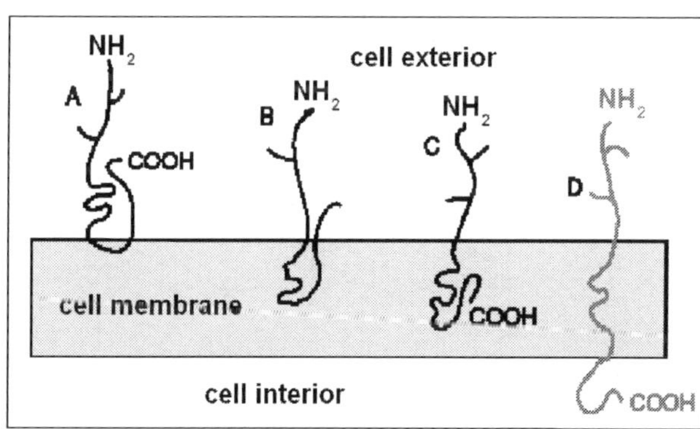

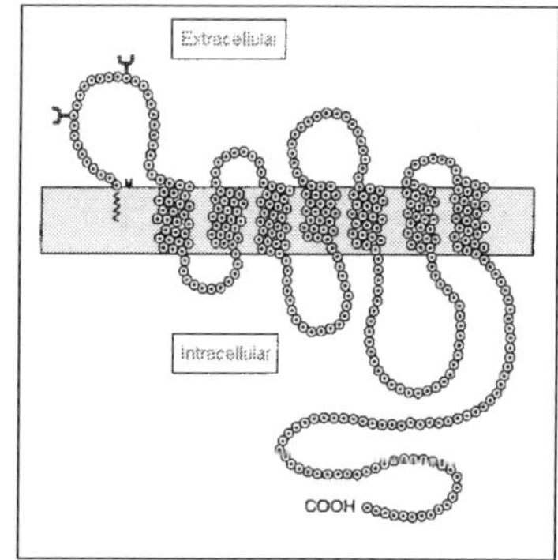

What Bretscher's discovery did for me, and for the whole field of complementary and alternative medicine, was to provide a missing link between the structures inside of cells and structures surrounding cells. I was able to make the diagram showing a cell, with its nucleus, connected via integrins to the extracellular matrix. The extracellular matrix in turn is the domain of the connective tissues, which form much of the structure of the human body. The connective tissues include the tendons, ligaments, the myofascial tissue surrounding muscles, cartilage, bone and the superficial fascia.

Most therapists learn that when they touch a part of the body, they are touching the whole body. The processes Chloe describes here – while they may be focused on a particular acupuncture point or chakra or other point – will have effects throughout your system. **Balance and coherence are contagious**. The integrins complete a picture of a whole-body system that extends from the top of your head to the tips of your toes. It reaches into every nook and cranny of the organism, including the interior of every cell and across the nuclear envelope into the nucleus with its DNA. In 1993 we began referring to this whole system as the living matrix. It is one of the main systems we are referring to when we use the term "holistic."

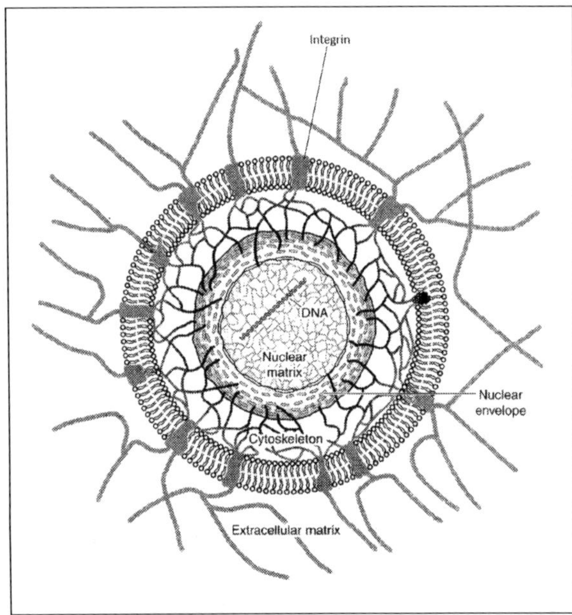

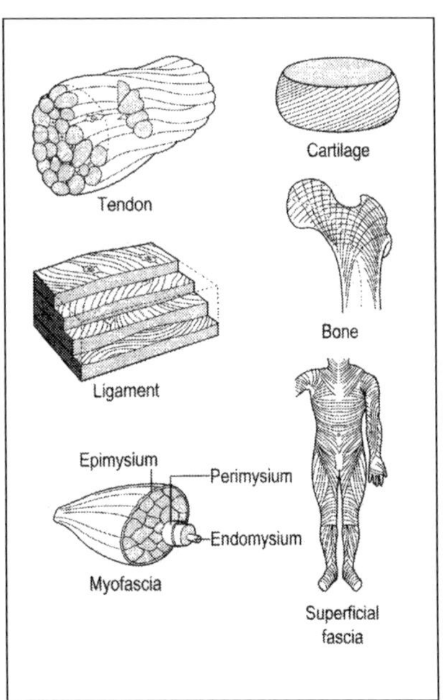

Research on integrins shows that there are many situations where the proteins go back and forth across the cell membrane many times. The parts in the membrane are helical. These are probably the places where essential oils, for example, have their effects. These are little helical antennas, picking up the frequencies of the oils and other subtle energies in the environment. These other subtle energies include the energies of those around us. This is why essential oils (and other Energizing Options) can have an immediate effect on our relationships.

Notice that this is a departure from the usual way of looking at how molecules affect living systems. The usual view is that the body is regulated by various chemical factors such as hormones, neuropeptides, growth factors, etc. that diffuse throughout the body and interact with receptors on the surfaces of cells. These molecules are thought to interact with their receptors via a lock-and-key mechanism. The signal molecule is the key and the membrane receptor is the lock.

Along with several other scientists, I regard this as far too slow a process to account for the speed and subtlety of living systems. It is especially slow when one considers how quickly the essential oils and other Options affect both emotions and many physical conditions. Chloe uses the term "warp speed" to describe how quickly some of these shifts can occur. She also reminds us that "it is not the speed of positive change that matters; it's the journey towards being our best and radiating our light that counts." Expect great changes, but be patient with yourself.

Our new view is that **regulatory molecules interact with their receptors via resonance, "the tuning-fork effect," using sound vibrations and electromagnetic fields conducted through the water system in the body**. We think the frequencies emitted by the essential oils and other modalities have direct effects on the receptors on cells, and the molecules in the oils do not have to actually touch the receptors.[5] This can also explain the effects of QiGong, external homeopathy, Reiki, Therapeutic Touch, Healing Touch, Polarity Therapy, and many other energy therapies. In external homeopathy, for example, the homeopathic remedy does not have to be taken internally and does not even have to touch the skin.

In researching this topic we were led to the work of Candace Pert and her colleagues who describe a "psychosomatic network."[6] This network joins the brain, glands and immune system and is probably the biochemical substrate of emotions. Key components of this system are the neuropeptides that affect opioid receptors that make us happy and reduce pain.[7] In the diagram below, the solid arrows are diffusing molecular signals, and the radiation patterns represent the proposed resonant photonic interactions. These are electromagnetic or photonic connections between cells and receptors.

With regard to resonance, it has been discovered that light frequencies have sub-harmonics extending down into the acoustic or sound spectrum.[8] If a light frequency is effective therapeutically but you do not have a source for that frequency, you can use music theory to determine an effective or equivalent sound frequency. (Music theory is similar to antenna theory in that dividing the wavelength by two increases the resonant frequency by a single octave. In the Western system of music notation, musical notes an octave apart are given the same note name – the name of a note an octave above A is also A. This is called octave equivalency.)

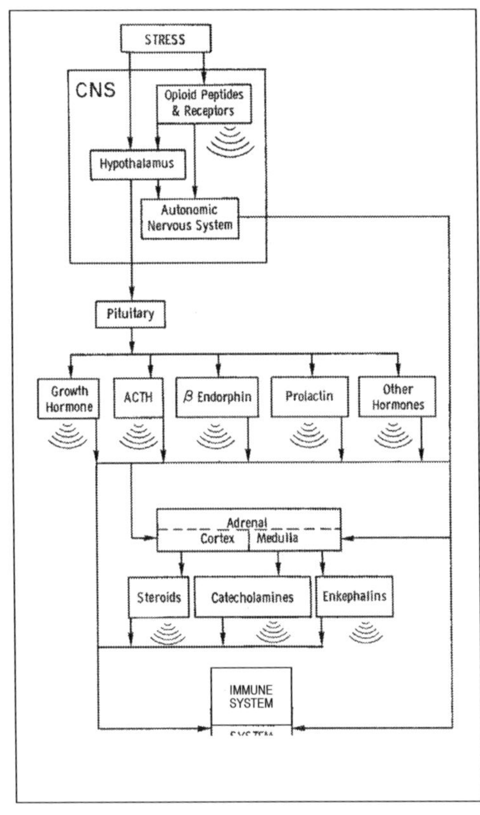

My interest in the subconscious, shared by Maurie Pressman, arose from mutual fascination with peak athletic and artistic performances and in therapeutics in which participants function at an extremely high level, sometimes referred to as "**the zone.**" This is a state in which individuals or groups have an extraordinary level of perception and coordination; or a state in which therapists develop a deep connection with their clients' repressed feelings or traumatic memories.

The role of the unconscious in peak performance was validated by Pressman's experiences with Olympic ice skaters, beginning in 1972. A detailed analysis of the possible energetic mechanisms was published in 2003 as *Energy Medicine in Therapeutics and Human Performance.*[9] There is a recognition that nerves do not transmit information fast enough to enable these kinds of extraordinary feats. There must be communication systems that operate faster than nerve impulses and diffusion of signal molecules. We think **the living matrix, electronic communication, resonance, biological coherence, and the frequencies of Energizing Options are all part of the story**.

When all of the diverse systems in the human body are integrated and coordinated and working together perfectly – when we are fully *Spiraled Up* – **remarkable feats become possible.**

In *Energy Medicine in Therapeutics and Human Performance,* I refer to this as *systemic cooperation.* Fritz-Albert Popp refers to it as *Gestaltbildung* or *cell coordination and communication,* when every cell knows what every other cell is doing and they all work together perfectly to accomplish your goals. Popp's research indicates that biophoton (light) fields are the primary coordinating system in the body. This is where the color and light options have their effects; but we need to recognize that sounds can have harmonics into the light spectrum, and light can have sub-harmonics into the sound range, and can therefore produce comparable or synergistic effects.

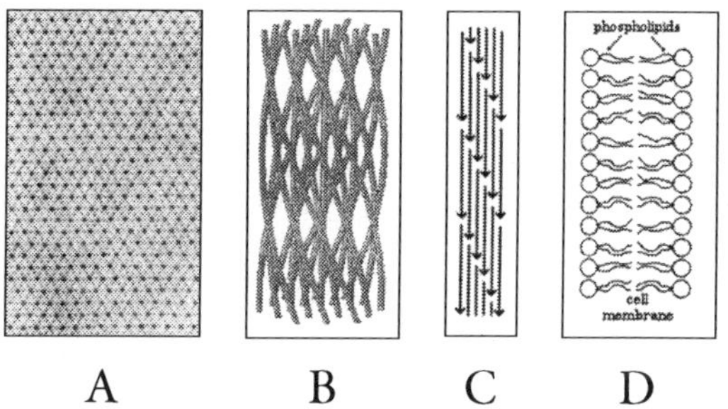

A B C D

It is important to emphasize that much of the living matrix, and therefore much of the human body, is nearly crystalline in form (see diagram above). We are referring to muscles (the crystalline packing of actin and myosin are shown in A above); DNA (B above), collagen (C above), and cell membranes, which are arrays of phospholipids (D). All of these materials are known as **liquid crystals** – they are partly liquid and partly solid. This is the profound discovery of Mae-Wan Ho in London.

Using a special polarizing microscope that she and her colleagues invented, Mae-Wan found beautiful color changes taking place within transparent microscopic organisms she had taken from a pond in her back yard (Daphnia, Cyclops, Artemia, Mosquito larvae, Rotifers, etc.). Every movement these little creatures make produces spectacular color changes, indicating changes in coherence. The color changes have been set to the musical track "Liquid Wormfat" by a musical group called Wormfat. She calls it "Quantum Jazz" and you can obtain a DVD showing this amazing aspect of life[10] or watch part of it on You Tube.[11]

These color changes represent shifting **domains of coherence**, which we will describe next. The living matrix is a huge "domain" in the human body, extending from head to foot, and body surface to the cell interior. In physics, a magnetic domain is a region within a magnetic material that is uniformly magnetized. Magnetism is thought to arise from the aligned spins of electrons. This means that the individual magnetic fields of the atoms are aligned with one another and they all point in the same direction, north to south. You could say their spins are coherent.

Here we are using the words "domain" and "coherent" to refer to spinning water molecules associated with biological structures. I used the term "domain" earlier in the context of the domain of connective tissue. Connective tissue will have various "sub-domains" such as ligaments, tendons, etc., as shown in the diagram, and additional ones not shown in the diagram, such as the collagenous capsules of organs, the partitions within organs, layers of cells in organs, and the various components within those cells.

Current thinking is that each of these domains is populated by a vast number of water molecules associated with the surfaces of membranes and proteins. **Coherent spinning of the water molecules energizes and informs the different domains so they function in a coordinated manner**. This is quantum coherence. It makes biological systems extremely sensitive and responsive to electromagnetic and other energy fields in the environment.

The linking of spinning water molecules is an aspect of a phenomenon known as *sync*. A very readable and delightful book on the subject has been published by Strogatz.[12]

And a remarkable amount of research has been done on biological coherence, initiated by a physicist, Herbert Fröhlich. This work is not very widely known, but it is profoundly important. A valuable resource is a book edited by Fröhlich entitled *Biological Coherence and Response to External Stimuli.* The book is out of print, but we have made a summary of it with commentary that brings it down to earth so ordinary people can understand it.[13]

One of the important aspects of biological coherence is:

> When the energy level in these liquid crystals reaches a certain point, the molecules begin to vibrate coherently, leading to the emission of coherent light.
>
> ~ Herbert Fröhlich

This emitted light has the capability of spreading coherence to other domains. When all of the domains are resonant and coherent, all of the water spins are synchronized and you have achieved the ultimate in *Spiraling Up.*

To understand the significance of biological coherence, there is an inspiring essay by Mae-Wan Ho entitled *Quantum Coherence and Conscious Experience*:

> I propose that quantum coherence is the basis of living organization and can also account for key features of conscious experience – the "unity of intentionality", our inner identity of the singular "I", the simultaneous binding and segmentation of features in the perceptive act, the distributed, holographic nature of memory, and the distinctive quality of each experienced occasion.
>
> ~ Mae-Wan Ho, 1997

Mae-Wan's article also includes a statement that describes the value of quantum coherence in liquid crystals:

> Liquid crystallinity gives organisms their characteristic flexibility, exquisite sensitivity and responsiveness, and optimizes the rapid noiseless intercommunication that enables the organism to function as a coherent coordinated whole.[14]

My aim in writing this little Afterword has been to let you know there is a lot of science that fits with the methods Chloe has described here. SPIRAL UP! has a wealth of approaches that you can use to resolve physical or emotional aches, pains and discomforts, and, at the same time, free yourself to be who you long to be and accomplish what you long to accomplish. Deep down inside, you know what you need, and it is great to know that you can find it here, in this book. I do not recommend that you try to do all of the processes described in this book. Instead, as Chloe says: "Find the options that speak to you, that make something in you 'light up' or cause you to take a deep breath of recognition. Listen to your responses and follow their lead."

I look forward to learning how people are affected by these Spiral Up Options, because medical science needs to know about this work.

James L. Oschman, PhD
Author of *Energy Medicine: The Scientific Basis*

ENDNOTES

1. http://www.nobelprize.org/nobel_prizes/chemistry/laureates/1977/presentation-speech.html
2. Oschman JL, Pressman MD. 2013. "An anatomical, Biochemical, Biophysical, and Quantum Basis for the Unconscious Mind." Chapter 2 in the *Clinical EFT Handbook: A Definitive Resource for Practitioners, Scholars, Clinicians and Researchers.* Church D, Marohn S (eds). Fulton CA: Energy Psychology Press: 25–39.
3. Ober AC, Sinatra ST, Zucker M. *Earthing: The most important health discovery ever?* Laguna Beach CA: Basic Health Publications, 2nd ed., 2014; and research papers at http://earthinginstitute.net/
4. "Human erythrocyte membranes: specific labelling of surface proteins." J. Mol. Biol., 58, 775–781 (1971); "A major protein which spans the human erythrocyte membrane." J. Mol. Biol., 59, 351–357 (1971); "Major human erythrocyte glycoprotein spans the cell membrane." *Nature New Biology,* 231, 229–232 (1971).
5. Oschman JL, Oschman NH. "Recent Developments in Bioelectromagnetic and Subtle Energy Medicine" in *Bioelectromagnetic and Subtle Energy Medicine.* (2nd ed.) Rosch PJ, ed. Taylor & Francis/CRC Press, 2013.
6. Pert CB, Ruff MR, Weber RJ, Herkenham M. "Neuropeptides and their receptors: A psychosomatic network." *Journal of Immunology.* 1985; 135(2):820s–826s.
7. The illustration is modified from Figure 1 from page 836s in Shavit Y, Terman GW, Martin FC, et al. "Stress, opioid peptides, the immune system, and cancer." *Journal of Immunology.* 1985; 135(2):834s-837s.
8. Boehm CA. *Method for Determining Therapeutic Resonant Frequencies.* United States Patent 7,280,874. October 9, 2007.
9. Oschman JL. *Energy Medicine in Therapeutics and Human Performance.* London: Butterworth-Heinemann.
10. The DVD "Quantum Jazz" is available at www.i-sis.org.uk
11. http://www.youtube.com/watch?v=oxKL4IPVZOM
12. Strogatz SH. *Sync: How Order Emerges From Chaos In the Universe, Nature, and Daily Life.* Hyperion: 2004.
13. Oschman JL, Oschman NH. *Book Review and Commentary on Biological Coherence and Response to External Stimuli.* Edited by Herbert Fröhlich and published by Springer-Verlag, Berlin, 1988; review published 1994.
14. Ho M-W. *Quantum coherence and conscious experience.* Kybernetes 1997:26, 265–276.

RESOURCES

Understanding the formatting prompts 297

CD suggestions for free movement 300

References and further reading for SPIRAL UP! 301

What can I do next? 302

Training in Resonance Repatterning 303

Seminar descriptions 305

Eight points of interest to clients 308

Repatterning Practitioners Association USA 309

The Vision of the Resonance Repatterning Institute 310

The Mission of the Resonance Repatterning Institute 311

Spiral Up supplies 312

LIVING IN TUNE – TURN YOUR PROBLEMS INTO JOY 316
52 web radio shows with Chloe Faith Wordsworth

About the author and contact us 321

The story behind SPIRAL UP! 320

Acknowledgments 322

UNDERSTANDING THE FORMATTING PROMPTS

SPIRAL UP! is used both by students and practitioners of the Resonance Repatterning System as well as by those who have not studied Resonance Repatterning but want to use the Energizing Options in their everyday life.

The three formatting prompts in the boxes that follow, and used throughout this book, are taught in the Resonance Repatterning seminars. These prompts are for students and practitioners of Resonance Repatterning.

If you have not studied Resonance Repatterning, whenever you see the prompts relax and tune in to your felt sense, your personal 'gut knowing' of what you feel you need. You may feel attracted to do a particular Option, or reading the name of an Option may make something in you 'light up' or cause you to take a deep breath of recognition. Listen to your responses and, if they feel balanced and rational, follow their lead. If in doubt, get help from a certified practitioner.

The bottom line is that any Energizing Option you are drawn to do inputs coherent energy and brings some kind of coherence to your body-mind.

Be aware that the Energizing Option you feel drawn to from your gut knowing may be different from the one that intellectually 'fits' or that you think you might need.

The three formatting styles are:

(mcs)
(•)
a.b.c. / 1.2.3.

(mcs) = muscle check yourself

If you have attended the first Resonance Repatterning seminar or have learned the muscle checking technique somewhere else, you can muscle check yourself (mcs) to identify the precise Energizing Option that will revitalize your body and mind energy.

You can also (mcs) to identify whether you are complete with an Option– that the purpose of the Option has been achieved.

(•)

Words in parentheses, with a dot (•) between words or phrases, offer choices – one or more of which may be needed. For example, (mcs) (Love • Trust • Courage) is needed? Your muscle checking will tell you which of these three options you need.

a.b.c. / 1.2.3.

a.b.c. When you see a.b.c. etc., it means that AT LEAST one of the items will be needed, if not all of them.

1.2.3. When you see 1.2.3. etc., it means that ONLY ONE of the items is needed – except in the Process Options, which always number each step to be completed in sequence.

In addition to the above three formatting styles, you will see *[**cr**] on the Four Ovals graphic. ***[cr] means Check for Resonance.** Checking for your own or a client's resonance is taught in the Resonance Repatterning seminars.

The practitioner uses the Resonance Muscle Check to confirm that the client no longer resonates with negative beliefs, feelings and attitudes, and that the client now resonates with positive life-affirming beliefs, feelings and attitudes for his/her optimal functioning.

You can successfully use SPIRAL UP! without checking for resonance. Just follow the directions.

CD SUGGESTIONS FOR FREE MOVEMENT

Earth Chakra CD Suggestions

- Brent Lewis. *Earth Tribe Rhythms.*
- *Afro-Latino,* #7. Putumayo World Music. *(Good for rumba rhythm)*

Water Chakra CD Suggestions

- Gypsy Kings. *Greatest Hits.*
- *Afro-Latino,* #7. Putumayo World Music. *(Good for rumba rhythm)*
- *The Best Cuban Album in the World – Ever.* Virgin Records.
- Luis Miguel. *Segundo Romance.*

Fire Chakra CD Suggestions

- Aretha Franklin. *Love Songs.*
- Beatles. *Abbey Road.*
- Ray Lynch. *Deep Breakfast.*
- Louis Armstrong. *A Portrait.*

Air Chakra CD Suggestions

- Wolfgang Amadeus Mozart. *Violin concertos.*
- Wolfgang Amadeus Mozart. *Clarinet concertos.*
- *Amadeus*
- Andrea Bocelli. *Romanza. (#7 for the Bolero rhythm)*

Ether Chakra CD Suggestions

- *Relax with the Classics,* Vol. 4.
- Wolfgang Amadeus Mozart. *(Piano Concerto Number 21 and his operas, symphonies and concertos)*
- The Swingle Singers. *Bach Hits Back.*
- John Rutter. *Gloria: The Sacred Music of John Rutter. (#13 is particularly beautiful)*
- *Brainwave Symphony. (Four CDs of music that activate beta, alpha, theta and delta brainwaves)* ResonanceRepatterning.net/estore/

REFERENCES AND FURTHER READING FOR SPIRAL UP!

Batmanghelidj, F. *Your Body's Many Cries for Water.* Falls Church, VA: Global Health Solutions, 1995.

Burmeister, Alice, and Tom Monte, *The Touch of Healing, Energizing Body, Mind and Spirit with the Art of Jin Shin Jyutsu®.* New York, NY: Bantam Books, 1997.

Clarke, Jean Illsey. *Growing Up Again.* New York, NY: HarperCollins, 1989.

Dennison, Paul, and Gail Dennison. *DLR.* Glendale, CA: Educational Kinesiology Foundation.

Essential Science Publishing. *PDR: People's Desk Reference for Essential Oils.* Essential Science Publishing, 1999.

Goldman, Jonathan. *Healing Sounds, The Power of Harmonics.* Rockport, MA: Element Inc., 1992.

Hale, Teresa. *Breathing Free.* London, UK: Hodder and Stoughton, 1999.

Hanna, Thomas. *Somatics.* Reading, Massachusetts: Perseus Books, 1998.

Jenny, Hans. *Cymatics.* Basler Druckund Verlagsanstalt: Basilius Presse, 1972.

Kilham, Christopher S. *The Five Tibetans.* Rochester, VT: Healing Arts Press, 1994.

Liberman, Jacob. *Light Medicine of the Future.* Santa Fe, NM: Bear and Company Publishing, 1991.

Maman, Fabien. *The Role of Music in the 21st Century.* Redondo Beach, CA: Tama-Do Press, 1997.

Marshall, Ian and Danah Zohar. *Who's Afraid of Schrodinger's Cat, An A–Z Guide to All the New Science Ideas You Need to Keep Up With in New Thinking.* New York, NY: Quill, 1998.

Ott, John. *Health and Light.* Alpharetta, GA: Ariel Press, 1973.

Omura, Richard S. *Katsugen, The Gentle Art of Well-being.* Lincoln, NE: Writers Club Press, 2000.

Pénoël, Daniel, M.D., and Rose-Marie, *The Guide to Home Use of Essential Oils.* Provo, UT: Essential Publishing, 2002.

Tomatis, Alfred A. *The Conscious Ear.* Barrytown, NY: Station Hill Press, 1991.

van der Kroon, Coen. *The Golden Fountain: The Complete Guide to Urine Therapy.* Amethyst Books, 1996.

WHAT CAN I DO NEXT?

For those of you who have enjoyed SPIRAL UP! and want more, you may be wondering, **"What is my next step?"**

- If you want a deeper understanding of Resonance Repatterning, you can **READ** Chloe Wordsworth's QUANTUM CHANGE MADE EASY. *See ResonanceRepatterning.net/estore/* and *spiralup127.com*

- If you want to study the 127 Energizing Options in more detail, you can purchase **CHLOE'S VIDEOS** in which she demonstrates each of the 127 Options and the **AUDIO downloads of the 127 Energizing Options**. More SPIRAL UP SEQUENCES FOR LIVING IN TUNE *see spiralup127.com* give you numerous ways for using the Options in your life. You can also check **CHLOE'S FREE VIDEOS and AUDIOS** *See spiralup127.com*

- Another important step for you may be to **LISTEN FREE** to Chloe's 52 LIVING IN TUNE web radio shows with their inspiring stories, themes and Repatternings; you can proxy into the sessions and also download, study and use any that interest you. *See spiralup127.com*

- Receiving Resonance Repatterning **SESSIONS** is an ideal way to receive support and discover for yourself what Resonance Repatterning is about. *ResonanceRepatterning.net > Sessions* gives you information on what sessions are about and provides a Practitioner Listing with Ads from students and practitioners at various stages of their training. Sessions can be in person, over the phone or by proxy.

- Resonance Repatterning **SEMINARS** with Resonance Repatterning Institute endorsed teachers and Chloe Faith Wordsworth: for those who want to learn Resonance Repatterning so they can use it for themselves and/or others, or simply for the joy of new learning. Seminars may be taken in-person or online.

TRAINING IN RESONANCE REPATTERNING

Schedule of seminars *See ResonanceRepatterning.net > Seminars* for the schedule of seminars, a description of each seminar and the contact information for all teachers endorsed by the Resonance Repatterning Institute. If you have any difficulty registering for a seminar, you may contact the teacher or seminar coordinator direct, or you may contact the RRI at info@resonancerepatterning.net.

Energizing and enjoyable All seminars are taught with music, movement and other Spiral Up Energizing Options for left- and right-brain integration and to ensure that learning is easy, enjoyable and energizing. You get to see, participate in and practice the RR processes, the Energizing Options and Repatternings along with informative, inspiring and practical learning.

THREE OPTIONS FOR TRAINING IN RESONANCE REPATTERNING

1. Attend **IN-PERSON SEMINARS**

   Take each seminar in sequence at your own pace and with any Resonance Repatterning Institute teacher endorsed to teach that seminar. In-Person seminars may involve traveling to different areas where the next seminar is being taught. Teachers sign the student's RRI Seminar Attendance for each seminar completed. If you like, you may apply for a Diploma of Completion once you have completed all requirements.

2. Attend **ON-LINE SEMINARS**

   This is an excellent option for those who cannot take time away from work or family, who want to study at home, or who live abroad where Resonance Repatterning seminars are not presently offered. Teachers sign the student's RRI Seminar Attendance for each seminar completed. If you like, you may apply for a Diploma of Completion once you have completed all requirements.

3. **WEBINARS along with Teacher Mentoring and practice** will be offered in the future.

   All three options are self-paced: some students like to digest what they learn slowly; others like to study the whole system quickly. All three options can lead to Certification by the USA Professional Repatterning Association, or the Association of your country.

Certification Students who have attended the basic seminars through to and including TRANSFORMING FIVE ELEMENT AND MERIDIAN PATTERNS may choose to complete their requirements for certification. In the USA the independent Repatterning Practitioners Association, and in Mexico The Resonance Repatterning Association, are responsible for certifying practitioners, maintaining standards and ethics, and supporting practitioners who want to be professionally successful. *See ResonanceRepatterning.net > Sidebar > Partners* for links to all certifying bodies, which provide information on their requirements for certification.

The Resonance Repatterning Institute Diploma of Completion is granted on the successful completion of all requirements: attending all Resonance Repatterning seminars with any of the RR endorsed teachers, completing assignments in the back of each manual and being observed.

SEMINAR DESCRIPTIONS

FUNDAMENTALS OF RESONANCE REPATTERNING

- This twenty-one hour seminar provides the foundation for all subsequent Resonance Repatterning seminars.
- In Fundamentals, you learn **the five Keys** that make all positive change possible and how to **transform unconscious belief systems** that result in your problems.
- You learn how to access your autonomic nervous system's muscle responses in order to re-align yourself with how you want to feel, who you want to be and what you want to achieve.

TRANSFORMING PRIMARY PATTERNS

- In this twenty-one hour seminar you go deeper into the Resonance Repatterning system for transforming the thoughts that create your reality.
- Applying the muscle checking technique, you change your resonance with the unconscious patterns relating to your **self-image**, how you **express yourself creatively**, your capacity to have the energy to **commit yourself 100%** to the different aspects of your life, and the **destructive thought patterns** that keep you stuck in anger, jealousy, fear, worry, infatuation and the "never enough" of always wanting more.

TRANSFORMING UNCONSCIOUS PATTERNS

- This twenty-one hour seminar shows you how the neural connections in your brain either free you or imprison you.
- You learn six powerful Repatternings to transform memory imprints, parental patterns and compensations that sabotage **how you want to show up in your life**.
- As you resonate with the coherent qualities associated with the seven major brain areas and the neurotransmitters needed for optimal body-brain functioning, you automatically spiral up to a higher frequency state: **happiness, relaxation** and **an optimistic attitude** are just a few of the results people experience.

TRANSFORMING CHAKRA PATTERNS

- This twenty-one hour seminar introduces you to the ancient Indian system of natural healing – to the seven major reservoirs of energy that determine your thoughts, emotions, life attitudes and actions.

- In this seminar you go to the root cause of any problem. You transform your resonance with your life stresses by re-aligning your energy field frequencies through four Chakra Repatternings and the Chakra Energizing Options.
- Einstein wrote, 'Everything is energy and that's all there is to it.' If we want positive change, we need to balance our energy. This seminar teaches you how.

TRANSFORMING FIVE ELEMENT AND MERIDIAN PATTERNS

- This twenty-one hour seminar introduces you to the Chinese Five Element and Meridian system of natural healing.
- This five-thousand year system of Acupuncture balances the flow of energy for maintaining harmony, optimal health, constructive thinking and emotional balance.
- In this seminar you strengthen the flow of Chi life energy through seven powerful Repatternings (including the Mu Point Repatterning for releasing fears and phobias). You also learn how to use tuning forks, north pole magnets and light on Acupuncture points for maintaining balance in your daily life.

PRINCIPLES OF RELATIONSHIP

- This twenty-eight hour seminar covers fourteen Repatternings for transforming yourself and your relationships.
- Any problem involving someone else, is also our problem – calling our attention to where our own personal transformation is needed.
- The three principles of positive relationship help you to re-align yourself so you resonate with harmony, respect, mutual empowerment, heart connection, safety and joy. What you resonate with is what you experience.

INNER CULTIVATION

- This forty-two hour seminar (six days), gives you an in-depth understanding of the 5 Element system of Chinese Acupuncture – using color and light on Acupuncture points in relation to twenty-five Meridian Repatternings.
- This seminar involves our inner work towards manifesting and living the Five Essences.

  The Shen Essence of consciousness that enables us to know and follow the truth of our heart.

  The Zhi Essence of our Will that leads to an unperturbed mind. The Will enables us to conserve our resources and direct them in actions that help us manifest our inner potential.

The Hun Essence governs our evolution and growth. It gives us an elevated perspective and the capacity to access the overall plan for our life that is stored in our depths.

The Po Essence is associated with peace – the inner tranquility that comes when we are connected to the Divine plan at every moment.

The Yi Essence makes it possible for us to extract nourishment from all sources (whether from food, ideas, relationships or life experiences) and living with integrity. Integrity provides us with the inner nourishment we need by aligning our words, thoughts and actions with the truth of our heart.

- With the Meridian Repatternings, specific acupuncture points, five Indian Mudras that are taught with each of the Essences, and the use of color and light, we aim to balance the five emotions and our Five Essences.

A NEW VISION

- This twenty-one hour seminar is about light, movement and memory images in relation to our vision (physical acuity, and how you see yourself, others and life).
- In this seminar you expand the narrow bandwidth of what you see.
- Through the Repatternings and Vision Energizing Options, you have the potential to free yourself from old patterns that inhibit your movements.
- You release non-coherent memory images.
- And you discover that the amount of light you take in to your brain and body through your eyes determines your thoughts, how you relate to others, your posture, breathing and how you move.

ENERGETICS OF RELATIONSHIP

- This twenty-eight hour advanced seminar introduces you to the four components of your electric circuit in terms of your relationships.
- Powerful Repatternings support self-healing from shock and trauma, balance the frequency field and help you build your energy when your reserves are drained through stress in your relationships.
- Other Repatternings support the natural development of long-term intimate relationship and help you sustain successful bonding in your relationships.

EIGHT POINTS OF INTEREST TO CLIENTS

We encourage clients to read the following eight points as they provide you with important information concerning your session, its scope, the level of training attained by your practitioner, and certain needs you may have.

1. **The Resonance Repatterning system** facilitates a natural state of well-being or coherence.
2. **Resonance Repatterning** is not a medical practice or a psychological method. It works at the frequency level by transforming your resonance with unconscious patterns, which creates physical, emotional and mental coherence or well-being.
3. **The Resonance Repatterning** muscle checking tool accesses what you resonate with and what will support a higher state of coherence and well-being for you.
4. **Your Resonance Repatterning Practitioner** only uses the muscle checking tool with your permission and in the context of your session.
5. **The muscle checking tool cannot be used** for making a decision – such as whether an operation is needed or not; to diagnose a disease condition; to identify if a medical prescription is needed; or to find out if an abuse experience "really happened." It checks for your resonance with these, and helps you transform the resonance for your own self-healing.
6. **In all Resonance Repatterning sessions**, you remain fully clothed.
7. **Be aware that RR students, Qualified Practitioners and Advanced Qualified Practitioners have achieved their own standard of excellence** based on the **skills** they have learned, their **experience** and their personal **wisdom**.
8. **We encourage you to see the Practitioner Seminar Attendance to appreciate the extent of a Practitioner's training, and their Practitioner Qualification / Advanced Qualification Diploma.**

REPATTERNING PRACTITIONERS ASSOCIATION USA

The Repatterning Practitioners Association is incorporated in the US as a 501(c)6 trade association. This professional membership organization has a Board of Directors elected by the members at large. The Repatterning Practitioners Association maintains standards in the practice of the Resonance Repatterning® system, sets criteria for and certifies RR students as certified practitioners, maintaining a registry of members who are Certified by the US Association, and produces a quarterly journal. *See RepatterningJournal.com*

Membership Membership is available and open to all at the Associate, Student, Student Practitioner and Certified Practitioner levels, and offers the opportunity for collaboration, connection and learning related to the practice of Resonance Repatterning. Membership benefits include an online community with quarterly journal, blogs, podcasts, and an annual virtual conference. The Association strives to promote the work of practitioners with the public through an online presence, listing a practitioner registry, and a variety of online events.

Certification To become a certified practitioner, candidates must join the Association as a Student Practitioner and meet the current approved criteria for certification. Student Practitioner membership includes the certification manual and online support. The process is intended to help candidates experience personal growth and transformation and to help them reach a level of competence and confidence in their own self-directed time line.

For additional information on the RPA Certification Program, please visit:

RepatterningPractitionersAssociation.com

Email: certification@rpamembers.org

Phone: 1-800-685-2811 Ext 3

For general articles, information and community links please visit:

RepatterningJournal.com

THE VISION OF THE RESONANCE REPATTERNING® INSTITUTE

We believe that the field of limitless life energy
that sustains and maintains life
is Spirit or unconditional love.

We believe there is a range of frequencies
at which our body and mind function optimally in the world.
When we resonate with this optimal frequency range
we are at our best at that moment in time;
we have the confidence to face life's challenges with equanimity
and to commit to our journey of self-healing and growth.

We believe that every positive change we make within ourselves –
each one of us being a minuscule part of the whole –
creates a ripple effect that benefits the whole.

This vision is based on the foundational understanding
that all matter consists of energy;
that what we resonate with determines what we experience;
that self-healing and extraordinary change are possible
when the frequencies of our body, emotions and mind
are coherent;
that no matter how hard the circumstances of our life may be,
there is always hope.

THE MISSION OF THE RESONANCE REPATTERNING® INSTITUTE

- To teach the Resonance Repatterning® system to all those who are interested – in a way that supports a solid grounding in the practice of Resonance Repatterning and the development of our personal and relationship best. All teaching supports joyful and creative learning through the use of color, music, movement and laughter, and inspires a high standard of practice with love, integrity and self-confidence.

- To support each student's personal self-healing and transformation through seminars, which also include individual and group RR sessions and demonstrations. Each student experiences for themselves the power of the Resonance Repatterning System to create extraordinary change.

- To inspire students and clients to live with renewed hope that they can make the Point of Choice, at any moment in time, to use the Resonance Repatterning System for being their best, giving their best, and appreciating the best that life offers.

- To promote Resonance Repatterning so its value and potential in the workplace, schools, social institutions and the family is appreciated and makes a positive difference in people's lives.

SPIRAL UP SUPPLIES

The following supplies include those referred to, taught and used in the Resonance Repatterning seminars. Suggestions for how to use each Energizing Option are given in Chloe Wordsworth's book, SPIRAL UP! 127 ENERGIZING OPTIONS TO BE YOUR BEST RIGHT NOW, in her videos and audios demonstrating all the Energizing Options and the Spiral Up Sequences for LIVING IN TUNE.

- The Resonance eStore is committed to Spiral Up Supplies of high quality, each personally endorsed by Chloe Faith Wordsworth and used in Resonance Repatterning seminars and her practice of Resonance Repatterning.
- For the complete list of Spiral Up Supplies available at the Resonance eStore, used in Resonance Repatterning seminars and sessions, go to ***ResonanceRepatterning.net/estore/***

CD OPTIONS

God's Cricket Chorus CD

This CD is a one-hour recording of crickets, slowed down to the equivalent of the human lifespan, and sounds like a chorus of ethereal voices, bringing uplift and a sense of awe before nature's beauty and innate harmony.

Resonance Repatterning CD

This moving CD offers an introduction to Resonance Repatterning by the Founder, Chloe Faith Wordsworth, along with teachers, practitioners and clients who share how Resonance Repatterning has reshaped people's lives. You may purchase while the stock lasts, after which it will be a DOWNLOAD item only.

Spirit of Love

An inspiring CD with songs like "The Rose" and "You Can Relax Now." Often used in the PRINCIPLES OF RELATIONSHIP and other RR seminars.

SOUND OPTIONS

Harmonic Overtone Guide

This book and CD by Nestor Kornblum is an example of overtoning at its best. The guide takes you step by step through the process of learning this powerful Energizing Option for yourself. Listening to this master of Harmonic Overtoning on Nestor's CD is a Healing Option in its own right.

Quantum Healing Codes™

Quantum Healing Codes are based on the discovery by Dr. Joseph Puleo of an ancient scale of six musical notes called the Solfeggio. Over 2,500 years ago Pythagoras knew the mathematical and geometric significance of the frequencies of these notes; the notes are also the basis of the original Gregorian chants. Quantum Healing Codes is often used in the Negative Thoughts Repatterning, the Reptilian Brain Repatterning, the Fusion and Diffusion Processes, and as an Option for general use as needed. Quantum Healing Codes includes a CD of the specific frequency notes and intervals created by the human voice, along with a fascinating booklet by Steven Linsteadt explaining the notes in relation to sacred geometry.

Om Tuning Fork

The Om Tuning Fork, tuned to 136.10 cycles per second, is thought to be a coherent frequency of universal significance for the earth. It can be struck and then held to the left and/or right ears; it can be moved over various body areas, particularly where there is tension, as in headaches; or the stem can be placed on the spine or specific areas of the body. Made in Germany of high quality stainless steel, the Om Tuning Fork is designed specifically for the purpose of vibrational well-being and is beautifully packaged in its own velvet satin-lined pouch.

Tuning Forks for the Complete Scale – C, C#, D, D#, E, F, F#, G, G#, A, A#, B

Made in Germany of high-quality stainless steel and packaged in a beautiful velvet satin-lined pouch, these twelve Tuning Forks make up the complete western scale. They are tuned from the diatonic pitch: A = 220 Hz. As an Energizing Option, you can listen to the vibration or use one or more of the Forks on or over any part of the body, on a Chakra, a Meridian point, a Jin Shin safety energy lock, a reflex point, the spine, etc.

Planetary Tuning Forks

These eleven tuning forks are mathematically tuned to the frequency of the planets, each of which has a particular frequency and is associated with its own characteristic qualities: the Sun, Pluto, Mercury, Mars, Saturn, Jupiter, Earth, Uranus, Moon, Neptune and Venus. Information on how to use planetary intentions, and the signs that may indicate a planetary tuning fork is needed, is provided in SPIRAL UP! 127 ENERGIZING OPTIONS TO BE YOUR BEST RIGHT NOW. *pp.41–50*

Chromatic Tuner

The Chromatic Tuner is used for quickly identifying the note or notes a person needs to tone. Each note (in a one-octave range) is listed on the tuner. When you press the note on the tuner, it gives you the sound you need to tone. The tuner is small and light and can be carried in a purse or pocket for use wherever and whenever you need to 'tune yourself up'.

COLOR AND LIGHT OPTIONS

Flower Pattern Cards

Photographed in India and South Africa, these flowers represent patterns found in sacred geometry. Flowers are said to be the language of the heart. Each flower carries a unique high-frequency note that is not audible to the human ear but is associated with its shape (a manifestation of sacred geometry), its fragrance, texture and its color. The Flower Pattern Cards encourage a shift in perspective as you see light and shadow, color and shape, depth and texture. Focusing on the flower pattern activates the right brain of imagination, feeling, creativity, global vision and receiving a new understanding of your present situation.

ColorYourWorld Glasses

This set of 13 pairs of lenses (and three plastic frames onto which the lenses fit) includes the twelve primary Dinshah colors, plus pink. Each color has a specific frequency and is made from Roscolene gels, as recommended by the Dinshah Health Society. Using the ColorYourWorld Glasses during a Repatterning or as an Energizing Option allows specific color frequencies into the brain-body energy field, often with a dramatic change in perspective, understanding and a sense of well-being. Many people use the CYW Glasses to fine tune their energy or to release stress, tension and depression.

Silk scarves

Nine silk scarves in the colors of the Chakras: red, orange, yellow, green, turquoise, indigo, purple, plus pale pink and white. In gossamer silk, they can be worn around the neck or used in a Resonance Repatterning session when a Chakra or Five Element Acupuncture color is needed.

ColorYourWorld Torch and 13 mini filter gels

The ColorYourWorld Torch comes in a box that includes a silver-mounted natural clear quartz crystal, a mini Mag-Lite with washer cap to hold the crystal and color gels in place, and a set of 13 Roscolene mini gels. The light and color are used to activate and balance the energy field by focusing on specific Jin Shin points, cranial bones, Mu Acupuncture points, Chakras, Meridian points and other body areas.

A book of geometric and Sanskrit gels to use with the CYW Torch is also available.

A Near Infrared Red Light (NIR) and LED Red Light

These powerful lights are shone in the nose and, based on Chinese research, have a direct effect on the brain for neurological conditions, memory, Alzheimer's, MS, migraines and other chronic problems. The LED red light is for other general problems such as allergies, insomnia, etc.

GRAPHICS AND MISCELLANEOUS OPTIONS

Geometric Pattern Cards

Geometric patterns represent the basic patterns or building blocks of the creation. When energy vibrates, the movement creates patterns that are universal – intricate patterns such as spirals and those seen in the movement of water and cloud shapes. Each frequency pattern, experienced as shape, creates coherence in its own unique way. The set of twenty-eight laminated Geometric Pattern Cards consists of six variations of the circle, seven types of spirals, eleven variations of the platonic solids and four crop circle patterns.

North Pole Magnets

The **Soother One** is a round two-inch negative north pole magnet disk that penetrates two inches and is used for relieving pain and tension; it can also be used on Acupuncture points, Jin Shin points and the cranial bones.

The **Ceramic Block** negative north pole magnet, 6" x 4" x ½", penetrates six inches and is used for issues involving organs such as the liver, spleen and kidneys. Dr. Philpott, M.D., renowned North Pole Magnet researcher, used the Ceramic Block magnet in cases of cancer and pain involving deeper areas of the body. The Flex magnet is the same as the Ceramic Block but is soft and flexible for wrapping round joints or other areas of the body.

The **Magnet Eye Mask** is a powerful way to activate Negative North Pole energy in the retina of the eyes that, along with the pineal gland and intestinal wall, are the only areas in the body that produce melatonin. *Info* VISION

For the above and other Spiral Up Supplies, posters of the Mandala and the Point of Choice poster, the Daily Empowerment Guide and Resonance Repatterning books go to ResonanceRepatterning.net/estore/

WEB RADIO SHOWS AND TRANSCRIPT DOWNLOADS

LIVING IN TUNE – TURN YOUR PROBLEMS INTO JOY WITH CHLOE FAITH WORDSWORTH

In fifty-two LIVING IN TUNE web radio shows, Chloe Wordsworth – founder and developer of the Resonance Repatterning® system – talks about different aspects of the body, mind and spirit in relation to Resonance Repatterning.

After sharing the theme of the week along with inspiring stories and powerful information, Chloe does a new Repatterning for someone who calls in during the first break, or she conducts a fascinating discussion with guests who are experts in various fields related to Resonance Repatterning.

- **Listen FREE to the shows in the Living in Tune Archives** at ResonanceRepatterning.net > Downloads
- **Create a LINK on your own website** to the Radio Show Archives
  Copy/paste the Archives hyperlink from the Home page of the ResonanceRepatterning.net website – or create your own in three easy steps:
  1. Go to the Archives
  2. Copy the 'url' or website address (in the address bar at the top of your screen)
  3. Paste it into your website
- **SHARE THE BENEFITS** Select a favorite show in the Archives, copy the hyperlink name of the show, paste it into an email and send to your friends or clients.
- **New Repatternings available to anyone** Chloe developed twenty-seven new Repatternings especially for LIVING IN TUNE. These new Repatternings are available in the transcripts of the shows, which anyone is welcome to download and use.

Go to ResonanceRepatterning.net > Downloads to listen to the shows or purchase a PDF download of your favorite shows.

INDEX OF THE 52 LIVING IN TUNE SHOWS AND REPATTERNINGS

LISTEN FREE AND DOWNLOAD TRANSCRIPTS

ResonanceRepatterning.net > Downloads

All the shows and Repatternings are with Chloe unless otherwise noted

NO.	TITLE OF RADIO SHOW	NAME OF REPATTERNING
1	Mastering Time	**Mastering Time Repatterning**
2	Uncomfortable in Groups – Finding Your Star Quality	**Group Oneness Repatterning**
3	Self-Mastery and Problems	**Problems into Opportunities Repatterning**
4	The Seven Opportunities in Every Problem	**Seven Opportunities Repatterning**
5	Infinite Possibilities – The Nine Steps for Transcending Limiting Beliefs	**Nine Steps for Transcending Limiting Beliefs Repatterning**
6	Trigger Reactions and Stress: The Five Steps and Ten Actions for Higher Brain Possibilities	**Stress Repatterning**
7	Five Secrets to the Winning Strategy	**Five Secrets Repatterning**
8	The Truth Within Your Goals	**Truth Within Your Goals Repatterning**
9	The Mystery of Your Power – Access It, Live It	**Mystery of Your Light Repatterning**
10	The Blessing of Anger – Quantum Leap to a New Way of Being	**Blessing of Anger Repatterning**
11	The Marriage of Your Yin and Yang: "Living Happily Ever After"	**Yin-Yang Spirit-Mind Repatterning**
12	The Power of Your Self-Image – Does it Limit or Express the Essence of You?	**Inner Nature Repatterning**
13	How Does Your Heart Reach the Heart of Another?	**Reaching the Heart Repatterning**
14	Your Breath – The Fascinating Miracle of Life and Health	**Breath for Life Repatterning**
15	Commitment to Your Self – The Challenge to Greatness	**Commitment to Greatness Repatterning**

16	Living Your Dreams	**Living Your Dreams Repatterning**
17	The Creative Life – Living Your Note	**Creative Life Repatterning**
18	Quantum Physics, the Nature of the Hologram and Resonance Repatterning	*Guest Host: Michael Fisher, Resonance Repatterning Practitioner*
19	Recession Proof Your Business	*Guest Host: Carolyn Winter, RR Practitioner & President, RPA* – Recession Proof Repatterning *by Carolyn Winter*
20	Turn Your Fear into Courage and Power	**Fear to Courage Repatterning**
21	Maturity and the Five Elements of Chinese Acupuncture	**Maturity in Relationship Repatterning**
22	True Abundance	**True Abundance Repatterning**
23	Communicating for Connection	**Communicating for Connection Repatterning**
24	Crack in the Vase – and the Secret It Holds	**Jealousy Repatterning for Radiating Your Light**
25	Depression – There Are Answers	**Depression Repatterning**
26	The Hero Within – Celebrating Our Journeys	**Hero Within Repatterning**
27	How Your Birth Journey Affects Your Life and Relationships	*Chloe interviews Guest: Ray Castellino, DC, Director BEBA*
28	The Secret of Your Ears – How They Recharge Your Brain	*Chloe interviews Guest: Billie Thompson, PhD, Director of Sound Listening*
29	Feng Shui and Resonance Repatterning	*Chloe interviews Guest: Sandy Sue Rector, Feng Shui Expert*
30	Facial Diagnosis	*Chloe interviews Guest: David Card, Author and Homeopath*
31	From Illness to Health – Transforming the World, One Family at a Time	*Chloe interviews Guest: Victoria Boutenko, Author and Speaker*
32	A New Look at Weight: The Hidden Message We Need to Hear	**Weight Repatterning**
33	The Song of Your Spine	*Chloe interviews Guest: Dr. June Leslie Wieder, DC*
34	The Healing Power of Magnets	*Chloe interviews Guest: Dr. Arthur Cushing*
35	Food and Disease, Food and Health	*Chloe interviews Guest: Dr. Brian Clement, Director of the Hippocrates Institute*
36	Healing Your Family System	*Chloe interviews Guest: Magui Block, Teacher of RR, Author and Therapist*

37	The 80/10/10 Diet	*Chloe interviews Guest: Dr. Doug Graham, Author of the 80/10/10 Diet*
38	Resonance Repatterning Practitioners and Teachers	*Guest Host: Ardis Ozborn, RR Teacher and Practitioner, interviewing four practitioners*
39	Jump for Health, Strength and Vitality	*Chloe interviews Guest: Dave Hall, Developer of the Cellerciser*
40	Reach for Your Vision	**Envisioning Repatterning**
41	Non-Coherent and Coherent Triangles in Our Relationships	**Triangle Repatterning**
42	Rediscovering the Intelligence of the Heart	*Chloe interviews Guest: Joseph Chilton Pearce, Brain Researcher & Author*
43	From Birth to Breast	*Chloe interviews Guests: Dr. Ray Castellino, DC and Mary Jackson, RN*
44	Healing Trauma and Abuse	*Chloe interviews Guests: RR practitioners Tabitha Crook and April Gonzales*
45	Healing Our Animals, Healing Ourselves	*Chloe interviews Guest: RR practitioner Jonathan Martin*
46	Resonance Repatterning in a Center for Domestic Violence	*Chloe interviews Guest: RR Practitioner Shirley Collins*
47	The Yequana Indians and What They Teach Us	*Chloe interviews Guest: Jean Liedloff, Author, The Continuum Concept*
48	Successful People with Big Dreams Talk About the Impact Resonance Repatterning Has on Their Lives	*Chloe interviews four clients of RR practitioner Mary Schneider*
49	The Nature of Trauma, How it Manifests and the Tools for its Healing through Resonance Repatterning	*Chloe interviews Guest: RR Teacher and Practitioner Michelle Bongiorno*
50	Underlying Issues of Weight Disorders, Pain and Physical Issues – the Point of Choice – Resolved through Resonance Repatterning	*Chloe interviews Guests: RR practitioners Liz Tobin, Dorinda Hartson and Jane Winne*
51	The China Study – Creating Waves for Positive Change in Our Health	*Chloe interviews Guest: T. Colin Campbell, Professor Emeritus Cornell University and Director/Author of The China Study*
52	The Nine Yequana Principles for a Joy-Filled Life	**Nine Yequana Principles Repatterning**

Listen to the Archives at ResonanceRepatterning.net > Downloads
Download the transcripts at ResonanceRepatterning.net > Downloads

THE STORY BEHIND SPIRAL UP!

For more than forty years Chloe has studied, practiced and taught the Spiral Up Energizing Options found in this book. She had the honor of studying with some of the greats in the field of energy medicine: in the 1970s with Dr. Randolph Stone, who created Polarity Therapy and opened the way for her to understand the Chakra energy system; in the 1980s with J.R. Worsely, a major player in bringing the ancient Five Element System of Chinese Acupuncture to the West; and Dr. Upledger, the first doctor to teach Cranial Sacral work to a non-medical public; even a few seminars in the late 1970s with the genius Moshe Feldenkrais, who taught how to re-educate the brain and body through movement. And so many more.

Studying Acupuncture at the Traditional Acupuncture Institute led to a full-time Acupuncture practice and time to think more deeply about the cause of stress, pain and lack of health. After years of searching for a panacea for human ills, failures and relationship conflicts, Chloe began to develop the Resonance Repatterning® System (initially called Holographic Repatterning™), which began to take shape in 1989–90.

She also began to write down in an easy How To format all the Spiral Up Energizing Options from sound, color and light, movement, breath, essential oils and energy contacts (from Jin Shin Jyutsu, Acupuncture, Chakra balancing and left-right brain integration). These pages of notes resulted in the present SPIRAL UP! book, which has been the mainstay for thousands of Resonance Repatterning students and practitioners all over the world since 1990.

ABOUT THE AUTHOR AND CONTACT US

Chloe Faith Wordsworth is the founder and developer of Resonance Repatterning® and author of QUANTUM CHANGE MADE EASY and eleven other books on Resonance Repatterning. She lives and writes in Arizona and teaches in the USA and abroad.

For more information go to *ResonanceRepatterning.net*

- To find **a practitioner**, go to*ResonanceRepatterning.net*
- For information on Resonance Repatterning **seminars**, go to *ResonanceRepatterning.net*
- For information on Resonance Repatterning **books and Spiral Up supplies**, go to *ResonanceRepatterning.net/estore/*
- For **videos and audios of the Energizing Options demonstrated by Chloe Faith Wordsworth and for Chloe's** LIVING IN TUNE **web radio show downloads** go to *ResonanceRepatterning.net* or *spiralup127.com*

ACKNOWLEDGMENTS

First, and most important, constant gratitude to my spiritual teacher and his successor. Their example and spiritual principles challenge me on a daily basis to live my highest and best; they are my north star as I travel this life's path, my inspiration to keep spiraling up!

Profound love and gratitude to my parents, John and Karis Guinness, who strived for the ideal and whose values are the foundation of my life's desire to teach people how to bring positive change to themselves and others.

I am deeply grateful to my sister Lindis Guinness, RR practitioner: she gave unstinting help for five years in the early 1990s, which made it possible for me to give my time and attention to developing and writing the early editions of the manuals and to teaching this work; my appreciation also for her passionate belief in Resonance Repatterning!

To my other sister, Anthea Guinness, RR practitioner and former RR teacher, much gratitude for our conversations over the years, which are a continual source of inspiration for me; and for editing, proofreading and helping design the 2008–2014 editions of all my books, including SPIRAL UP! How to thank you for helping me reorganize SPIRAL UP!, which changed everything. You continue to raise the bar for me, pushing me to go the extra mile with all the books and manuals.

This book could not have been written without the knowledge I gained from so many teachers and in my travels around the world. To name, with appreciation, just a few of my teachers in the healing arts: Dr. Randolph Stone; Professor J.R. Worsley and the teachers of the Traditional Acupuncture Institute; Sharry Edwards (for an introduction to Sound frequencies); Dr. Paul Dennison and Gail Dennison (for introducing me to Edu-K); Patti Steurer who introduced me to the idea of the 'Balance' format; Moshe Feldenkrais, Dr. John Upledger, Mary Burmeister, Ann Wigmore and so many more wonderful beings.

I would like to thank the following people who have contributed to my learning and inspired me to adapt Energizing Options from their work: Jean Illsley Clarke, author of *Growing Up Again;* Gary Young of YoungLiving essential oils; the Flower Essence Society in Nevada; Fabien Maman, author of *The Tao of Sound,* for his research on the pentatonic modes and his seasonal and Five Element correlations; and Elizabeth Keith my Awareness Through Movement and Bones for Life teacher, for reminding me why I love what Moshe Feldenkrais created. And all the other writers and teachers I have acknowledged throughout SPIRAL UP!

I would like to thank each of the Resonance Repatterning teachers for their continued commitment to teaching Resonance Repatterning and the unique quality each of them brings to their teaching; also for their feedback, questions and suggestions that kept me moving forward. Thank you for the joy of working with you: Rosario Aziri Avendano, Michelle Bongiorno, Karine Bourcart, Mary Cameris, Beatriz Godinez, Jennifer Johnson, Didac Mancera, Ana Signoret Marcellin, Bobbie Martin, Clara Olivares, Ardis Ozborn, Leopoldina Rendon Pineda, Sylvi Salinas, Elisa Sanchez and Judith Urbina. And to Magui Block, former RR teacher, for integrating her Family Systems work into the Resonance Repatterning model and deepening RR students' understanding through her seminars. And my love and appreciation for our past teachers who have moved forward in their own creative direction, but gave so generously to Resonance Repatterning in their time.

My gratitude to Maggie Honton and Lori Forsyth for suggestions and proofreading of earlier editions of this book; Victoria Benoit for proofreading a previous edition; Susan M. Brooks, for editing the information on the Jin Shin Jyutsu Safety Energy Locks; Roman Yaworsky, medical illustrator, for his illustrations of the Jin Shin and Mu points; Bobbie Martin and her designer Teresa Mandala for re-energizing the Point of Choice graphic with its color and dynamism and inserting fear and trust in the Power of Your Point of Choice graphic; loving thanks to RR practitioner and former RR teacher, Helen Peak, who gave me the idea for the Fusion Process; to Ardis Ozborn, RR practitioner and teacher and past president of the RR Association for many years, for her constant support in those early days, for feedback on bits and pieces and chapters I sent her, for friendship and her persevering vision to get Resonance Repatterning 'into the world'; and Shady Sirotkin for our friendship, wonderful conversations and her ever-ready wisdom and support.

Heartfelt gratitude and love to Carla ElDorado for doing the graphics for SPIRAL UP! and preparing previous editions for publication, as well as years of hands-on support with books, DVDs, computer know-how and so much more. Great appreciation to Carol White, for doing the composition and design of the 2008–2014 editions of all the Resonance Repatterning books and for being an indispensable help over the years, always there when I need her – and for coming up with the design for the SPIRAL UP! book cover. My thanks to George Foster for completing the cover design in his masterful way.

Special thanks to James Oschman for writing the afterword to SPIRAL UP! and his chapter on the science of spirals, and the foreword to my first book, QUANTUM CHANGE MADE EASY. His brilliance and clarity, and his belief in Resonance Repatterning, add so much that I am grateful for.

My appreciation to the non-profit Association Board members in the USA, Mexico and Spain (and in the UK and South Africa in the past), for volunteering ideas, energy and commitment so generously and for maintaining the standards and ethics of Resonance Repatterning practitioners. Loving thanks to Karine Bourcart who poured her energy into establishing RR in Mexico and, with her support team, continues to create a firm foundation for RR in this wonderful country; also to Lourdes Fernandez Palazuelos for teaching and supporting many RR students in the early days of establishing Resonance Repatterning in Mexico.

Much gratitude to the team of translators who have made Resonance Repatterning available to so many: Leslie Pascoe Chalke, Margara Graf, Karine Bourcart, Jennifer Justel and Carmen Marcela Orozco for their Spanish translations, and the translators who are now volunteering to translate this book into German and Portuguese.

For all the seminar organizers, going back to the early 1990s when no one knew we existed, who inspired people to learn Resonance Repatterning in South Africa, Spain, the UK, Taiwan, Australia, New Zealand, Canada, the USA, Mexico, Chile and India. They brought new possibilities to so many through the Resonance Repatterning seminars they organized: my gratitude and great appreciation to all – too many now to name. And to my friend of more than forty years, Netta Pfeifer, who was in charge of our Spiral Up supplies eStore – my appreciation for managing it (and me!) with love, laughter and efficiency. Gratitude to Gail Glanville, my co-author of Quantum Change Made Easy, who, with Carolyn Winter supported the Resonance Repatterning Institute and the Association at a critical point in its growth.

Finally and far from least, my appreciation to all Resonance Repatterning students and practitioners for the pleasure of seeing you light up, and for brightening the lives of all those you do Resonance Repatterning with. I love your passion for this work, your joy in the deep transformation it has brought to you and your families, and your commitment to making your own unique 'ding' in the universe!

Made in the USA
Las Vegas, NV
14 April 2022